OUT OF THE FIRE

A Life Radically Changed

"Is not this man a burning stick snatched from the fire?"

Best Wishes!
David Hobbs

David Hobbs

4L Press

All of the persons and events recorded in this book are true. Some names and minor details have been changed to protect the privacy of the individuals involved.

Out of the Fire
Published and Copyrighted © 2009 by 4L Press,
P.O. Box 5975, Marysville, CA 95901
ISBN-13: 978-0-615-28481-1

Cover Design by **James Davis**

Special thanks to the team:

Beth Ward for technical assistance in preparing the ms.
Bill Crocker and **Kara Davis** for editing.
Patti Thomas for accounting.
Kara Davis for publicity and advising.
Dave McCreary for website hosting
John Zemko for IT Services.
Ken Miller for photo restoration.

Printed in the United States of America
1st edition: July, 2006
2nd edition: Jan. 2007
3rd edition: June, 2009

Copies or comments–outofthefirebook.com
Or 4L Press, P.O. Box 5975, Marysville, CA 95901

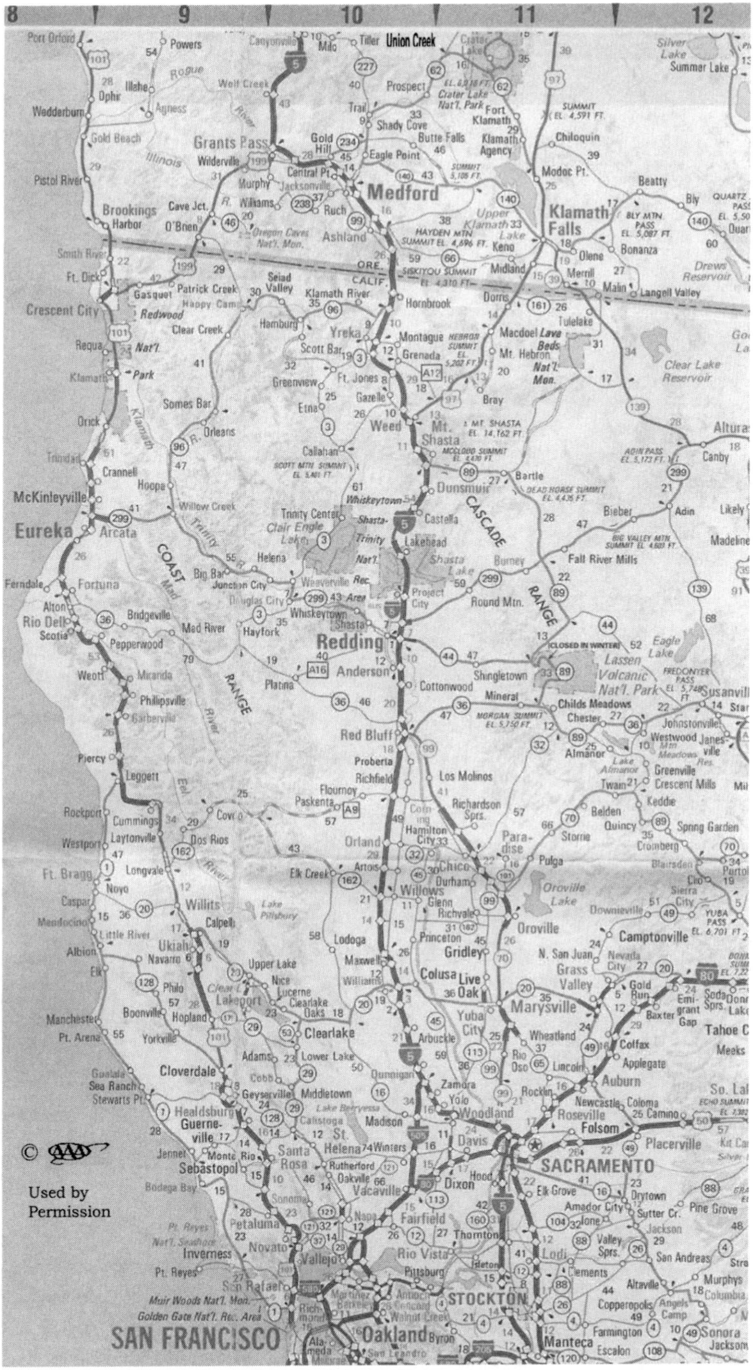

8
9
10
11
12
Port Orford
Powers
Union Creek
Crater Lake
Silver Lake
Summer Lake
Prospect
Crater Lake Nat'l. Park
Fort Klamath
Chiloquin
Wedderburn
Gold Beach
Grants Pass
Gold Hill
Eagle Point
Butte Falls
Medford
Jacksonville
Central Pt.
Shady Cove
Klamath Agency
Modoc Pt.
Beatty
Bly
Pistol River
Brookings
Harbor
Cave Jct.
O'Brien
Ruch
Ashland
Oregon Caves Nat'l. Mon.
Upper Klamath Lake
Klamath Falls
Keno
Olene
Bonanza
Drews Reservoir
Smith River
Ft. Dick
Crescent City
Gasquet
Patrick Creek
Seiad Valley
Klamath River
Hornbrook
Midland
Merrill
Malin
Langell Valley
Dorris
Tulelake
Redwood Nat'l. Park
Clear Creek
Hamburg
Yreka
Montague
Grenada
Macdoel
Lava Beds Nat'l. Mon.
Mt. Hebron
Clear Lake Reservoir
Requa
Klamath
Scott Bar
Ft. Jones
Greenview
Gazelle
Etna
Bray
Somes Bar
Orleans
Weed
Mt. Shasta
Orick
Trinidad
Cranell
Hoopa
Callahan
Dunsmuir
Bartle
Alturas
Canby
McKinleyville
Eureka
Arcata
Willow Creek
Trinity Center
Castella
Lakehead
CASCADE
COAST
Bieber
Adin
Likely
Madeline
Helena
Big Bar
Junction City
Weaverville
Burney
Fall River Mills
Ferndale
Fortuna
Alton
Rio Dell
Scotia
Bridgeville
Mad River
Hayfork
Whiskeytown
Shasta
Project City
Round Mtn.
RANGE
Redding
Anderson
Cottonwood
Shingletown
Lassen Volcanic Nat'l. Park
Eagle Lake
Susanville
Pepperwood
Weott
Miranda
Phillipsville
Garberville
Platina
Mineral
Childs Meadows
Chester
Westwood
Johnstonville
Red Bluff
Proberta
Richfield
Los Molinos
Almanor
Lake Almanor
Greenville
Crescent Mills
Twain
Keddie
Piercy
Leggett
Flournoy
Paskenta
Richardson Sprs.
Belden
Quincy
Spring Garden
Rockport
Cummings
Covelo
Laytonville
Dos Rios
Westport
Orland
Hamilton City
Paradise
Storrie
Cromberg
Ft. Bragg
Longvale
Noyo
Artois
Chico
Durham
Pulga
Elk Creek
Willows
Caspar
Mendocino
Willits
Glenn
Richvale
Oroville Lake
Downieville
Sierra City
Little River
Calpella
Oroville
Camptonville
Albion
Ukiah
Lodoga
Princeton
Gridley
N. San Juan
Grass Valley
Nevada City
Elk
Navarro
Upper Lake
Maxwell
Williams
Colusa
Live Oak
Nice
Lucerne
Philo
Clearlake Oaks
Marysville
Gold Run
Emigrant Gap
Soda Sprs.
Manchester
Boonville
Hopland
Lakeport
Clearlake
Yuba City
Wheatland
Baxter
Tahoe City
Pt. Arena
Yorkville
Arbuckle
Lower Lake
Rio Oso
Lincoln
Colfax
Meeks
Applegate
Adams
Cloverdale
Dunnigan
Zamora
Auburn
Gualala
Sea Ranch
Stewarts Pt.
Geyserville
Middletown
Yolo
Rocklin
Newcastle
Coloma
So. Lake
Healdsburg
Calistoga
Madison
Woodland
Roseville
Camino
Guerneville
St. Helena
Winters
Davis
Folsom
Placerville
Jenner
Monte Rio
Santa Rosa
Rutherford
Oakville
SACRAMENTO
Sebastopol
Vacaville
Dixon
Hood
Elk Grove
Drytown
Bodega Bay
Sonoma
Napa
Fairfield
Amador City
Sutter Cr.
Pine Grove
Petaluma
Ione
Jackson
Novato
Vallejo
Rio Vista
Thornton
Lodi
Valley Sprs.
San Andreas
Inverness
Pt. Reyes
Isleton
Pittsburg
Clements
Murphys
San Rafael
Martinez
Antioch
STOCKTON
Altaville
Columbia
Muir Woods Nat'l. Mon.
Golden Gate Nat'l. Rec. Area
Richmond
Berkeley
Concord
Walnut Creek
Copperopolis
Angels Camp
SAN FRANCISCO
Oakland
Byron
Farmington
Sonora
Alameda
San Leandro
Manteca
Escalon
Jackson

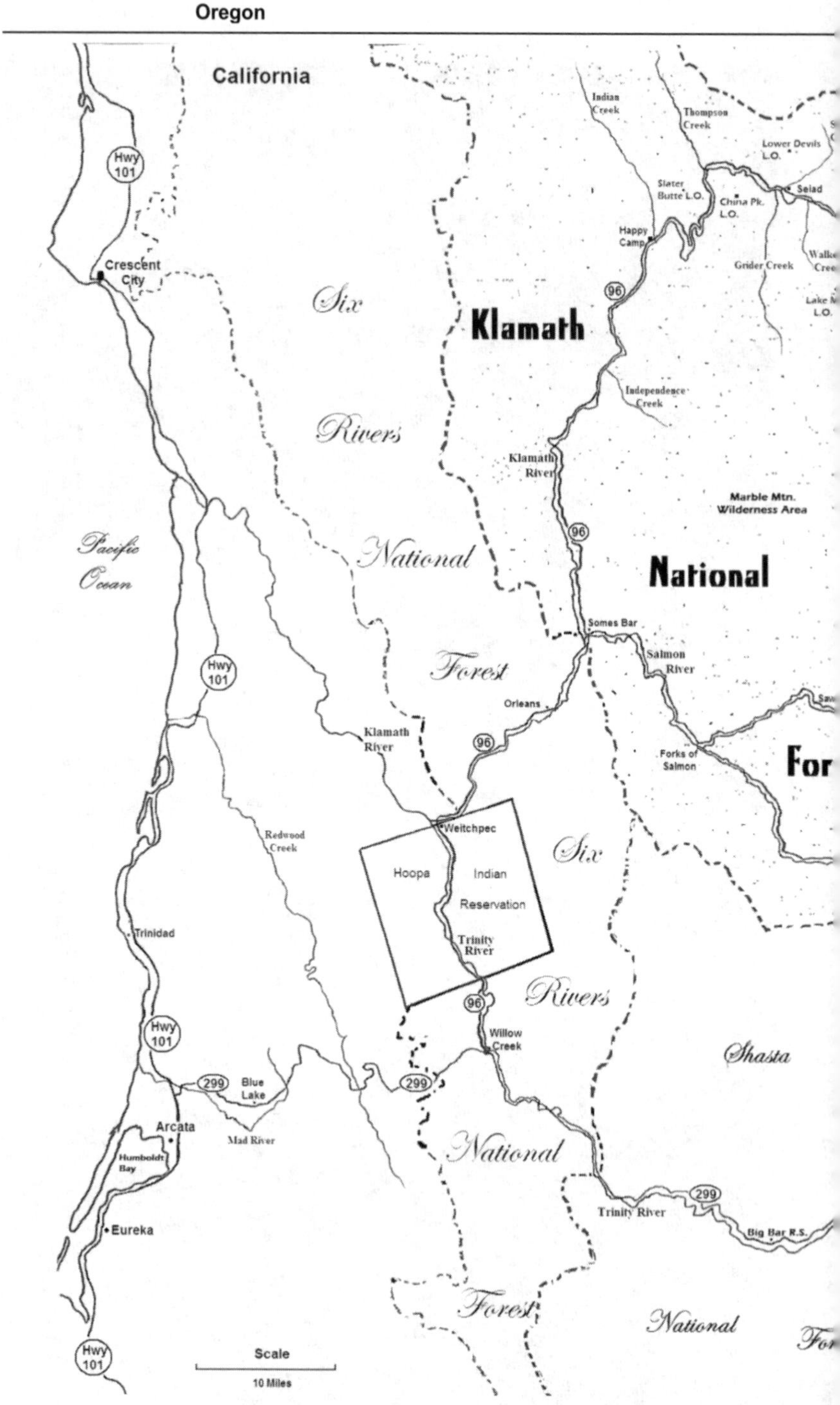
Oregon
California
Hwy 101
Crescent City
Six Rivers National Forest
Klamath National Forest
Indian Creek
Thompson Creek
Lower Devils L.O.
Seiad
Slater Butte L.O.
China Pk. L.O.
Happy Camp
Grider Creek
96
Independence Creek
Klamath River
Marble Mtn. Wilderness Area
Pacific Ocean
Somes Bar
Salmon River
Orleans
Klamath River
Forks of Salmon
Weitchpec
Hoopa Indian Reservation
Redwood Creek
Trinity River
Trinidad
Willow Creek
Shasta
299
Blue Lake
Mad River
Arcata
Humboldt Bay
Eureka
Trinity River
Big Bar R.S.
National
Scale
10 Miles

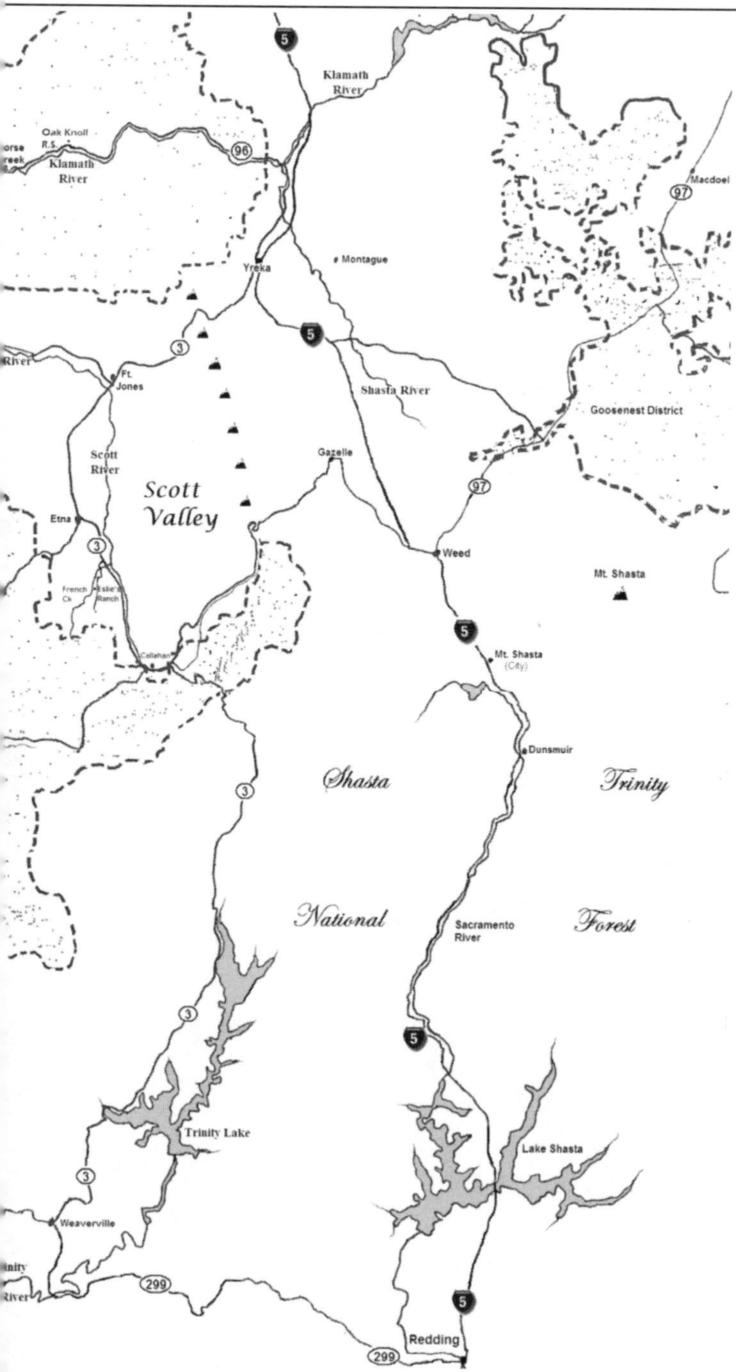

Klamath River
Oak Knoll R.S.
Klamath River
96
Macdoel
97
Montague
Yreka
3
Ft. Jones
Shasta River
Goosenest District
Scott River
Gazelle
97
Scott Valley
Etna
3
Weed
French Ck
Eske's Ranch
Mt. Shasta
Callahan
Mt. Shasta (City)
Dunsmuir
Shasta
Trinity
3
National
Forest
Sacramento River
3
Trinity Lake
Lake Shasta
3
Weaverville
299
Redding
299

TABLE OF CONTENTS

Year Title Page

Year Title Page

Year Title Page

THE BEGINNING

September 1965

"Here, take this, you might need it." It was my father speaking. He had hurried up behind me as I was walking along the train to the boarding area. A strange look of intensity was on his face. Overcome by feeling, he looked away as he stuffed a twenty dollar bill into my hand. His number two son was about to board the train that would take him away to college on the other side of the country. My dad had never been an emotional man. I can't remember him ever saying "I love you," hugging me, or getting mushy. But now the words seemed to catch in his throat. They were barely audible, and were the only sign this dear, quiet man had been overcome with emotion, a tenderness I had never seen.

Only later did I realize he was grasping the true significance of the moment: his son, who he had raised for eighteen years, was leaving for California to start a new life, 2,500 miles away. And though I would return, it would only be as a visitor. That incident remains one of my most precious memories of my dad.

As for me, when people asked why I left Ohio for California, I would glibly reply, "Because it was as far away from home as I could get!" Not that I hated home, but I had an adventurous spirit and longed to get out on my own, and the West was calling. I was going out to major in forestry at Humboldt State College in far Northern California and then go to work for the Forest Service, a dream I had carried all through high school.

I was not a stranger to California. My mother was born and raised there, and we traveled there every five years to see her family. One of the only relatives left was her father's brother Eslie Cory, who lived alone on the old family ranch in Etna in the remote Scott Valley area of far Northern California.

After a last, emotionless "Hobbsian" goodbye, I was off in pursuit of my dream.

Out of the Fire

In San Francisco, I got on a bus for the all-night ride to Arcata.

The bus ride was 290 miles of twisting, deserted Highway 101 along the rivers and over the mountains of the rugged north coast redwood forests. We left at 9:00 p.m. and finally got there around 6:00 a.m.

From the bus station, I had to walk over a mile uphill through the cool morning air to the college dorm where I was to stay. Then life was a blur of freshman orientation, a new roommate, signing up for classes, buying books, and getting homesick.

One Thursday, I returned from class to find a notice posted on the dorm bulletin board. Forestry students were needed to help the Forest Service burn some slash over in the Willow Creek area that weekend. Excited, I called the phone number and was plugged into a carload of students going. We left Arcata Friday afternoon for the hour's drive to Willow Creek's ranger station, forty miles inland.

"What is this 'slash' that we're supposed to burn?" I asked the guys I was riding with.

They explained it was the limbs and tops of trees left after logging. "They dry out over the summer and the Forest Service burns them in the fall to clear the ground for replanting."

We spent Friday night on cots set up in the warehouse.

Saturday we split up. Two of us went with a Forest Service regular to check on some previous slash fires. But when we got there, the fires were already out. There was nothing to do the whole day but hang out in the woods.

From our vantage point in a logged over area high in the mountains, we could see a column of smoke from a forest fire on another district. There was a steady stream of retardant-carrying planes flying overhead and talk on the radio. Our crew leader called the dispatcher to let him know we were available. The dispatcher told him to "stand by," that is: "stay where you are and keep tuned to the radio." I thought it would be exciting to get sent to the fire but didn't know how we could get back to school by Monday.

The dispatcher never called us back, which made our crew leader disgruntled. "You'll find the Forest Service is not nearly as together as they'd like everyone to believe," he said dourly. Since I neither knew how together the Forest Service was, nor how together they wanted everyone to think they were, I kept quiet.

We came down from the mountains in time for dinner. Afterwards, the foreman asked if any of us wanted to go up and help them burn a slash block that night. Another fellow and I readily agreed. Soon we were crammed into a pickup with a couple of regulars heading up the darkening mountain roads to the block.

There are two basic ways to burn slash. If the slash is thick enough, it is burned where it lays. Otherwise, it is burned in piles pushed together by caterpillar tractors called "cats." Back east I had always called them bulldozers. The piles are called "cat-piles."

We had a series of cat-piles in this block. By the time we got there to relieve the day crew, they already had the piles burning.

The block was forty acres in size, spread out over some rolling terrain near the top of a ridge. One of the Forest Service regulars walked me to the other end of the block. He said they expected some trouble in this far corner. It had some of the biggest piles in the block, and its comma shape made it nearly surrounded by forest. If the fire got going too intensely and the wind began swirling around, it could easily spew sparks into the forest.

We each carried a fire fighting hand tool. In addition, my partner had a rubber "bladder bag" with a hand pump filled with five gallons of water strapped to his back. This would be ideal for squirting out sparks falling outside the line.

We passed through the block along a one-lane dirt logging road that snaked its way through the burning piles. Darkness had fallen completely; there was no moon to light the sky and no light from civilization near or far. All the eye could see was burning piles of slash surrounded by darkness and silence. Some we could see up close as we walked by, with their flames and smoke leaping toward the sky, the embers hissing and popping as they burned fiercely. Others were just flickering red and yellow lights far away in the midst of the darkness.

From the crest of a small rise, we could see new fires spread out over the rolling landscape below. On the horizon was a fire burning hotly, sending off showers of sparks and clouds of smoke: a whole convulsing world of its own, yet with no one to experience it, to care about it, or even be affected by it. In other places, less intense fires burned, easily overlooked, yet each just as much a world unto itself. And in between them all, and around them all, and beyond them all was the darkness. It was a scene of fascinating beauty yet utter desolation, devoid of life, inhabited only by fire and smoke, and presided over by silence.

Walking through the slash block was like walking through the classic depiction of hell: a stark place of darkness yet fire, devoid of anything soft or beautiful, the abode of disorder, confusion, oblivion. Not that I believed in a literal hell. Atheist that I was, I believed that when you died you were dead.

We walked to the far corner of the block, to the place where they anticipated there might be trouble. We settled in to see what would happen as the fires increased in intensity. No problems arose, however. The fires burned vigorously but tamely. No winds arose to whip them and no sparks escaped into the forest. Like my life, it was burning quietly and contained, with nothing yet to send sparks and flames out into uncharted territory

By the time we were ready to head home Sunday night, I had been on the job for almost thirty-two straight hours, during which time I had done almost nothing. "That's got to be some of the easiest money I've ever made!" I thought, "And some of the most exciting!"

We left the lights of Willow Creek behind and started up the winding, mountain road towards the top of the first of the three ridges between Willow Creek and the coast. To our right was a drop-off into a ravine, on our left the wall of the mountain. We were going up a short, straight stretch when suddenly a car, approaching at a high rate speed, came careening around the turn in front of us, crossing well over into our lane. Before we could act, the driver swerved back out of our lane. But he over-corrected, going completely through his lane, off the highway, and into a shallow ditch. Crossing the ditch, he smacked into the rock wall of the mountain with a grinding crash just about the time he was opposite us, who were watching bug-eyed. Without even slowing down, he bounced off the rock wall, came up out of the little ditch, back onto the road behind us, continued down the highway, and exited around the next bend, leaving the road as dark and deserted as before.

We were beside ourselves with amazement. "What was that?" we practically yelled.

Our driver alone was unperturbed. He shrugged off our urgent request for an explanation of this frightening event. "Ahh, drunken Indian. Reservation's just a few miles down the road."

We had come to burn slash, a potentially risky operation. But our only danger had come in almost being killed by a drunken driver on our way home. So life is not always what we expect. Just when it seems tamest, its dangers can arise suddenly without warning .

DORM LIFE

Excited by my first experience doing something I had always dreamed about, I was soon applying to every national forest in the state, eager to get on a fire crew for the upcoming summer.

Meanwhile, my roommate Mike Orford also got me excited

about the music of Barbra Streisand. We bought all her albums, and I even went so far as to make a "Barbra Streisand for President" sign that I put up in our dorm window.

I had become a militant atheist in high school. Madalyn Murray became my great hero after I read an interview of her in *Playboy Magazine*. In my zeal, I composed a bitterly anti-religious "epic" poem, attacking the sins of the church down through the ages. In writing it, I drew on the spirit of Mrs. Murray and the anti-establishment folk singer Bob Dylan, who included the religious establishment in his bashing.

I also eagerly embraced the "God is Dead" movement that had arisen dramatically in the mid '60s. I didn't know anything about it except that I could resonate with its name. Soon I took down the "Barbra Streisand for President" sign and put up a "God is Dead" sign in its place. Actually, dorm policy prohibited all signs in the students' windows, but at the time it wasn't being enforced. My "God is Dead" proclamation strained this policy of non-enforcement. And later, when I put up my third sign regarding our governor, "Pat Brown Should be Dead!" all hell broke loose.

Being away from home gave me the opportunity to get into binge drinking. We began to party on the weekends, getting desperately drunk. Though I had occasionally gotten drunk during my high school years, I never drank so much as to make myself physically sick—by violently throwing up. Though it was a horrible experience, it began to happen fairly regularly.

At this point in the narrative I could regale the reader with stories such as sitting on the bank of a drainage ditch in lower Arcata with my new roommate Larry Miller, so drunk I didn't even realize I was holding my beer can upside down and all the beer was running out. Or the story of our secret beer party in our dorm room. Since we didn't want anyone to know we were there, we couldn't leave to go down the hall to the bathroom. So we peed in a three-pound coffee can. By midnight, the can was full and so were we. We made a dash for the bathroom, hoping nobody would see us at that late hour. In our haste and drunkenness, we kept sloshing the can's contents on us and the hall floor. Or the time I returned to the dorm from a party dead drunk, tried to take off my sweater, and suddenly threw up all over the place, then passed out on my bed, leaving the mess for my first roommate Orford to clean up.

There are many such stories that could be told. But though humorous in retrospect, all they did at the time was lead me away from things that were truly important. A lot of what happened at this time in my life was influenced by my new roommate and best friend, Larry Miller, who moved into my dorm room when Mike Orford suddenly moved out. Larry influenced me greatly. Though he was my friend, he tried to get me extra drunk, wanting me to get sick and to throw up. He thought it was funny! He encouraged me in the writing of my anti-Christian poem and cutting classes. Even though he was my best friend, Larry used to mock me for my meekness and my stuttering. His favorite word for me was "obsequious."

I went along with Larry in most things, including how we lived as pigs! He was utterly slovenly. But because his personality was dominant, I went along with him, never thinking about going in a different direction. I had no moral standards or absolutes—no moral compass with which to orient my life. I was a moral vacuum, ready to be filled by whatever was at hand. And Larry was at hand.

We never picked anything off the floor or put anything away. Then one day late in February he decided it was time to do a spring housecleaning. We cleaned everything up and put it all in order, taking all Saturday to do it. To celebrate, we decided to skip the dorm food that night and go to the student union for a pizza. We brought a big one back to our room, invited some friends over, and had a party in honor of the cleaning of our room.

But old habits reasserted themselves quickly. Before we knew it, the room was back to its usual mess, in fact even worse than before. You couldn't even see the floor! Finally, when it came time to pack up and leave for the summer, we were forced to clean the room again. We gradually worked down through the layers of mess. At last the floor came into sight. The very last thing at the bottom of the pile was an old, flattened cardboard box. Larry picked it up and looked at it. "I wonder what this is from?" he mused.

Suddenly, I flashed on the answer. "That's the box we got that pizza in last winter after cleaning our room!" And so it was.

GETTING THE JOB

I began getting responses back from the Forest Service, some saying I was under consideration, most that I was not. February was rapidly passing without anything definite.

Then, unexpectedly, one evening late in February, I got a call on the pay phone down the hall from a Zack Walton on the Seiad (*Cy-add*) district on the Klamath National Forest. He said two of the men they had expected back weren't returning. He wanted to know if I was interested in a job. He said there was a position on the helitack crew and one on the slash crew. Naturally I accepted on the spot, and then ran to find a map to see where Seiad was located. It was on the Klamath River, just south of the Oregon border. That was the same forest in which my great uncle Eslie's ranch was located! But Eslie lived in the southern part while Seiad was in the north.

That turned out to be the only job offer I got from all my applications, and I wouldn't have gotten that one except two men dropped out at the last minute. Breaking into something for the first time can be hard. But the break had come, and I could hardly contain my excitement!

GETTING STARTED

June 1966

I arrived in Seiad in the first few days of June, the first "college student seasonal" to arrive.

Seiad was in a valley made in the shape of a "T"—about a mile long and three-quarters of a mile wide at its widest point—where Seiad Creek flowed into the Klamath River. It was ringed by the steep Siskiyou Mountains through which the Klamath had cut a path to the ocean, about fifty miles due west. A county road branched off Highway 96, going up Seiad Creek. Just up this road was the booming Seiad lumber mill. It and Chick Lucas Logging were the major employers in town.

The town was smack in the middle of the valley, on the bank of Seiad Creek. The sign on the road said the population was 250, but who all those people were was a mystery. There was a general store with a lunch bar on one side of the highway, and a gas station on the other. On one end of the store was a tiny post office facility, while adjacent to that was a small trailer court with a Laundromat. Half a mile down the highway was a bar called the Wildwood, and another little trailer court.

Just up the highway was the Forest Service's Seiad Ranger Station, its front yard well shaded with tall trees, my new summer home. The office was a tiny structure containing only four small rooms in which the entire staff worked.

One of the first people I met was Zack Walton, the fire control officer who had called me on the phone. Zack was hale and hearty, the epitome of the western cowboy with his tall stature, rugged good looks, and ever-present cowboy boots.

He introduced me to Dick Leslie, the nervous-mannered ex-military lifer who was fire dispatcher for the district. After he and the two secretaries completed the paperwork for my hiring, Zack took me on a tour of the rest of the ranger station.

The driveway circled a flagpole in front of the office, and then continued back along the right perimeter fence, past Zack's house and a trailer. Next was the compound, a roughly hollow square of buildings clustered around an oiled-gravel parking lot. Most of my time at the ranger station—eatin,' sleepin,' workin,' and "funin'"—would be spent right here on the compound.

The main building that paralleled the highway and went across almost the entire property, was the warehouse-shop building. The warehouse housed the tanker and all the firefighting equipment, while the shop was… well, the shop.

Down the far leg of the square was a multi-vehicle garage; while on the near leg of the square was the building housing the barracks and cookhouse. Like all the buildings, this one was small and old, painted "Forest Service brown" with "Forest Service green" trim. They were probably all built at the same time in the '30s. Beyond the barracks was an open area of lawn and trees and then an old decrepit trailer where big Wilbur Straight, the tanker operator, lived.

Making up the final leg of the square, at the end of the property farthest from the highway, was an old horse barn, still serviceable, but leftover from another era. In front of it was a small corral. The barn was now used mostly for storage.

The driveway continued past the end of the barn, leaving the ranger station property through a fence and over a small irrigation ditch. From there, it wound around some huge piles of dredger rocks, ending up at the heliport, a small, level area made by flattening out a pile of the dredger rocks. The Forest Service leased it for use by the helicopter based there in the summer.

Zack told me I would be working on the "helitack crew" when the helicopter arrived in about a month. I had been chosen second man on the two-man crew that went with the helicopter to fires and oversaw everything the Forest Service did with it. There were only two districts on the forest that had a helicopter, and I was chosen for the only seasonal position on one of them. I felt fortunate indeed!

As I was completing the tour and depositing my duffel bag in the bunkhouse, Zack introduced me to Fred Clark, an ex-navy lifer, who was station foreman. Fred was short and stocky, in his 40s with a deeply lined face. Friendly and gruff all at the same time, Fred supervised most of what happened on the compound.

Fred then outfitted me with the standard Forest Service issue—a hardhat, knapsack, first aid kit, snake bite kit, and bedding. Fred also loaded me up with fire fighting training manuals to read in my spare time, of which I had a lot in the first few weeks. I devoured them eagerly, trying to get a quick handle on this new occupation.

The next morning my forest service career began. I started by staining picnic tables we were building for the campgrounds, to replace those washed away in the devastating 1964 flood.

I soon discovered I was working with some real characters, all older men. First there was Jack Byers, the station carpenter. Jack was a sixty-year-old right-winger and soul-mate to Archie Bunker. Always current on the latest conspiracy theory, he loved to grouse and complain and take the most negative slant on things.

Next was Jim Stevens, an affable sixty-year-old who took care of the public campgrounds on the district. Jim was a real teaser and a classic "dirty old man," always interested in the love lives of the younger guys.

Then there was Frank Fazakas, the slash crew foreman, another ex-navy lifer. In his fifties going on seventy, Frank was the classic bureaucratic type. His first priority was getting along in the organization and not displeasing his boss. His next priority was his own personal comfort. His last priority was getting any work done.

Last but not least was Bud Flack, a cantankerous codger who had worked for the Forest Service many years. Unlike the rest, Bud was native to the Klamath River area. He limped around on a bad knee, harboring bitterness regarding whatever had caused it.

We worked together on the picnic tables, building them out of huge timbers. I was enjoying myself immensely, a dream come true. When 10:00 a.m. rolled around, Jim Stevens shouted over to me that it was time for a coffee break. That concept was foreign to me, and since I was having so much fun, I just happily kept on working.

As I was working away, Fred came over. I forget what he said exactly, but it slowly dawned on my naive brain that I was violating a sacred ordinance—*nobody* refrained from joining in the coffee breaks. It was written in stone from the foundation of the world: "At 10:00 a.m. and 3:00 p.m. *there will be* a ten minute coffee break that will last fifteen minutes with all employees back at work by 10:30 and 3:30."

In all my seasons at the forest service, I've never seen anybody opt out of the coffee breaks. And to think, on my first day there, I almost defied a solemn tradition that went back to time immemorial. I shudder to think at how close I came to an offense that would have branded me forever as outside the bounds of civilized society.

The coffee break is a time rich in variety and meaning: coffee is consumed, junk food is eaten, gossip is bandied about, information is exchanged, news is announced, opinions are freely exchanged on a variety of topics, and work is rarely discussed.

These conversations would be picked up again at the noon lunch break and the afternoon coffee break. However, at 5:00 p.m., it all ended as the men clambered into their pickups and drove away, leaving the compound deserted while the shadows of the sunset slowly climbed the surrounding mountains.

At the beginning of the summer, life was lonely after work. Everyone went home leaving just a few of us on the compound.

I had never lived so hemmed in by mountains. On the one hand, they were beautiful and so close at hand! Their presence was protective and reassuring. But on the other hand, they limited, they closed in, they made the world small. In the evening, the sun went down much earlier behind the high mountains. Likewise in the morning, the mountains shut out the sun until well after dawn.

The seasonals hadn't arrived yet and there was no social life. I was too young to hang out at the bar like Wilbur, and I had no car to go anywhere. So I spent many evenings wandering down by the Klamath River, checking out the old dredger piles, and singing plaintive songs from the D. Hobbs Songbook.

FRED, WILBUR, AND TOM

Fred Clark was an interesting guy to work for. I'm sure he was the navy's equivalent to an army sergeant. He was comfortable dealing with men, used to being in charge. He was often loud and sometimes pugnacious, partly because of his personality, and partly because he was deaf in one ear. Only five feet six, Fred could be intimidating by the force of his presence alone. He once had two great addictions in life—cigarettes and coffee. But now, although his face was deeply lined from a lifetime's smoking of unfiltered cigarettes, he had quit smoking and was down to only one addiction—coffee—which he consumed in prodigious quantities.

I liked Fred. He became like a father to me. I readily submitted to his gruff ways, finding underneath an honest, caring man.

I was fascinated by his way with men. He understood how to manage them in ways I had never seen. For instance, we might be standing on the compound talking, when one of the other crewmen would wander over to see what we were talking about. This would irritate Fred, yet he would say nothing, ignoring the other person completely. Instead he would trail off talking to me and look down at his notes on the clipboard he always carried, studying them more and more intently. And thus we would stand frozen: me, puzzled and waiting; the other fellow, trying to figure out what was going on; and Fred, totally engrossed in his notes as though they revealed the secret formula of Coke. Finally, the attention span of the newcomer would wane, and he would wander off again, looking for something more interesting. No sooner would he be out of earshot when Fred would look up from his notes and resume the conversation exactly where we had left off as if nothing had happened!

This was Fred's subtle approach, but by no means his only one. If involved in a more urgent discussion, or if the interloper was out of Fred's graces, he could bark with the best of them, "Don't you have something you should be doing?" But the subtle approach was more classically Fred, and he used it to perfection.

Fred didn't show any obvious favoritism. He was diligent and a hard worker and he expected everyone else to be the same. But in his gruff way, he maintained a friendship with me that went beyond the working relationships he had with the other summer help, to many of whom he seemed authoritarian and old fashioned--out-of-step with the new generation.

In addition to the older, mostly ex-military men, there were two younger men to whom the Forest Service was their primary career: Wilbur Straight, the tank truck operator, and Tom Beers, the helitack foreman. Wilbur was at least six feet tall and weighed over 300 pounds. He had been a star football player in high school. Tom was barely five feet tall and probably weighed less than 125 pounds. But their differences went deeper than size. Wilbur could fix you with a scowling stare that could stop the boldest man in his tracks. Tom on the other hand was friendly and harmless. Wilbur didn't say much. He had to make an effort to be friendly and polite, whereas to Tom it was second nature. Wilbur was a loner-bachelor while Tom was a contented family man, doting on his wife and young children.

But in spite of these differences, both were energetic and equally dedicated to their Forest Service jobs: Wilbur driving the tanker truck, and Tom on the helicopter.

When the bunkhouse got full Wilbur asked if I wanted to take the other bedroom in his trailer. That made me feel good, because it meant he considered me the least weird of all the guys who had come so far. So I moved into Wilbur's place, which offered more peace and privacy than the bunkhouse.

Though I lived with Wilbur all summer, I never got to know him well. He didn't eat with us in the mess hall. Instead, he cruised by nearly every night in his pickup to the Wildwood for his supper and night's entertainment of drinking beer and watching TV. Then just about the time I was going to sleep, he would return, causing the whole trailer to shake, and me to jump awake as his 300 pound frame hit the attached metal step outside the door.

MY FIRST FIRE

Upon my arrival, Fred had given me all kinds of books to read on forest fire fighting. Among the equipment he gave me was a knapsack, in which he told me to make up my own fire pack, including a change of clothes, extra pairs of socks, blanket, jacket, map, and any other personal items I might want to take with me on a fire. He had stressed the importance of time, that “once the fire alarm goes off, grab your stuff and run, and you might not be back for two weeks." So I diligently made up my fire pack and hung it on a hook in my locker. It had everything but my hard hat, which I wore around the station.

It was my second week on the job, and there hadn't been any action. The fire danger was still in the *moderate* range, so the few temporaries who were there were working on the slash crew with Frank Fazakas. It was a quiet day in the middle of the week. Wilbur was off; in fact even our tanker was away in Yreka at the maintenance shop being repaired. In its place, they'd chained a 500 gallon water tank to a three and one-half ton flatbed truck, with a water pump and some fire hose hooked up on the back. We also had this antique fire truck, a skinny model from back in the '30s that still worked if you could get it started.

It was midmorning, and I was puttering about my work when suddenly the fire alarm went off. Immediately my mind went to panic mode, and I started running around like a chicken with its head cut off. The words "Fire! Fire!" were going through my brain, and I started running toward the tanker bay. But as I was running, suddenly the words "Hard hat! Hard hat!" took over in my mind, sending me running to where I had left my hard hat. But after grabbing that and heading back toward the tanker, the words "Fire pack! Fire pack!" started firing in my beleaguered brain, and I had to turn around again and dash back to the barracks, scrambling through the clothes hanging in my locker to fish out my fire pack.

By the time I got out of the barracks with my hard hat *and* my fire pack, and headed toward the tanker bay for the third time, Fred already had the makeshift tanker roaring down the driveway in a cloud of dust. For a second, I felt like the guy who missed the train going home for Christmas. Luckily, I was able to jump into a pickup truck driven by Charlie Feheley, the Horse Creek Guard.

We raced off through town in hot pursuit of Fred in the slower tanker. We gained on him steadily as he headed up Seiad Creek for about a mile and caught him just as he was turning into the driveway to someone's house.

Pulling up to the house, we were primed and ready to spring into action even before getting the vehicle stopped. Yet the house was strangely quiet, with no sign of anything amiss: inside, outside, or around the back. There was no fire or even a wisp of smoke.

We parked and jumped out as Fred was dismounting from the tanker. Behind us, Zack was coming up the driveway in his pickup. A sheepish looking woman appeared on the wooden porch. "The dryer," she said, "in the laundry room..." she made a vague waving gesture toward the house. We rushed into the laundry room, but there was nothing. The woman was apologetic. "I'm sorry," she said. "I turned on the dryer and the room filled up with smoke, so I called you." Something had shorted out in the dryer and some insulation had burned off the wires, filling the room briefly with smoke before the fuse had blown.

We reassured the woman that she had done the right thing by calling us, and we had all been fortunate that no fire had occurred. Then Zack called on the radio and cancelled the alert, and we headed for home. Just as we were pulling out of her driveway, Jack Byers came driving up in the old antique fire truck. He had struggled getting it started, and even running its ancient engine had no power, but he had gotten it there. We gave him the raspberry for not arriving until the call was over. Finding himself the butt of the joke, he unleashed a tirade of cursing at the hapless tanker, and we all went home.

Though it had been a false alarm, I was impressed with the speed and the *size* of the Forest Service's response. Not only were all the forces available at our station dispatched, but our dispatcher called the Forest Dispatcher in Yreka, who alerted the other districts and put a fire restriction on the radio channel so it couldn't be used anywhere on the forest for anything other than our fire. If the fire danger had been *high* instead of *moderate*, both the Happy Camp tanker to our west and the Oak Knoll tanker to our east would have automatically been dispatched, and the air tanker at the Montague airport would have been sent with a load of fire retardant. "Boy," I said to myself, "these guys don't mess around!"

I had waited a long time for this moment, but still hadn't been ready when it had come. And when it did come, it turned out to be a dud! But none of this mattered. My feet were wet; I had crossed the line; I was a real live fire fighter.

THUNDERSTORM

All of my life, I had heard Smokey Bear say that nine out of ten forest fires were caused by man. But one look at the forest service's own statistics at a training session in Yreka revealed just the opposite: the vast majority of forest fires were started by lightning.

I developed the habit of watching the sky as the cumulus clouds developed during the course of the day. Due to the dryness of the air, they usually didn't turn into thunderheads, but dissipated in the evening when the sun went down. But when conditions were right, look out!

Twice a day the dispatcher in Yreka read our weather forecast over the radio, including the chance of thunderstorms.

When the chance was high, and the clouds were building, a tension came over the ranger station. The lookouts were consulted on how the clouds were looking up there. If the weather continued to deteriorate, work crews were called back to the station, lightning packs were loaded into pickups, and canteens were filled.

It didn't take me long to experience my first thunderstorm. It came in June, even before our helicopter arrived. The weather forecast was grim, clouds had been building ominously all day. By afternoon the tops started flattening out into dark and menacing thunderheads.

Normal work was forgotten around the compound. Fred was busy showing us how to check the lightning packs and batteries, yet he stayed close to the crank phone in the warehouse, listening for the different rings as the lookouts and Dick Leslie talked back and forth to each other. Usually, the many rings of the phone were ignored, but on a day like this, when he heard a lookout call the office, he surreptitiously picked up the phone in the warehouse and listened in on the conversation. Then he would announce to us, "China Peak's seeing thunderheads over the Marble Mountains," or "Lower Devils reports buildups south of Horse Creek." We also listened for static crackles on the little AM radio in the warehouse that indicated flashes of lightning.

About 4:00 p.m., we got reports that one thunderstorm was moving out of the Marble mountains towards us and another one was moving through the Horse Creek area, about fourteen miles upriver. We could see the dark clouds around us and hear distant rumbles. The slash crew had been called in but wasn't back yet, and the timber people were still out in the field, so there were not a lot of us at the station. Wilbur Straight was the first up, with a seasonal. This was unusual because the tank truck operator (TTO) normally wasn't sent out to fight lightning fires. He was kept at the station in case the tanker was needed for fires near the road or structure fires. However, the choice of veterans was thin. Both Tom Beers and Zack Walton were off the district at the time, having been sent down to the huge Wellman Fire on the Los Padres National Forest in Southern California.

So Wilbur and a temporary were sent out on the first report of a fire in the Grider Creek drainage, close to the Marble Mountain Wilderness. There was no road up Grider Creek, only a trail. But there were logging roads up Walker Creek, the next drainage over. They planned to drive up one of these logging roads to a spot on the ridge between the two creeks, and then hike back to it from there, hopefully finding it before dark.

Next to go was Charlie Feheley, the Horse Creek Guard, who was sent with another fellow to the first fire reported in the Horse Creek area, his beat.

At that point, Fred told me that Chuck and I would be next. Both of us were rank rookies, but Chuck had grown up around Horse Creek, the son of a local rancher, so was at least familiar with the area. And he was a good head. I think Fred had a measure of confidence in us, not based on our experience, but on each having a degree of intelligence and common sense. Anyhow, they didn't have a lot of options that early in the season with so many people gone.

Not long after came a call from Dick Leslie that a local rancher had spotted a smoke near Horse Creek and to send out the next crew. After some last minute instructions from a worried Fred and an equally concerned Dick, we were off. Though I had read the fire fighting manuals given to me by Fred, neither one of us had ever been on a fire. We were to drive up to a gravel road just past Horse Creek where the rancher would meet us and take us to the fire.

Chuck was driving the Forest Service pickup barely under the speed limit. We were both pretty excited. We got to Horse Creek and found the rancher, an older fellow in an ancient pickup. We followed him up the gravel road for three-quarters of a mile. He pulled over on a turn in the road and pointed. There it was, rising out of the canopy of trees a distance away: a straight blue/white plume of smoke! Our adrenaline leaped. Then he took us up the road to the spot he figured was nearest the fire. We parked, unloaded our gear as he drove off, and we were on our own.

The fire was only one-quarter of a mile off the road on roughly the same level. It was burning briskly in the pine needles and duff of the forest floor in a circular area about twenty-five feet in diameter. Fortunately, the ground was fairly level and the forest was open with no large concentrations of fuel to worry about. We did what all the books told us to do—scraped a fire line down to mineral soil around the fire as close to the burning edge as we could and then sat back and let it burn out inside the line.

Once things were under control, we started looking around. I was amazed when I found where the lightning had struck. It hit a dead, half-rotten old snag with such force that the tree literally exploded, sending chunks of wood and bark up to 100 feet away. For some reason, the tree that was hit didn't catch fire. If it had, we would have had some real problems, since we didn't have a chain saw, and it would have burned like a Roman candle.

As it was, one of the exploding pieces apparently caught fire during the explosion and started the fire where it fell, a good distance away. And we got there before the fire could burn back to the snag .

As darkness fell, we kept one little part of the fire going for a warming fire and used it to heat some C-rations for supper. We used one of the empty ration cans to warm some water for tea. By this time, the fire had burned down to scattered, glowing embers. I experimented with the pee-pump in Chuck's lightning pack by putting the suction line in my canteen and attempting to spray a fine mist of water over the still-glowing coals. But I couldn't get the pump to work.

We reported in on our radio that everything was under control and asked what we should do. Dick told us to come back in whenever the fire was out. We were also listening in to the radio conversations of the other crews. It sounded like there were a lot of fires, and many of them didn't seem to be going as smoothly as ours.

We were still excited and wanted to be back where the action was. We figured if we stayed out all night on this fire, as soon as we got back in the morning we would be sent to bed instead of back out on another fire. It seemed a better plan to go in that night and get a few hours of sleep. Then we would be fresh in the morning and ready for a new assignment.

About 10:00 p.m., we started back in. There was not a breath of wind, nor had there been all evening since the thunderstorm had passed. Under the light of our flashlights the fire looked dead, but if you turned off the flashlights and stirred it with a stick, it would pop and bright coals would flash, showing there were still hot spots under the thin layer of ashes. However, with nothing else to burn inside the fire line, and no way to get out of the fire line, it seemed safe enough. So we left and headed for home, being careful to flag our way out with white plastic flagging so the fire could be checked later.

Later we realized that if the experienced fire fighters had known what we had done, they would have flipped a lid! We weren't aware how important it is to *never* leave a fire until it is dead out. If a wind had sprung up that night and fanned some of those coals to life and blown them over the line into fresh fuel, the fire could have taken right off again! However, we were both young and zealous and ignorant of the fine points of fire fighting. It seemed safe and in most cases would be quite safe. We were fortunate that this was not the exception. No wind came up, and by morning the fire was cold.

We got back to the station between 11:00 p.m. and midnight, but the lights were still on in the office. We reported in to Dick Leslie and got an update on the other fires. Wilbur hadn't found his fire on the ridge above Grider Creek and had ended up getting lost and going straight down into Grider Creek. He found the trail along the creek and followed it downstream to the gravel road that crossed it near the Klamath River. Since his pickup was back on top of the ridge where he and the seasonal had started, he had to call on the radio for somebody to come over and pick them up. Frank Fazakas had just been dispatched to get them. Meanwhile, nobody knew what Wilbur's fire was doing.

Other than that particular odyssey, things were mostly under control. We were the first crew back in from a fire. Dick told us to get some sleep and be ready to go at 5:00 in the morning.

As I walked back to the compound, I noticed all the lights on and people walking around in the warehouse. It turned out to be men from the neighboring Happy Camp District, on standby in case any other fires showed up that night.

THUNDERSTORM, continued

The next morning at 5:00, in the first light of dawn, we assembled. Wilbur and his partner had been safely retrieved from the "jungles along Grider Creek," although their pickup was still up on the mountain. That fire had never been found, so it was top priority this morning. Also, there was another fire Wilbur had found on his way to the main fire, near where they had parked their truck. It was small and they had scratched a line around it and left it to look for the main one. So this fire too had to be checked and manned. Another guy and I were sent with Bud Flack to man the lesser fire, while a five-man crew was being sent with a forester by the name of Dick Pak to find the main fire. Jack Byers went with us to retrieve Wilbur's pickup.

It was about an hour's ride in the early morning mist up the mountain logging roads to the crest of the ridge between Grider Creek and Walker Creek. We turned off the main logging road onto a little spur road and found a place to park, right by Wilbur's pickup! Dick Pak's crewmen were already unloading their gear and getting ready to head down the ridge to try and find the fire that still had not been manned twelve hours or more after it had started. Lower Devils Lookout could still see its smoke, so there was no chance it had gone out!

We easily found our fire. It was in the thick woods right by the little spur road. It was still smoldering in deep duff within the fire line Wilbur had scratched around it. Bud directed us in strengthening the line, then in using our shovels to spread the smoldering embers out inside the line so they would lose heat and go out faster.

I was standing in the middle of the fire as I worked, raking the coals around with a shovel. Bud grunted and pointed at my feet. "You're going to burn your boots by standing there on that hot ground," he criticized.

I looked at my feet. The lug soles were thick. It wasn't as if I was standing in the midst of flames or even on a bed of red-hot coals. The fire was mostly out. Besides, my feet weren't even hot. I resented his criticism. Who did he think I was, a rookie?

"Oh I'll be all right," I assured him. Be gentle with him, I thought. After all, he's old, probably close to senile. . . . I kept working away. Besides, Bud wasn't even in the fire area; I wanted to get the fire out.

About five minutes later, I smelled something funny, like something burning. At the same time the heat began to penetrate the soles of my boots; my feet were getting hotter and hotter! The soles were starting to melt and my feet were starting to burn. At that point, I hurriedly "hot-footed" it out of there to find a place to sit down to take the pressure off the hot soles of my boots. Bud was highly amused at me sitting there with my feet stuck up in the air and didn't miss his chance to say, "I told you so."

The day passed slowly and uneventfully. We finished work on our fire in a couple of hours and then it was just a matter of waiting for it to go out.

Early in the afternoon, we had a surprise when one of Dick Pak's crew, another rookie, walked into our little camp. He told us they had found another small lightning fire just over the ridge as they were hiking in. Dick left him behind to attend it. It was even smaller than this fire, and he had built a line around it and waited for it to go out. Then he walked back to where we were, not sure what to do next, but wisely not attempting to set off alone after his original crew.

Along about 4:00 p.m., Bud began to get the idea of leaving. Our fire was out by this time, and there didn't seem to be any point in waiting longer. Arriving at the station after 5:00 p.m., we no longer had to worry about Fred putting us to work! And we didn't want to miss supper! However, before we left, since the other guy was a rookie, Bud wanted to check his fire out. So we set out, with the other fellow leading the way.

The thunderstorm had apparently traveled right down the ridge, sending down a bolt of lightning every few hundred yards, some of which started fires and some of which didn't. This other fire was right on a line with ours, maybe 300 yards away. However, it was over the top of the ridge on the Grider Creek side, whereas ours had been on the Walker Creek side.

As we came out into the open and looked over the Grider Creek Valley, suddenly for the first time we could see the main fire. It was at least a mile away, on the far side of a lateral ridge rising up from Grider Creek, sending up a convection column with a great quantity of smoke!

As soon as we saw the convection column, we knew there was trouble. As we watched, an air tanker flew over and dropped fire retardant on it, another sign that it was out of control. We watched for awhile, then walked down and checked the other fire. It was out; he had done a fine job. Then soberly, we headed back to our pickup.

As we arrived at the pickup, another crew pulled up in our

ancient "crummy"—a van-like vehicle with two bench seats and a cargo area in back—with Frank Waldo at the wheel.

Frank was the second-in-command under the District Ranger. He was taking in another six men to help Dick Pak. Radio communication had been lost with Dick early in the afternoon. I was learning that our old army surplus radios and GSA-supplied batteries were a constant source of trouble. No one down at the station knew what was going on, though it was apparent from the convection column of smoke that the fire, which had been named the "Bark Shanty Fire," so far was winning.

The sun was sinking in the west as we watched them march off into the trees, just as the sun had been rising in the east as we watched Dick Pak's crew march off into the same trees that morning. We wondered what was in store for them that night. I don't think any of us was anxious to trade places with them.

We drove back to the ranger station, had warmed-over supper, and caught up on the news. Everything on the district was in good shape except for the Bark Shanty Fire. That fire had the Fire Control office in Yreka worried. Zack Walton, our own head fire fighter, and Tom Beers were gone, and Dick Leslie our dispatcher was new. All our seasonals were rookies. Then there was the fire itself. Even twenty-four hours after it started, it was still mostly an unknown quantity. Frank Waldo hadn't gotten in until dark, but his initial report was that the fire was on very steep terrain that made fighting it difficult. Then his radio started malfunctioning too.

In the face of the continuing difficulties in handling the fire, that night the decision was made to upgrade the status of the fire from a simple lightning fire to that of a campaign fire, and to start committing resources to it on a large scale, lest it get away from us completely.

Therefore, still another, even bigger crew was put together to go in first thing in the morning. It would be led by Walt Robinson, probably the most woods-wise, experienced man on the district. Walt had grown up in Seiad. He was a quiet, powerful man who worked forest-wide as a "cat skinner."

There were nine on Walt's crew, including some brought in from other districts, and me! So I would make the fire after all! We were the third crew sent in to the fire, each one bigger than the last, none of which had yet come out!

So once again in the early morning mist, we were disembarking at the spur road high on the ridge. But this time, I was heading to the fire myself, crossing the line from observer to active participant. It was a feeling both scary and exhilarating.

As we headed down the ridge, we came to the same open clearing where we looked out and saw the smoke from the fire the previous night. This early in the morning, there was just drift smoke.

The fire was on the far side of a large spur ridge that came off at right angles to the main ridge on which we were standing. To go directly to the fire would have entailed hiking down into a deep ravine that separated us from this spur ridge. Instead of that more direct route, we continued along the main ridge at almost right angles to the fire, until we came to where the spur ridge joined. Then we turned down it, always staying on top where the walking was easier and there were no steep downhill or uphill climbs. This was an important lesson—to stay on top of the ridge, even if it meant going the long way around. The steep slopes, brushy bottoms, and rocky outcroppings made this wisdom irrefutable.

Under Walt's expert guidance and steady pace, we arrived at the fire in about an hour. The first thing we saw was smoke rising in the trees ahead of us on the crest of the ridge. The trees were thick, so I could never see the entire fire at once. But it stretched about 100 yards along the crest of the ridge and then several hundred yards downhill, something like four to seven acres in extent.

The night crew under the direction of Frank Waldo had done a good job in knocking the fire down. It was still pouring out smoke, but there was little active burning.

We soon learned firsthand the problem posed by the extremely steep slope. A 100% slope is a forty-five degree angle. This slope was about 90%. In some places it was impossible to walk uphill unless you first cut steps in the soft earth; otherwise you would slide back down as fast as you went up. That's how they had lost the fire the day before. Burning material, especially pine cones, kept rolling out of the bottom of the fire, carrying it ever farther down the slope. So our first job was to dig a huge trench under the fire, deep enough to catch all the rolling material so that wouldn't happen again during the heat of this day.

With all of us fresh troops there at just the right time, we were able to jump on it quickly and keep it from coming back to life. Some worked at digging the trench and improving the fire line, while others fanned out through the fire, knocking down hot spots and beginning the process of mopping up. Then it was only a matter of time until the job was done.

Meanwhile, others began constructing a helispot on the ridge just past the lower edge of the fire. They wanted to bring in a helicopter to establish dependable communications, ferry in a fire camp, and take out Dick Pak's crew who had been there for twenty-four hours.

By noon the fire lines were all built. Cutting down the burning trees was the only problem remaining. This provided some excitement however, as when this yahoo named Stan from another district decided to fall a massive, dead, burning tree. The best procedure was to fall it uphill, since the falling distance would be less and there would be less danger of it getting away down the steep slope. But trees on a slope have a tendency to lean downhill, which makes falling them uphill difficult. However, this Stan fellow "knew what he was doing," and he spurned all the attempts of others to caution or counsel him.

He put his undercut in on the uphill side, just like in the book, and then started his back cut, meanwhile yelling at us watching above him to get out of the way because the tree would be coming at us. Because of its obvious downhill lean, we found that hard to believe, but we dutifully moved back a little.

As his back cut progressed, he put wedges in the cut to keep the tree from settling back on the saw. Then we heard the loud pops of the heartwood snapping and the tree began to fall. It began to fall all right, right back at him! He had to fling the saw aside and run for his life as the tree hurtled downhill, hitting the ground with a tremendous crash, and then sliding right out of its bark! It took off downhill like a giant battering ram for a hundred yards or so, uprooting small trees and crushing everything in its path, until it crashed into a giant boulder and thudded to a stop. It ended up adding an acre to the size of the fire by forcing us to extend the fire line down to where the tree had finally come to rest. We joked that if the tree hadn't been stopped by the boulder we might have had to chase it all the way to Grider Creek!

The crew finally got good communication established between the fire line and the ranger station. By afternoon, the helicopter was able to land and start ferrying in men and equipment. It was a tight spot, however, with only one way in and out. The pilot had to fly in over the pad and turn 180 degrees in the hover position before landing. Then he was in position to fly out the way he had come in.

The first order of business with the helicopter was to fly the fire camp in and Dick Pak and his crew out. They had been the first on the scene, had valiantly fought the fire all during the heat of the day yesterday, through the night and again today, and were exhausted. They were sent out and even more men brought in to replace them.

I was excited to see the helicopter up close. We hadn't gotten ours yet, so one had to be brought in from somewhere else. I couldn't wait for us to get our own and start working with it.

With fire camp set up, we got a hot supper instead of rations and then tried to find a flat spot to lay our paper sleeping bags out for the night.

The next day at last it was my turn to be flown out. I had never ridden in a helicopter. It was an amazing sensation to hear the engine wind up and see the rotor-wash blow forest litter in all directions, then to feel the slight lurch of the seat beneath me as we came off the ground, and finally to be out in the air over nothing.

The forest dropped rapidly away as we flew out over the canyon. For a few breathtaking minutes, we had the greatest view of the forest imaginable, truly the "eagle's eye view." But then, all too soon, we were approaching the ranger station.

The journey from ranger station to fire had taken almost three hours by pickup and on foot. Therefore, it seemed we must be in the middle of nowhere. This made the quickness of the return surprising. Only minutes after takeoff, the pilot was setting us down in a field beside the ranger station—he didn't seem to know about our heliport—and we had a joyous reunion with Dick Leslie, Fred, and others.

I got back filthy, hungry and tired, but having the time of my life. Then, for the first time I had to make that tough but glorious choice that became so familiar but no easier over the years—what do I do first: shower, eat, or sleep?

If life never got any more complicated than that, I could have lived "happily ever after" right there.

THE HELICOPTER ARRIVES

Having a campaign fire on the district so early in the summer caused no small stir in the Forest. Especially chagrined were Zack and Tom, who came back from Southern California to discover what they had missed right on their own district! But there was no time to mourn; the helicopter was due to arrive, and we had to get ready.

Back on the station, I told Fred about my experience with the pee pump not working. He let me check the pumps in all the lightning packs, and I found that many others didn't work either. For a full day, I worked on all the broken pee pumps in the station. Those I could fix, I did. The rest we threw away and ordered more. Now at least we knew they all worked.

As soon as Tom returned, we busied ourselves checking our equipment and preparing for the helicopter's arrival.

Out of the Fire

The guiding force behind the "cherrying out" of the base heliport was, of course, Tom Beers, the helitack foreman.

Tom loved to dote over every little detail and get it all just right. Fred Clark was incredulous at some of Tom's touches, like the "Seiad Base Heliport" sign, complete with its own little roof to keep the rain off and the painted plywood boxes to cover our fire extinguishers from the weather. Many times when I told Fred what Tom was having me do, he would shake his head and bite his tongue to restrain himself from railing against such "frivolous projects."

At last the day came for the helicopter to arrive. Late in the afternoon, we heard the first faint beating of the rotors in the distance, growing louder and louder. "It's the helicopter," Tom shouted, and we raced on foot over the road around the rock piles to the heliport. The helicopter came in with a rush of sound and wind as the pilot guided it to the huge red metal "H" on the middle of the raised pad with the windsock whipping crazily in the rotor wash. He shut off the engine and climbed from the bubble cockpit. Ducking the still spinning rotor blades, he came out to greet the impromptu, assembled crowd.

We were greeted by a shock of surprisingly blond, wavy hair over the smooth, round, boyish face of Dave Dreyfus, a friendly fellow still in his 20s. As soon as I saw him, I thought, "Now there's a Californian for sure." He looked like he had stepped right out of one of the surfer movies. Later, when the mechanic arrived by company pickup, he turned out to be even younger.

Both of them were single. They were not only young and handsome, but had glamorous jobs and were from "out there"—from the bigger, more exciting world beyond the narrow confines of the Klamath River. This made them instantly the most eligible bachelors on the river.

With the helicopter in place, a whole new phase of training began. I learned to use hand signals to communicate with the pilot over the sound of the rotors and engine. I learned all the gear associated with the helicopter: "D" rings and "O" rings; parachutes and cargo slings to get supplies into small lightning fires. Especially important was the 110-gallon "L.A." water tank that attached between the skids, which Dave could use to drop water like the big air tankers.

SAWYERS BAR FIRE

One warm July evening, we were on standby playing our usual volleyball game, when Dave Dreyfus came running down the driveway towards the compound shouting, "Fire! Tom! We got a fire! We got a fire, Tom!"

His words had an electric effect. Wilbur spun around and started running towards the tanker bay. The guys started scurrying around for hardhats and fire packs. Fred was yelling at Dave, trying to figure out the details of the fire. But Dave was still yelling at Tom, and Tom and I were racing toward the heliport. At this point, nobody but Dave knew anything about the fire, and Dave was running toward the heliport with us, shouting orders to his mechanic and leaving the tanker crew behind milling in confusion. As we were running through the gate at the rear of the compound on the way to the heliport, we finally made out what Dave was yelling between gasps, "Sawyers Bar's burning, Tom. The whole town's on fire."

Sawyers Bar was due south of us, beyond the Marble Mountain Wilderness area on the Salmon River.

Dave already had the helicopter fired up before Tom got enough information out of him to realize we hadn't even been dispatched yet.

Tom knew his protocol. "We can't leave without a dispatch," he cautioned.

But Dave wouldn't be denied. "Just tell 'em we're on our way," he shouted happily. He was revving up the engine now, going through his preliminary checks for take-off.

We had everything ready to go anyway. The empty, aluminum water tank was attached underneath; the pump, gas can, hose, and powdered fire retardant were all secured in the cargo baskets.

Tom was non-plussed, caught between Dave's enthusiasm and proper Forest Service procedures. He tried to get a direct answer via the radio from Yreka. We were waiting.

But Dave's enthusiasm knew no bounds. "Just tell 'em we're on our way," he shouted again over the roar of the engine, pulling upward on the "collective" in his left hand to increase the pitch on the rotor blades. I saw the rush of air beat the ground on the pad, dislodging small pebbles. Then we were off the ground in a hover, feeling how the machine responded to its load and the air conditions. Tom looked at me helplessly; I raised my eyebrows and shrugged. It was out of our hands.

Totally absorbed in the art of flying, Dave cautiously pushed the cyclic stick in his right hand forward, tilting the main rotors so they began to push some of the air behind us, edging us forward. We moved ahead slowly out over the miniature parking lot, and then picked up speed steadily over the small rocky field beyond. Crossing the dilapidated barbed wire fence that marked the property boundary, he pulled back slightly on the cyclic stick, the translational lift kicked in, and we were airborne. We were over the Klamath River turning up Grider Creek when we finally got official orders to go to the fire!

Grider Creek is the most direct route into the Marble Mountains. It runs pretty much in a straight line from the Marbles down to the Klamath, emptying into it just downstream from the ranger station.

It was a spectacular sight flying up Grider Creek in the still evening air, with the late afternoon sun reflecting off the white granite of the Marble Mountains. It was the first time I had seen their beauty, and the position of the sun and the vantage point of the helicopter couldn't have been more dramatic. As we got into the mountains themselves, we could see the high mountain lakes spread around the bases of the peaks.

We had gained quite a bit of altitude flying up Grider Creek and over the lakes, but as we approached the crest of the Marbles, the ground got closer and closer as it rose steadily to meet us. We were approaching a magnificent white rock face that was the pinnacle of the mountains. We were gaining altitude, yet the top seemed still above us. Higher and higher and closer and closer we got. Then we rushed over the very peak of the mountain with only twenty feet to spare! For one breathtaking moment, I could make out every feature on the ground below: every rock, every stunted bush.... Then we were past.

The first thing that caught our attention, once we looked up from the ground falling away rapidly beneath us, was a huge convection column of smoke dead ahead. Excitedly, we pointed it out to each other. "Man oh man it's really burning," Tom exclaimed. The origin of the smoke was below the tops of the ridges out of sight, so we couldn't see any flames—only the smoke boiling up from the caldron below that had been Sawyers Bar.

Sawyers Bar was an old gold mining town built on the Salmon River. It was never very big, but was the only town for miles in either direction. Back in those days, the "highway" was a winding gravel road along the bottom of the Salmon River Canyon, paved only through the town itself. It was about twenty-five miles from Sawyers Bar up over Etna Mountain to the town of Etna and civilization, or twenty-five miles downriver to the practically nonexistent town of Somes Bar—the so called "end of the universe" where the Salmon River emptied into the Klamath.

There had been a bad fire in Sawyers Bar's recent past, when half the old town had burned to the ground. This time, the other half was burning, especially the historic hotel. I never heard the cause of the fire.

By the time we topped the last ridge and descended into the Salmon River Canyon near the town, the old buildings were completely gone, just heaps of fiery coals. The modern buildings that had been built since the last big fire were still intact, but the destruction of the historic town was complete.

The problem that faced us was that the fire, having consumed the buildings, was roaring through the forest outside of town, heading up the face of the canyon toward the top of the ridge. Our immediate task was to set up a pumping operation from the Salmon River and start making water drops on the leading edge of the fire to help the hand crews on the ground stop its forward progress.

We set down on a gravel bar by the river and immediately unloaded our equipment. We took the gasoline-powered pump to the water's edge and threw the heavy drafting hose with its one-way valve into the river. I began thrusting it into the river rapidly and repeatedly, forcing the water farther and farther through the drafting hose until it reached the pump. When it did, the pump was ready to be started.

In the meantime, Tom had stretched out a fifty-foot section of one and one-half-inch fire hose from the pump to the helicopter and hooked on the special mixer nozzle. The nozzle was a device that let us mix a powdered fire retardant called "Gel-gard" into the water as it was pumped into the helicopter's tank. Gel-gard was a seaweed material dried and powdered as fine as flour and dyed red. When it was mixed with water each particle expanded to many times its size and the water in the tank became like soupy tapioca.

In only a few minutes we were set up and filling the helicopter's tank. Soon it was full and ready to head for the fire. I yanked the nozzle out of the tank and fell back while Tom gave Dave the thumbs up hand signal meaning, "clear for takeoff."

With 800 pounds of water in the tank, Dave was fully loaded. But the river served as a great "runway" for him to build up air speed and altitude before heading up the ridge to the fire. For a couple of hours till dark finally stopped us, we kept up the process. By each of us working together perfecting the system, we got to where Dave was able to make a round trip in six minutes, meaning that we were able to strategically place about 1,000 gallons of retardant on the advancing edge of the fire every hour.

The fire boss had Dave dropping the retardant along the top of a spur ridge where they hoped to stop the fire. With the bright red dye in the retardant showing him where he had made his last drop, he was able to lay a line of retardant right up the ridge. He started out dropping where the ground crews were working, greatly helping them knock down the flames as they scratched a fire line up the ridge trying to catch the fire's moving front. Then he gradually moved out ahead of them, knocking down the fire beyond them and slowing its advance, allowing them to catch up with it.

At one point, we had to shut down briefly when a big air tanker arrived to make its drops on the fire.

An air tanker working in mountainous country is an awesome sight. But these big airplanes have very limited maneuverability and have a hard time flying in and out of canyons.

I recently saw a Hollywood fire-fighting movie that included a lot of footage of air tanker drops. These shots showed the air tankers flying down inside the forest canopy, dodging trees and surrounded by licking flames, even hitting an occasional burning snag! Such ridiculous Hollywood fantasizing tends to trivialize the very real drama that these planes and their pilots engage in every day. The danger is real enough and the flying skill required is high. These huge, lumbering planes are loaded with 3,000 gallons of retardant. They skim the treetops as slowly as they dare to get their retardant right on the edge of the fire where it's needed.

In a real situation like this, where they are dropping on a ridge, the planes will come limping down the ridge with full flaps, getting so slow they are almost at stall speed, which is still over 100 mph. Just when you begin to wonder if they can ever make it out, they will drop 500-1000 gallons of retardant and hit full throttle, every nut and bolt in the plane groaning as the pilot tries to pull his plane back into the sky. Off he will go down the river valley a long way, gradually building up speed and altitude to pull up out of the canyon and start his long turn around. Then, 5-10 minutes later, there he will be again, limping back down the ridge, ready to drop another 500-1000 gallons at just the last minute.

These big planes, like the B-17s, carried 3,000 gallons, usually in six 500 gallon tanks, which they could drop one, two, or more at a time. They were very ponderous and gave up a lot to the helicopters in flexibility and maneuverability. However, if you're the fire fighter on the ground trying to stop a hot fire, there's nothing like 1,000 gallons of red slurry cascading through the trees onto you and the leaping flames. An accurate drop can knock down a lot of fire!

While at first we thought we would have to shut down because of the air tanker's activity, its long, slow runs gave us the idea of working together with it, making our drops while he was turning around. Dave could hide below the ridge with his helicopter until the tanker was safely past, then sneak in behind him and drop his load!

When the darkness finally shut us down for good, we secured our equipment and caught a ride into town—or what was left of it—for a bite to eat. They gave us a government meal chit. The maximum for dinner was $3.00, which in those days was pretty good.

As we were eating in the restaurant, many of the fire fighters who had been out on the line came up to us, excited over how our drops had helped them stop the fire. Then the district FCO came over and told us the same thing. Dave, especially, was on cloud nine, so excited over what he and his helicopter had been able to accomplish. We were a smashing success, which was a great feeling.

By the combined efforts of the air tanker, our helicopter, and the ground crew, we had stopped the fire at the ridge. Since fires usually slow down at dark, the night crew had no problem completing the task of bringing the fire under control. By the time morning came with the next burning period, the fire was fully throttled, left in the hands of mop-up crews to finish.

We spent the night in paper sleeping bags on the gravel bar by the helicopter. The next day we were on standby in case anything happened. This was also a good opportunity for the "big wigs" to get recon flights in the helicopter to "inspect the fire scene from the air." Towards the end of the day, they released us to fly home, arriving back in Seiad Valley about suppertime, full of tales of glory.

Those back home on the tanker crew were disgruntled. They had missed the whole thing! They had gotten only as far as Cade Mountain, the high point between Seiad and Happy Camp, to cover for Happy Camp whose tanker crew was sent farther south to cover for the Ukonom District, whose tanker was called to the fire. They sat on the tanker on Cade Mountain for several hours till dark and then were sent home.

"Hey, Dave, do me a favor," Wilbur growled at Dave Dreyfus, "the next time you hear something on the radio, don't come running back through the compound yelling, 'Fire!'"

What had been a great adventure for us had been a painful disappointment for them. I was being favored with a lot of exciting experiences, but the question "why me?" or who was behind it, never crossed my mind.

THE GOOSENEST

One morning, the forest dispatch center in Yreka sent the helicopter off to the Goosenest District on the east side of the forest. I was to follow in the helitack truck. Since I didn't know how to get there, I was to go to headquarters in Yreka and "report to a man by the name of Lee Morford. He'll tell you how to get to the Goosenest."

The forest went through a remarkable change as I progressed the fifty-odd miles upriver from Seiad to Yreka. With every mile, I got farther from the ocean, the source of the forest's life-giving moisture. By the time I reached Yreka, the vegetation was mostly dead grass and brush with only scattered, stunted pine trees left to remind me of the towering forests of Seiad and Happy Camp.

It was almost noon when I reached the forest headquarters. Because it was Saturday, the front doors were locked and I had to use the back entrance. Down the hall was a sign over an open door that said "Fire Control." I walked in, but the office, dominated by a huge radio console and speakers on every wall, was empty. There was another door open on the side of this office. I went over and looked in. Inside was an older man sitting at a desk frozen in absolute stillness. I stood there looking at him with wonder. He was frozen in an unnatural position, like someone had hit him playing "freeze tag." Then his eye happened to look up and see me standing there. Seemingly without moving a muscle in his body, he pursed his lips in a silent "shhh" sign. I didn't know if the Russians had landed, if there was a cat burglar in the next room, or what.

Suddenly, his hand shot out in a blinding flash at something on his desk. "Got him!" he exulted triumphantly as he held up a squished fly, "got him!" This was Lee Morford.

Lee Morford was the Assistant Fire Control Officer for the forest. He was in his 60s and readying for retirement, though his face behind his rimless "granny glasses" still had a boyish shine of excitement to it. His glasses helped give him a scholarly look, an impression enhanced by his pale complexion and slight figure.

The scuttlebutt was that Lee was still living in the world of yesterdays, oblivious to present-day realities. I wanted to have an open mind, but the fact that he was totally immersed in catching flies while the east side was on fire from lightning didn't do anything to build my confidence that things were well in hand while Lee was holding down the fort.

I told him who I was and he drew me a simple map of how to

get to the Mt. Hebron Ranger Station. Then he gave me a meal ticket for lunch and sent me on my way. His boyish enthusiasm and disarming friendliness to me, a total stranger, made me feel guilty for thinking such negative thoughts about him, yet without altering the underlying reasons for those thoughts.

Past Yreka, not only was the vegetation different, but the topography changed abruptly from the steep slopes and narrow canyons along the Klamath River to broad valleys interspersed with widely separated mountain ranges. These broad valleys offered a much more expansive feeling than the hemmed in, cloistered feeling down on the Klamath.

I traveled south to Granada, then east through the wide Shasta River Valley. Turning north on 97, I went over a mountain range and dropped into Butte Valley, a wide expanse of high desert containing the tiny town of Macdoel and the Mt. Hebron Ranger Station, the headquarters of the Goosenest District, the largest on the forest.

The Goosenest District, at its extremities, was approximately thirty-eight miles wide and another thirty-eight miles long, so it existed in an area of almost 1,450 square miles. There was always a lot of fire activity on the Goosenest. It was drier in climate, and it consistently received more lightning strikes than the rest of the forest.

I arrived from my 100-mile journey all fired up, ready to save the forest, only to find the helicopter parked and Tom and Dave inside drinking coffee and telling war stories with old Vern Lewis, the weather-beaten FCO. There had been lightning that morning which had started a few fires, but the fires were all manned and under control. Maybe Lee Morford catching flies in Yreka was all right after all.

The spirit at the Goosenest was easy going—a world apart from the rest of the forest. The Goosenest's most distinctive feature was district ranger George McCloskey, a pure westerner from his cowboy boots and faded jeans to his cowboy hat. George was a thoughtful man who spoke in a good-humored drawl. He smoked filter-tipped cigarettes and had a peculiar way of chewing on the filters and rolling them around in his mouth as he talked. He used to join us in the afternoons as we sat on the tree-shaded lawn in the shadow of the ranger station, watching the thunderheads build around us. He'd sit and talk with Tom and Dave, chewing on his words as he chewed on the filter of his cigarette, watching the clouds and telling war stories.

This was my first experience out in the adult world of work and "real life," and I was subconsciously studying everybody I met to see if that's who I wanted to be like. Did I want to be a homespun philosopher like George, a highly moral man like Tom, a dashing adventurer like Dave...? Who was David Hobbs supposed to be?

NEVER A DULL MOMENT

Because our helicopter was the only helicopter around, and because a helicopter had many uses in such rugged and inaccessible terrain as the Klamath National Forest, we were often called upon to perform duties other than fire fighting. Other branches of the Forest Service had an occasional need of our services, such as the engineers going into a remote area to survey a new road. We would fly in, build a helispot and then ferry them in with their supplies on Monday and out again on Friday.

We were sometimes called upon by private industry for their work crews in much the same way or for aerial reconnaissance.

So, whether it was the engineers, private industry, or fires, we were always on the go. It was the perfect job, and the perfect mix of fun and adventure, more than I could have asked for.

We were not only on the go a lot, flying all over the forest, but being away from the station gave Tom and me some pleasant "slack time." Dave would drop us off in some remote spot near where he was working and then we would have nothing to do but sit and talk while we awaited his return.

I remember one time somewhere on the Happy Camp District. We were perched high on a wide spot in a logging road at the top of an old, replanted logging block, with nothing but the grass and young trees below us and the sweep and roll of the mountains off into the distance. In such a panoramic setting, sitting on some rocks waiting for the distant beat of the helicopter's rotors to signal his coming, we talked about the important things of life. Our hearts opened up as we relaxed in the warmth that comes from hearty friendship.

Tom was a person who ran deep. Things *meant* something to him: the forest meant something. His family meant something. His job meant something. Doing what was right in a given situation meant something. He looked out over the sea of green forest below and said, "Dave, when I sit here and see all those green trees below, and think that I had a part in keeping them green—protecting them from a devastating fire... you know that's what life's all about." Most people today would assume he was a religious fanatic, but as far as I could tell, he didn't even have a religion. He was just a very moral man.

In many ways I envied Tom. His convictions seemed to satisfy him and give purpose to his life. Looking at life through Tom's eyes made it look simple and clear. Though I was having a great time and enjoying many exciting experiences, I wasn't any closer to figuring out life's enigmas, or even how to become a guy with such clear-cut convictions like Tom.

LIVING ON THE EDGE

As the fire danger gradually increased throughout the summer, there was a similar rise in tension among the fire fighters. Each day the forest was a little drier. If a fire started, it would spread faster and burn hotter than yesterday. There was a combination of mental stress from always being under the threat of fire, with the physical stress of working seven days a week without a break, starting in July and lasting into September. Whether we were on the payroll or not, still, like a soldier in wartime, we were always on alert. The fire call could come at any time. And when it came, whether we were on duty or off, we went.

When on duty at the station, we had to be able to be on the fire truck and out the gate within two minutes of a fire call, no matter what we were doing when the call came. Off duty we were allowed a longer response time: five to ten minutes. But even in the middle of the night, should the forest dispatcher call and dispatch us to a large fire 800 miles away in Southern Calif., we had to be dressed, packed, and ready to go within fifteen minutes. With that hanging over our heads, it is no wonder that tension and stress became a part of everyday life.

It was not unusual for us temporaries to be out cruising logging roads in somebody's car on a warm summer's night, relaxing, drinking a few beers, and listening to eight track tapes. Then, on our way in for bed about 10:00 p.m., to notice the lights on in the dispatcher's office. There would be Dick Leslie making up a list of people to send to the Angeles or the Los Padres for a fire that we hadn't even heard about yet.

The threat was always there, for fires locally or for campaign fires far away. The lookouts in their towers felt the tension too, as they were the first line of defense in detecting fires on the district.

As a helitack crewman, I didn't have to worry about being sent at night off the district, as the helicopter couldn't fly at night.

This didn't apply to local on-district fires however. One night I was dead asleep about two in the morning when a boot hit the outside step of the trailer, the door flew open, and Zack's voice boomed out, "Wilbur, let's roll, we've got a fire! You too Hobbs, let's go!"

Instantly I went from a deep and peaceful sleep to a mad scramble to don shirt and pants and the almost impossible task of quickly lacing up my high topped, lug-soled boots. Wilbur didn't bother lacing his boots, but rumbled past me with laces flapping wildly. When I caught up with him, he was rolling up the tanker door, with others straggling out of the bunkhouse, while Zack was telling him that a motorist passing by in the middle of the night saw a fire along the highway west of us. He had driven right through the ranger station to Zack's house and pounded on his door, waking him, and Zack, in turn, had come back to roust us.

We headed out on the back of the tanker in the cool, damp air, not knowing what to expect. Even though at this time of night the fire danger was low, still, a fire was a fire. The potential was always there. And if it was a structure fire... they were dangerous any time!

When we found the fire, however, we were surprised and relieved to find only a sleeping bag smoldering on a pile of rocks between the highway and the river. How it came to be there burning I'm sure would make an interesting story, if it could only be known. As it was, all we could do was roll out the rubber "hard-line" hose and douse the ruins of somebody's night's sleep.

The next day, the fire prevention technician would go out and try to obtain evidence on how the fire started. In the meantime, we would head back and resume our troubled night's sleep.

We arrived back to the station to find the lights on and Dick Leslie in his office. Fred Clark was also there—called from his home in Hamburg—and Frank Fazakas: all for a burning sleeping bag on a pile of rocks! "These people don't mess around," I marveled for the "nth" time. I was awed at the instant fire fighting power that had been assembled even in the middle of the night.

The tension on me was not as great as it was on Zack or Tom. I felt the pressure day by day, but mostly I found it exciting. I was needed, I mattered. In fact I mattered so much that the dispatcher wanted to know where I was at all times, even off duty. I was needed so much they wanted me to work seven days a week. This was heady stuff in an impersonal society where almost no one really seemed to matter, where even births and deaths were noted only in tiny squibs in the newspaper. Here I was important; here there was excitement; here we were living on the edge; here I was fighting a foe in a war in which we were always the good guys. I wouldn't have traded that summer for anything.

RISING TENSIONS

From the very beginning, 1966 had started out to be a bad fire season. There had been low rainfall that winter and a warm and dry spring. The summer's weather was near normal, which is dry and hot. Temperatures along the river customarily rise into the 90s during the afternoons, and during hot spells, into the 100s. The humidity is low and there is very little rain from May 1 to Oct. 1, leaving the forest continually drying during the summer.

Other factors like thunderstorms and chance fires were about normal. But what proved the greatest threat that summer was the wild card of arson. The forest did indeed have some arsonists working, and the worst seemed to be in Happy Camp.

We began to pick up arson fires there from the middle of the summer on. As the forest got drier, they grew progressively worse. Forest Service investigators had a suspect in mind. It was a secret investigation, so I didn't know any of the details. But they were playing a cat and mouse game with him; tailing him, trying to catch him in the act. Sometimes we would hear the investigators talking cryptically on the radio, "going south down the creek," or "just lost him," etc.

Still the fires continued. And, as the forest became drier and drier, the increasingly serious fires were stretching our resources to the limit.

In the meantime, we kept perfecting our helicopter initial attack strategy pioneered at the Sawyers Bar Fire, with the three of us flying to the fire with the empty L.A. Tank attached and the pump, hose, and powdered fire retardant in the cargo baskets.

Upon arriving at the fire, we would search out the nearest water source, set up and start shuttling hundred gallon loads of retardant to the fire, knocking down the hottest spots until the ground crews arrived with hand tools.

We made one crucial adjustment after a fire in Ukonom, which is a one and a half hour's drive from Seiad. Before the fuel truck could get to where we were working the fire, our two and a half hour fuel supply in the helicopter was exhausted, and we had to shut down and wait. After that we started packing four 5-gallon "Jerry

Cans" of aviation gas in the cargo baskets to every fire.

There was a particularly bad fire in Happy Camp in August, caused by arson. It started on a hot afternoon and almost blew up on us. We hit it with everything we had. Our helicopter dropped retardant along with air tankers from Montague, Medford, and Redding while ground tankers and crews from surrounding districts arrived as fast as they could get there. Because the fire was on fairly level ground, we were able to bring in cats from nearby logging crews. But even with all this fire fighting power and the organization working flawlessly, the fire got up to one and a half acres in size and almost got away. Once the speed and intensity of a fire reaches a certain "break-out" point, it becomes unstoppable. It doesn't matter what kind of organization or resources you have. All you can do is let it run and stay out of its way!

This fire was similar to other fires we had been picking up around the forest, many of them also arson. Tom recognized this trend and commented on it after the fire: "We've been doing pretty good picking up these fires before they get away. The whole [fire fighting] organization's been working just right. It's like a well-oiled machine. But each fire seems to get a little closer to taking off. Any one of these fires could have blown up into a major fire, but we've managed to hold them all to an acre or so. The question is, how long can we keep holding them before one finally gets away from us?"

Tom was prescient. We were outstanding as a fire fighting organization. But our margin for error was approaching zero. As the forest got drier and the fire danger increased, it was taking everything we had to stop the fires barely in time. But could we hold on for the balance of the summer and prevent the "Big One" from happening, or would our luck finally run out?

Such was the tension as we approached the end of August and the first of September. The fire danger was reaching its climax. The forest was tinder dry from the pine needles on the forest floor to the middle of the big, decaying logs. Humidity was at a dangerously low level. The days were hot and the late summer winds were blowing over the ridges. All conditions were reaching their climax as we entered the month of September.

On the other hand, the inevitable turn of the season was approaching. Summer couldn't hang on forever. The days were getting shorter and the sun was getting lower in the sky. Sooner or later the weather had to break and the fire danger ease. The end was almost in sight, but could we reach it?

If it was just a question of waiting out the danger of chance events or the possibility of a thunderstorm, there was a good chance we could. But the evil of arson is that it's not chance. It is intentional and so is likely to occur at exactly the worst times. Knowing we were looking for him with all our resources, would the arsonist hold off? Or would he defy us and strike again? The forest was tense as we awaited the answers to these questions.

THE BIG ONE

Labor Day, Sept. 5th, dawned just like any other day. The fire danger was high and the temperature was hot. Logging and most of the activities in the forest had been shut down because of the fire danger. All the seasonals were on the station, ready to go at a moment's notice. The forest was tense. Yet people went about their daily chores.

During the afternoon, a hot, dry wind sprang up, blowing up-river from the west. At our 3:00 p.m. coffee break, we were sitting in the shade at a picnic table by the barracks, listless in the heat, when Wilbur came back from the office and announced, "Happy Camp's gone into *extreme* fire danger; their fire index just hit 100!"

This news jolted us out of our doldrums. A fire index of 100 is the highest fire danger measurement! *Extreme* was as high as the fire danger could go! A tense hush settled over the forest. Even Fred Clark didn't seem interested in whether or not we were getting any work done.

Wilbur went over to the tanker bay to monitor the tanker's radio, while our break lengthened in the shade. Only a half hour later, Wilbur suddenly shouted over to us, "Happy Camp's got a fire!" Almost simultaneously the station fire alarm went off and pandemonium erupted. Most were running for the tanker, while I was running the other direction toward the heliport.

It was much later I found out from Tom that the investigators had grown weary of the cat and mouse tailing of their suspect. Several fruitless weeks had gone by since the last fire. It looked like he was aware he was being watched and was being good. Finally, they decided to drop their surveillance. The very next day the hot, dry wind hit, the fire danger "pegged the meter," and the blood red "EXTREME" fire danger sign was hung out to warn the public. It also officially advised the arsonist that the best time of the summer for arson had arrived. Not thirty minutes after the sign was hung, he went into the woods near Indian Creek and torched it off. The "Big One" had begun.

Out of the Fire

We raced to the helicopter and cranked it up. Underneath the 'copter between the skids was the L.A. Tank. In the two cargo baskets were five 5-gal. cans of aviation gasoline and our water pump, hose, pump gas, and retardant.

With a full tank of gas in the helicopter, the extra gas and pumping equipment in the cargo baskets, and the full complement of people, we were heavily loaded. The day was hot with the temperature near 100, which also lessened the helicopter's lifting power. But with the strong headwind blowing up the river, we had no trouble taking off. Dave picked us up off the pad, skimmed over the parking area and the small rocky field beyond to pick up air speed, and then zoomed over the broken down barbed wire fence and into the sky towards Happy Camp.

We headed westward down the Klamath River, gradually picking up altitude as we went. Approaching Happy Camp, we came to a place where the river looped far to the south to go around a high ridge of mountains called Thompson Ridge. Here the road turns south following the river for a number of miles, then finally crosses the ridge south of a peak called Cade Mountain, hitting the river again as it loops back north, and then on into Happy Camp. Between Cade Mountain to the south and the Slater Butte lookout to the north, there was a dip in the ridge called Shinar Saddle. We could see the smoke from the fire westward through the saddle, several miles north of Happy Camp.

We had enough altitude to fly over the saddle, but as we approached it, we seemed to go slower and slower. Dave pointed to the altimeter gauge, which showed we were sinking! The wind, which was whistling out of the west right into our faces, was being funneled through the saddle, increasing its speed even more. But as the wind crossed the saddle, it followed the slope down on the other side, creating a monstrous downdraft that was sucking us earthward. Dave already had the helicopter's power maxed out. We were helpless before the greater power of the wind.

"I can't get over the ridge," Dave shouted in frustration. "The downdraft's too strong. I'll have to go back and take another run at it." He turned the helicopter around and crossed the river to the slope up the other side, gaining altitude quickly as we hit a strong updraft. Now the wind was helping, lifting us with it as it blew up the next ridge.

Fortified with seemingly plenty of altitude, we started back over the river towards the saddle once more. But as we approached the ridge, this time far above the saddle, again our ground speed stalled, again the altimeter started to drop. We were up against an impenetrable wall of air!

Dave began loudly cursing himself for not thinking of offloading the five cans of aviation gasoline before leaving the station. Since we were only going to Happy Camp, the cans were not needed. The fuel truck would arrive in thirty minutes. All the while, we could see the white smoke churning into the sky from the fire directly ahead of us over the uncrossable ridge of mountains. The obvious urgency of the situation only heightened our frustration at not being able to get over this "one little ridge."

"We'll have to follow the river around." Dave finally accepted defeat and embraced the only alternative. We turned south and followed the loop of the Klamath along the steadily descending ridge until we finally reached a point where it was low enough that we could scoot across and head back north. We skirted east of Happy Camp, turned west, and approached the fire head-on in our original line.

It was an awesome sight. We never reached the main fire, which was a furnace of boiling smoke over another ridge near Indian Creek. But already on the forest floor beneath us were numerous spot fires caused by burning embers raining out of the sky, landing an incredible one-half mile in front of the main fire that was just getting started! Each spot fire had an orange-red intensity of its own, like the lurid glow of a road flare. And each one of these little spot fires burned with an intensity that would have been hard to stop were it the only fire in the forest! And yet they were everywhere. And they were only the spot fires—the advance troops, as it were, of the roaring main fire that was still in its first half hour of existence! "The Big One" was here.

We didn't bother getting any closer to the main fire; we had seen enough to know what lay before us. We turned back and landed on a gravel bar near the Klamath River southeast of Happy Camp and started the same pumping and dropping operation that had proved so successful all during the summer. We filled the helicopter's water tank again and again as Dave made strafing runs at the fire. But this time it was to no avail. "I might just as well be peeing on it," he said discouragingly during a break to refuel.

Down on the river where we were, we couldn't see the fire, but the column of smoke it generated got bigger and climbed ever higher in the sky. The tremendous amount of energy being released by the fire's intensity caused the water vapor near the top of the column of smoke to condense into a towering thunderhead—the sign of a major fire!

As ineffectual as our water drops were, still, there was nothing better to do. Since we hadn't been given any other orders, we continued until evening.

When we could fly no more due to darkness, we shut down the operation, drove into town, checked in at the ranger station and picked up some meal tickets. Next, we headed to a local restaurant to get some supper.

During the hours of darkness, forest fires usually "lay down for the night" as the heating power of the sun is gone, temperatures fall, the wind diminishes, and relative humidity rises. The Indian Ridge Fire, however, was not like most fires. Starved for moisture during the winter and spring, then baked mercilessly by three months of summer heat, the forest litter was ready fuel for the roaring fire that even night couldn't stop. The sun was gone, but the wind continued fresh, the humidity remained low and the temperature warm, especially on the western slope of the ridge where the fire was burning. As we somberly left the restaurant in Happy Camp to drive back to Seiad for the night, we could see the flames leaping into the air unchecked on the mountains east of town, their fiery glow lighting up the whole night sky.

The Forest Service had been steadily mobilizing men and equipment all that afternoon and evening. As we drove back to Seiad Valley, we passed vehicle after vehicle loaded with men and equipment en route to the fire. It would be a sleepless night for them and many others. Now it was their turn to be called out in the middle of the night and sent far away to our fire.

For us though, there would be sleep. But as we each lay down in our respective beds that night, in my case in Wilbur's trailer, we had no idea how close the events of the next day would make this to be our last night's sleep on the earth.

BLUE PAINT AND SPLINTERS

The next morning, we continued our totally ineffective retardant drops on the raging fire, which had burned unabated throughout the night. The weather was a carbon copy of the previous day, and things looked grim indeed. I guess we can be glad the arsonist started the fire in a place where the winds would carry it away from town. If he had started it west of Happy Camp, the whole town would have burned to the ground.

Late in the morning, the order came down to halt our water dropping. Those in charge were going to try another strategy. They were going to pull back and try to stop the fire on Thompson ridge, the one with the saddle we couldn't cross the previous day. They wanted us to relocate our operation to the top of the ridge and fill our helicopter's tank from a mother tanker. The mother tanker was capable of filling our helicopter's tank many times over. The tanker would be our source of water, instead of having to fly water up from the river a couple of thousand feet below. Meanwhile, as we slowly emptied the first mother tanker, a second mother tanker would be ferrying water up from the river.

So we loaded everything into the cargo baskets and headed to the top of the ridge. The smoke was awful, but we finally found where the heliport had been constructed with the mother tanker sitting beside it.

Pandemonium reigned supreme, as it always does on a rapidly spreading fire. The fire fighting forces were already strung out over at least ten miles of dirt logging roads and fire trails. Communications were poor, and in some cases, non-existent, yet plans had to change rapidly because of the fluidity of the fire situation.

By the time we landed at the top of the ridge, the plans had changed again. The new set of orders stated that we were to leave our pump and gas with the tank truck operator and fly back to Happy Camp. They had decided the smoke was too thick to fly near the head of the fire, and anyway, they wanted to use the helicopter to reconnoiter the fire instead. It was spreading so rapidly it was hard for them to keep track of.

As it turned out, the stuff we had to unload was all from the left cargo basket on the pilot's side. With the cargo in the left basket gone but the right basket still full of other stuff, the helicopter was out of balance. Seeing this in a moment of time, we realized we had to switch all the gear from the right cargo basket to the left to bring the helicopter back into balance.

The cargo baskets were made of aluminum tubing, crisscrossed at intervals on the bottom and sides. The tubes were not close together, meaning small articles like hose fittings could fall through. To protect against this possibility, we had cut a piece of plywood the size of the cargo basket bottom, about four or five feet long and maybe two feet wide. It was stout plywood, three-quarters of an inch thick, and fit so snugly into the basket that you had to jam it in to get it to the bottom. We had painted it blue as another of Tom's little touches.

In our rush to move the equipment from the right basket to the left, we didn't even think about this board on which all of the gear had been sitting. We didn't need it in the left basket, and since it was hard to remove anyway because of its tight fit, we just left it where it was. We didn't even bother strapping it down, since it certainly wouldn't shake loose, and the force of the wind blowing down from the rotor blades would also help to hold it in the basket.

So in a flash, we moved the cargo to the left basket and strapped it down with bungee cords. Then we lifted off from the ridge and sailed out over the trees, which dropped away quickly down the steep slope. To get under the smoke streaming over the top of the ridge, Dave cut power to the helicopter and we lost altitude quickly also, staying a few hundred feet above the trees as they descended toward Thompson Creek. With minimum power, the engine noise was muted and we could hear the wind whistling up through the rotor blades.

Suddenly there was a tremendous crash and the whole helicopter shook. We jumped out of our skins! For one tense, agonizing moment we froze, waiting to see what would happen next. What had broken? What had been disabled? What would disintegrate?

Flying a couple of hundred feet above the tops of 200 foot tall trees on a 70% slope is not where you want to be with helicopter trouble. To crash land into such a canopy would mean almost certain death. You would hit the tops of the trees, break apart, and then free-fall 200 feet to the ground.

But the engine kept running. The rotors kept turning. There was no other explosion or noise. There didn't seem to be any fire. Once that Eternal Moment passed, the questions came, the wondering started. What had happened? Tom and I looked questioningly at each other, worry and perplexity all over our faces.

Suddenly Dave blurted out, "Is that board still in the cargo basket?"

Since I was on the outside, I leaned out the door and looked down at the cargo basket. It was empty! I was flabbergasted. "No, it's gone," I shouted back over the noise of the engine and rotors.

Dave was furious. "You #%&'s are trying to kill me!" he screamed.

We were totally chagrined as Dave quickly brought the helicopter back to the heliport on top of the ridge and shut off the engine. When the rotor blades finally stopped, there it was! A streak of blue paint about five feet long ran the entire width of one of the blades! The force of the wind from our rapid descent had hurled the board into the blade, and the blade had struck it with such force that it had actually transferred the paint from the board to the rotor blade!

Fortunately, the main rotor blades on a helicopter are incredibly strong. If the blade had been damaged at all by the board, it would have become unbalanced and the resulting vibration would have thrown us out of control and out of the sky. We were also very fortunate that on the right side of the helicopter where the board hit the blade, the blade was traveling forward, hurling the debris from the board harmlessly in front of the ship. If it had been on the other side where the blade was going backward, the blade would have hurled the debris into the tail rotor, a much smaller rotor spinning many times faster. Because it is smaller and lighter, it is much more easily damaged, and because it spins so fast, the slightest damage to it would have resulted in a tragic imbalance that again would have made the helicopter un-flyable and cost us our lives in the forest below.

We had been spared, by something beyond our power, to live another day. But I'll never forget Dave's anguished scream—"You guys are trying to kill me"—torn from the depths of his soul in a sudden, horrendous revelation.

Dave was not really accusing us of trying to kill him. But those words, torn from the depth of his soul as he faced eternity, were not entirely wrong. In that moment, he was more prescient than we were, as I was to find out later.

STALL OUT

The Indian Ridge Fire burned out of control for two days. The plan to stop it at the top of Thompson Ridge was all in vain. As long as the hot, dry wind blew, nothing could stop the raging flames. Not long after our harrowing brush with death in the helicopter, the fire came roaring up the ridge and the futility of the fire bosses' plan became obvious. Fred Clark had been sent with the tanker to try and save Slater Butte Lookout. He told me at the spot the main fire hit the top of the ridge, the flames were leaping 200 feet into the air. But even before the main fire got to the ridge top, spot fires were already starting on the other side, sending burning material rolling all the way to Thompson Creek, and burning back up toward the top. With fire approaching the ridge top from both directions, hurried orders were given for everyone and everything to get out.

But not all were able to make it. The only escape route was the south end of the logging road along the top of the ridge. On the north, the road didn't go through. Some crews farther in couldn't get out before the advancing flames overran the road. Turned back by the flames, they followed the road in the other direction until they reached the dead-end.

They were trapped! Cut off from their escape route, out of touch by radio with fire camp, blanketed by dense smoke, with out-of-control fire raging all around them, for agonizing hours that afternoon their fate was uncertain. Were they dead or alive?

Finally, late in the afternoon, word came that they had been found! At the end of the logging road was a cut-block, an open area that had recently been logged and cleared. They were able to huddle in the middle of the cut-block while the fire roared around them. A couple of Forest Service vehicles, including Zack's pickup, and a bunch of loggers' trucks, including a fuel truck, went up in flames. But the men were spared. They all walked out alive!

Then, after two days of extreme fire weather and uncontrollable fire advance, the weather abruptly changed. The long-hoped-for break in the weather had come. The jet stream high above shifted and started blowing out of the north, bringing cool, moist, Canadian air down over Northern California. The fire lay down. It continued to burn, but only creeping slowly through the forest—its wild, untamed days were over. Now it was the fire fighters' turn to advance and bring it under control. We had come just two days short of getting the forest through the whole fire season practically unscathed!

Since the Thompson Creek drainage into which the fire had come was steep and without roads, helicopters played a major role in setting up field fire camps at strategic spots along the ridges and flying men and supplies in and out.

The fire bosses had been calling for more helicopters just like more of everything else. By now there were five. All but one were the small three-seaters like ours. We set up a base heliport along the Klamath River on an old gravel bar. We used this as a ferrying point to the many helispots and small fire camps in the interior. For days, we worked every daylight hour, ferrying men and supplies in and out.

In those days with such small helicopters, it was a laborious process. The small Bell and Hiller helicopters couldn't carry more than two passengers at a time, or a 300 lb. sling load of cargo. Men flown into a portable fire camp would have to stay for days at a time, working up and down the fire line, while we kept them supplied with food, water and sharp tools. Even so, the first thing every morning, there would be a line of men stretching far off into the morning mist, waiting to be flown into one of the fire camps. The line kept coming until noon.

We were on the go all the time. I spent a lot of time up in the mountains at various helispots, loading and unloading men and cargo, and directing the helicopters in and out with hand signals. Other days, I was down at the base heliport, loading and unloading the helicopters and making up sling loads of supplies.

All this was new to us. Helicopter use was in its infancy in the Forest Service, and we were learning as we went along. One time, they wanted us to sling in a chainsaw to one of the crews on the line. To get it down through the trees, we tied about 150 feet of nylon line—which has a lot of stretch—to the saw which we arranged in an accordion fashion to let it play out as the helicopter lifted off. A pilot named Tom Pfeiffer was going to fly it in.

We all watched as Tom lifted off in his helicopter. One helitack crewman stood in front, giving him hand signals, while another stayed by the cord as it played out in case it snagged. Tom kept rising higher and higher. But the higher he rose, the faster he went. Soon the line was whipping out like fishing line hooked on a whale. The helitack crewman by the line leapt back as he realized the thing was out of control and the cord was reaching terminal velocity. Then suddenly, the end of the cord was reached where it was attached to the saw. The saw sprang fifty feet into the air in one mighty jerk, and then bounced up and down wildly as the rope stretched like a rubber band.

Tom said later that he had gotten so high, he had lost sight of the crewman directing him. No one had anticipated the problems of trying to sling that long of a load. Since Tom had no way of telling when he reached the end of the rope to lift the saw off the ground, he just pulled power and took off flying, letting whatever happened happen.

None of us realized at the time what a danger Tom had been in. It wasn't until several years later that we heard what happens when a sling line breaks. When the line is suddenly released from the tension of the load, it can spring all the way back up into the rotor blades and disable them, like hitting a bunch of rope with a lawn motor. Without the main rotor blades, the helicopter falls out of the sky like a rock. There are no survivors in those accidents. We were all incredibly fortunate that our small nylon cord didn't break under the sudden strain of jerking the heavy chain saw into the sky!

The weather continued cool, even sprinkling rain at times, but the job of building a fire line around the fire and actually putting it out was immense. The fire had spread so quickly and started so many spot fires that there were fingers of fire spread over the entire ten to twelve square miles of Thompson Creek drainage. Since a fire could not be considered controlled until there was no unburned fuel within the fire line, all these fingers had to either be individually encircled with fire lines, which would have been a tremendous task, or all the unburned areas left in the whole drainage had to be burned out. This second alternative would be the easier of the two, but the weather had changed so much that now we couldn't even *make* the unburned portions burn; all they did was smoke and smolder! Whatever happened, only the winter rains and snows could finish what man first couldn't stop and now couldn't extinguish.

Late one afternoon a week or so into the fire, I was down at the heliport. We were getting ready to quit for the day. Thankfully the days were getting shorter and shorter because of the advancing season. The last job—ferrying men and equipment out of a small camp high up on a narrow ridge—was almost complete. The mood was somewhat festive. We had been working hard for a week or more, but things seemed to be in pretty good shape. We might even get to finish early that day!

I was the only one not in a festive mood. I was grumpy because I couldn't get anyone to help me with the equipment that was being flown in from the helispots—all the dull fire fighting tools, cooking gear, etc. Everyone wanted to stand around and "jaw"—telling war stories and goofing off. I wanted to get the work finished first and then relax. I'd ask someone to help me. They'd help for a while and then drift back to the crowd.

There was only one more trip: to pick up the last two men from the helispot and bring them back to base. Ron, a pilot with a Hiller from another forest, agreed to get them while the other helicopters shut down for the night. Ron was light on fuel, but had enough for the trip up to the helispot and back.

As Ron was making his approach to land at the helispot, his engine suddenly threw a rod and quit running—he was without power, with nowhere to go but down.

When an airplane loses power, it has fairly good glide characteristics. It might be able to successfully crash land if it could glide to a suitable place. But a helicopter does not glide like a plane. It has no wings. If you ever take your hands off the controls of a helicopter in flight, you will be out of control and heading for the ground in seconds. Flying does not come naturally to a helicopter, but must be achieved by the continually exerted skill of the pilot.

However, the helicopter does have one advantage over the

airplane: it has the capability of auto rotating down to a single spot to land. But it is a difficult feat to accomplish, especially in the forested mountains, where safe spots to land are few and far between.

To auto rotate, the pilot must first take all pitch off the main rotor blades, letting them spin freely in the wind, their speed being maintained by the air rushing through them, like the wind will spin an unplugged fan. Without power and with the rotor blades turning freely, the craft will drop quickly, much faster than a plane. This will limit his choices of landing places. But, if he has aimed the craft correctly and reaches a spot where he can land, full pitch must be put back on the rotor blades just at the last minute, converting the momentum of the heavy, spinning blades into one shot of lift.

There is no second chance. If he pulls pitch too soon, he will stop the craft's descent somewhere in the air above his landing spot, only to have it free-fall the rest of the way. If he pulls pitch too late, the craft will crash before its descent has sufficiently slowed, destroying the helicopter, and in all likelihood, the pilot. And finally, unless he stops the forward motion as well as the downward motion simultaneously right before touchdown, the craft may tip over on impact, with the rotor blades beating it to death against the ground.

Ron's best chance, if he could make it, was to crash-land at our heliport. He did have some things working in his favor: the helicopter couldn't have been lighter, with no passengers, no cargo, and very little fuel. If it had happened after he picked up the two men, or if he had filled up with fuel first, he would have ended up as debris on the mountainside.

Also in his favor was the exceedingly steep terrain. The spot where he was to pick up the two men was thousands of feet higher than the heliport, but not far in distance, giving him a better shot at reaching the heliport—his best hope for survival.

Down below, we were completely oblivious to the life and death drama unfolding in the skies above. Nobody was listening to the radio anymore. Everybody was relaxed and having fun. Ron's urgent "Maydays" went unheeded.

Unheeded maybe but not completely unheard. There were two crewmen from the other Klamath helitack crew, 100 yards away at the backside of the heliport, sitting in their truck talking with their radio on. They heard Ron's urgent calls as he was careening through the skies towards us and his date with destiny. They heard his pleadings for a report on the wind direction, and the imminence of his crash landing, but inexplicably did nothing. Later they would say they thought we, at the front of the heliport, had everything under control, in spite of the fact that no one from our radio responded to Ron's calls.

I think they were caught, unable to shift gears and respond to the suddenness and urgency of the crisis that no one expected or was ready for. Our leaders, who certainly would have been able to respond if they had known of the crisis, were also caught off guard by their letting down and loosening control over themselves and their jobs too soon. Like so many crises, the failings of men merely set the stage for the crisis to be played out in full without outside intervention—it was just Ron and God.

Ron was approaching the heliport downriver. The reason he was desperate to know the wind direction was if the wind was blowing upriver, he could come straight in, with the wind providing lift and slowing his forward speed until touchdown—or crash down! On the other hand, if the wind was blowing downriver, he would be coming in downwind and would have to come in with enough speed and maneuverability left to do a last minute 180-degree turn to land into the wind, adding one last twist to what was already an almost impossible feat. And the wind had been blowing downriver most of the afternoon.

If only someone had been alert enough to respond, Ron would have known that in fact, the wind had died down to nothing, and he could have come in any way he wanted. Since no one was, Ron was left to guess, with his life hanging in the balance.

Routinely, off in the distance, we heard the beat of the rotor blades, the first sign that the helicopter was returning. Tom Beers casually walked out onto the flattened pile of river rocks we were using for a pad to direct him in. My own senses were so dulled by my frustrations over the lack of help loading the gear that I didn't notice that there was no engine noise to go with the rotor pop. An alert observer would have noticed that other than the beating of the rotor blades, Ron was coming in with an eerie silence!

Assuming the worst—that the wind was still blowing downriver—Ron came in low and fast over the heliport, then suddenly banked the helicopter at a sharp angle into a 180-degree turn right over our heads. Because of the steep angle of his bank, I was able to look right into the cockpit and see Ron at the controls. I still didn't have a clue what was happening... until I saw his face! Suddenly my blood froze as my gaze was riveted to his face—he looked like a man who had just seen a ghost! His face was tense and ashen with haunted eyes, like a man staring into eternity.

I had no time to reflect on this however, as events moved with lightning swiftness. Ron had to come in fast enough to be able to make his 180-degree turn. But as he yanked maximum pitch onto the rotor blades, he had to use this last shot of lift to slow not only his descent, but also his forward speed. This required more momentum than his rotors had.

Tom Beers, out in the landing zone, was not as unaware as I was. He had noticed there was no engine noise from the helicopter. And as he saw the craft bank steeply over the crowd and come around straight at him he knew immediately that everything was wrong and dove headlong into the rocks.

The helicopter hit the pad with a resounding crash. The rotor blades flopped down from the force of the landing and smashed into the tail boom, sending the tail rotor whizzing off the back of the heliport at over a hundred miles an hour, too fast even to see. They found it the next day a quarter of a mile away! Though he hadn't been able to adequately slow the descent of the craft, he had been able to kill off most of its forward speed, allowing him to right the craft so that it landed flat. This saved his life and some of ours as well because the helicopter did not tip over.

With the engine dead, the tail rotor gone, the remaining force of the main rotors expended on the tail boom, and the helicopter sitting flat on its skids, there was little left that could happen. For one breathless moment, we stood frozen in place as the last shaking of the rotors died away and a few whiffs of smoke came from the engine compartment. Then, in the silence that followed, Ron climbed shakily out of the mangled remains of his Hiller—from the cockpit, the only part of the helicopter left intact, and we surged toward him.

It was a miracle! Everything about it was miraculous! We had failed, yet all had been spared. There were so many things that could have happened. Undoubtedly, by keeping the front of the helicopter toward us and the tail boom toward the back of the heliport, Ron had saved lives. Otherwise the tail rotor would have flown towards us instead of away, decapitating people so fast they wouldn't have known what hit them. If he hadn't been able to land the craft upright, but had tipped it over so that the main rotors smashed the ground, debris would have flown everywhere, a fireball might have erupted, and again lives would have been lost, including his. And, of course, he had the fortunate circumstances of the engine failure happening at a time when he was as light as he would ever be, and at a place where he had a fighting chance to reach the heliport.

Still it must be said that Ron was a good pilot, one of the best. Later, other pilots flew up to where he first lost power and tried to duplicate his feat. Not one of them was able to make the heliport!

After it was all over, and another helicopter had gone to pick up the two men still waiting on the ridge, all the pilots trooped the badly shaken Ron off to a bar in Happy Camp to buy him a drink. The mangled helicopter was left where it came to rest, scaring the bejeebers out of the crews that came out in the first misty light of the next morning to be flown to their places on the line. To them, it was jarring evidence of the dangerous uncertainty of this mode of transportation on which they were about to embark.

The symbol was quite different for those of us who knew the whole story, however. To us, it was a monument to the mercy of a Power beyond ourselves. The trapped men had been spared on Thompson Ridge the second day of the fire. Tom, Dave, and I had been spared the same day when our helicopter made blue splinters out of the plywood board. Tom Pfeiffer had been spared when he jerked the chainsaw into the sky with the thin line that didn't break. And now Ron had been spared most miraculously of all in this crash that destroyed his helicopter but harmed no person. It should have been enough to cause me to reconsider my atheism, but I have no recollection that it did. Miraculous escapes can foster an illusion that life is more secure than it really is. Sometimes it's only when tragedy strikes close enough that we feel the grip of its icy fingers—like it did to Ron—that we are forced to re-think our theology.

A HOUSE OFF CAMPUS

September 1966

The weather had changed; the danger was gone. But the task of fully extinguishing the sprawling, smoldering, 12,000-acre Indian Ridge Fire would go on until the snow flew. But the time had come for me to switch gears from firefighter to college student.

If I were only allotted one season for my Forest Service career, the 1966 season would have been the perfect one. I fell into the right job at the right time, and the fire season itself had perfect symmetry. It started with building picnic tables and steadily escalated to the fitting climax of the Indian Ridge Fire—a blowout right on our doorstep. It had caught me up and carried me along like a mighty wave of the ocean that was ready to deposit me back on the shores of Humboldt State. It was a fulfillment of all I had hoped for.

But, whether we end up in a wearisome valley or on an exhilarating mountaintop, life goes on. And so it was that I found myself once again at the Arcata bus station with a piece of paper in my pocket directing me to an address on Wilson Street.

Ron Dupuy had been in charge of finding us a place to live in the fall. Toward the end of the summer, I got a letter from him saying that he and another dorm friend of his, Mark Pahuta, had found a house to rent on Wilson Street. Did I still want to live with them?

Lately, I had become enamored with Bob Dylan's music. I especially liked his penchant for dark and obscure lyrics. So when I responded to Ron's letter, I thought I'd be cute. I adapted some lyrics from Bob Dylan's "Desolation Row" in a typically Dylanesque, obscure fashion. The Dylan version had gone something like this:

Well I received your letter yesterday
About the time the doorknob broke
When you asked me how I was doing,
Was that some kind of joke?
Right now I don't read too good,
Don't send me no more letters no,
Not unless you mail them from, Desolation Row

So I responded to Ron by paraphrasing:

Well I received your letter yesterday
About the time the fire danger broke
When you asked if I still wanted to live with you,
Was that some kind of joke? (Meaning "of course I do")
Right now I don't read too good,
Don't send me no more letters no,
Not unless you mail them from The Wilson St. address doo(r).

Which meant: "Get the house; I'll be there soon."

I thought the meaning would be perfectly clear, but to Ron, it was absolute gibberish. He had no idea what my intentions were. But he and Mark decided to go ahead and rent the house anyway. Mark found the house through his aunt, a single mom who lived on Wilson Street with her twin teenage daughters. It was a rental house behind the house of her next-door neighbor Jerry Ward.

Meanwhile, all I had was an address on Wilson Street, and I didn't even know where Wilson Street was! I didn't want to pay for a

cab, so I walked the couple of blocks from the bus station to the police station and asked where Wilson Street was. The desk clerk didn't know where it was either, though later that year they would sure find out! He had to look it up on the city map hanging on the wall. It turned out to be a mile north in what they called the Sunset Addition. Once more I put my baggage in a locker at the bus station and walked to the address.

Boy were the guys surprised to see me and hear about all my adventures! Ron chewed me out good for my obscure message. Because of doubt about whether I was coming, they had given my spot to someone else. But they graciously made room for me in the smaller bedroom. I soon found a bicycle to ride the mile to school, and year number two was underway.

DRUGS

Things were afoot in the fall of 1966 that would profoundly alter the fabric of American life. The war in Vietnam, that I kept thinking would end, continued unabated, dragging us ever deeper into its morass. At the same time, the student protest movement that had started as the civil rights movement in the early '60s, had evolved into the anti-war movement and was growing stronger.

But the most powerful force of all was quietly bubbling and building up steam in the Bay Area of California. Soon the volcano would erupt in a mighty social upheaval that would rock the nation. I'm talking about the drug revolution.

My first acquaintance with the drug craze came while I was still home in Ohio. I read an article in Life magazine about college students taking LSD at Berkeley. The article intrigued me. I knew nothing about LSD—or marijuana either—but it sounded like something I might like to try.

In my first year at Humboldt, I had taken a mandatory health class that included stern admonitions against the evils of taking drugs. The class' most powerful tool was a movie showing a dramatization of some young men after supposedly using marijuana. These guys were lurching around outside in what looked like an alley of a big city, laughing uproariously, looking like they were staggering drunk. Then they got out some bottles of Coca-cola to drink. But they were too drunk from the marijuana to get the bottle caps off the Cokes. Instead they broke the tops off the bottles on the cement stoop and began drinking right out of the jagged stems. Soon blood was flowing everywhere as the razor points of the broken stems sliced up their lips and faces. Yet even with their own blood flowing profusely over their bodies, they were still lurching around convulsing with laughter and reveling in their "drug experience."

I found the movie shocking. The thought that this marijuana could cause people to mutilate themselves so terribly without even being aware of it was horrifying.

Later in the fall, Larry Miller came up for a visit. He was living in Berkeley with his high school friend Terry White and taking classes at Hayward State. Larry was excited because he'd just gotten turned on to marijuana. And he'd brought some up for us to try!

We were all initially skeptical. We'd heard the warnings. "I'm not gonna go slicin' myself up with no broken coke bottle."

"No, no, no," Larry kept insisting, "It's all a big lie. Drugs aren't bad; in fact they're great."

In spite of the fact that Miller was our leader, we were still skeptical. Of the four of us, I was the only one willing to try it with him. That article I had read in Life magazine had stimulated my curiosity, and I tended to be the most willing to try new things.

So Larry and I went back to the bathroom. He lit up a joint and passed it to me. He showed me how to suck it deep into my lungs, holding it as long as possible before exhaling. Even though I was used to smoking cigarettes, the marijuana smoke was harsh. Still, if it got me high, it would be worth it.

Miller got high, but I didn't. I couldn't tell any difference. With the power of suggestion, I could probably have psyched myself into something, but I couldn't say for sure that anything had happened.

When we returned to the front room where Ron and Mark were, they looked me over like an exhibit in a freak show, waiting for something to happen. They took turns saying sarcastic things like, "Well, do the colors look any brighter? How bright does my shirt look? Are you hallucinating yet?"

I was disappointed that nothing happened after smoking the joint, but Larry said not to worry. He said this was normal, that most people had to use it several times before turning on the first time. He suggested that I come down and visit him some weekend in Berkeley and try it again.

Soon, an opportunity arose for that very thing. Mark was going to the Bay Area to visit a relative and would drop me off at Miller's.

Larry lived in a house on Haste Street that had been divided into apartments. It was only a few blocks from the university that Terry attended, a hothouse for the revolution of the '60s.

Their apartment had been fixed up with a little flair, which probably reflected Terry's influence. The kitchen with its sink full of encrusted, dirty dishes definitely reflected Larry's influence. In a corner of the main room, they had a giant aquarium with a backdrop of the painting of the Last Supper. Over the entrance to the hall to the bathroom, there was a curtain of beads, making it look like the curtain to a stage. The living room was typical "college student": a couch, some chairs, a TV, and a stereo.

On the first evening after getting there, we smoked some joints, but again nothing happened to me.

This marijuana smoking, I discovered, had its own trappings. Each time before smoking it, they would light some pungent incense that filled the room with smoke. "What's that for?" I asked Larry.

"That's to hide the smell of the marijuana smoke."

Thus were millions of pounds of incense burned during the drug days of the '60s!

Another of the absolute essentials of drug use was the stereo. Listening to music seemed to be the favorite pastime of stoned people—"grooving" they called it.

The TV was not used much—it contained a lot of silly sitcoms that may have made sense to the average American, but not to the druggie. In fact, the banality of these programs seemed to be the essence of what my generation was rejecting.

The next morning after breakfast, we sat around and tried it again. This was typical of the drug culture, where the usual activity was to sit around and get stoned. Unless you had something pressing to do, like going shopping or studying for a test, you just sat around and got high. Again nothing happened to me, though Miller and White seemed to be enjoying themselves immensely.

I felt like such an outsider! After getting high, they would talk and even giggle together over things only they could understand. It was like some kind of secret society from which others were excluded.

After lunch, White had to run an errand and Larry and I stayed in the apartment and smoked some more. Again I didn't experience anything. I felt like I must be the only person in the world immune to marijuana's effects.

That evening we all sat around again to get high. Once more the incense was lit, the joints were rolled and smoked one at a time, each being continually passed around so somebody was sucking on it at all times. I was smoking away, drawing it deep into my lungs and holding it there as long as I could each time the joint came around, while the latest Lovin' Spoonful, album "Do you Believe in

Magic" was playing on the stereo.

Then it happened. A fog began to rise and come over my mind. My voice sounded different and far away. The music seemed to be coming from inside my head. I was smiling and couldn't help it, just like the lyrics of the song:

> **Just go and listen it'll start with a smile**
> **It won't wipe off your face no matter how hard you try**

"Hey, he's got it. He's got it!" Miller's voice reached me through the fog. "He's got the eternal smile!" Miller was pointing me out to White. That made me self-conscious, which momentarily brought me down. But he was right, I couldn't stop smiling. Somebody said something. I started to laugh. The fog completely enveloped me, and I broke out on top. I was high.

It was an incredible experience. The music had taken over my brain. Even in the subdued lighting, what colors that could be seen were lush and breathtaking. Also, there was a difference in my spatial perception—distances seemed magnified! Looking out through my eyes in my head was like standing on top of a great mountain, surveying the room spread out below. The coffee table was a long ways down, though it too was the top of a mesa set far above the plain of the floor. Then there was an ocean of vast space across the carpet until finally another huge structure rose up that turned out to be Miller's chair with the giant trunks of his legs in front. My eyes traveled slowly from the floor up his legs to the bend in his knees, then up to his lap. "Boy' he's big!" I thought as my eyes continued up his torso to his neck at the top of his shirt, then to his chin and mouth, through his mustache, up his nose to his eyes, only to find his eyes looking intently back at me, and had been all along. Our eyes met and bridged the gap between us and I laughed, giggled really like he and White did.

"Wow!" We were both high, and we both knew it and shared it together. Then I realized that though it had seemed like an eternity while my eyes traveled across the floor and up his body to meet his eyes, in truth it had all happened in a brief moment.

It was a new world to explore. Everything about it was new. Everything I had already experienced in life I had to re-experience while high. TV was different. Sitcoms that we might have watched before and thought amusing seemed incredibly stupid. Watching pro basketball with those grotesquely huge men running and leaping in a frenzy seemed the height of bizarre.

Music was different. The self-pitying whine of country music seemed ridiculous. On the other hand, classical music gained a new appreciation. It was so pure, clean, and light, with many textures and nuances of sound.

The ocean and the beach had to be re-experienced. The breakers were fascinating in their ever-changing varieties of motion; they could be watched forever. Mountains had more grandeur; I could sense their massive size.

Merely going through the kitchen cabinet was a new experience, as I stood fascinated by the bright colors of the various food packages. A person could really get lost in a supermarket! Wandering the aisles overwhelmed by the sheer volume of brightly colored packages calling out to you... a straight person might have to go in and get you out!

Even the simple action of smoking a cigarette was captivating, as I watched the smoke swirl up in endless patterns from the glowing tip, or as I blew a huge cloud from my lungs, and watched it spread out in a billowing fog to fill the whole room.

Music especially had a deep impact on my soul. It was as if the stereo speakers were inside my head. Listening through headphones was incredible! I completely entered the world of the music and became oblivious to my surroundings. I heard things in songs that I had never heard before: different parts and harmonies and sounds that were always there, but I had never noticed.

After grooving to music for awhile, Miller went into the kitchen and brought out some snacks. Junk food was indescribable. Potato chips melted in my mouth as my teeth ground them into buttery particles that dissolved in a rush of flavor on my tongue. Delighted, I wanted to go on to other treats like ice cream, and chocolate, and hot buttered toast covered with honey. Then Miller opened up a bottle of Coca-cola and passed it around. "Here Hobbs, try this." The effect of the carbonation in my mouth was an explosion of tingling fizz. "Wow!"

Time seemed to stretch out, but certainly not to drag. With my senses so stimulated, it seemed like a lot of time had passed, but in fact only a little had. My high seemed to last forever: grooving to music, exploring the intricacies of the smoke rising from my cigarette, gorging on junk food. By the time I noticed I was coming down a little, Larry was already firing up another joint. Finally, we wound down as bodily fatigue overcame the effects of the high.

Many years later, I heard a narcotics officer describe the drug scene as, "a bunch of people in an endless pursuit of trying to recapture their first high." He made a good point: the first time was fantastic, never quite reached again.

Out of the Fire

When Mark picked me up the next day to go back to Arcata, I was overflowing with excitement over the effects of getting high. I was also amazed at how the older generation and "The Establishment" had tried to trick us into thinking that marijuana was harmful. After my experience, I heartily concurred with Miller's assessment, "It's all lies man; it's all lies!"

Now the modern music culture made sense to me—the vibrant sound, the lyrics, the drug allusions of musicians like Bob Dylan and the Rolling Stones,—these people had turned on already and were celebrating it in their music.

With my enthusiastic testimony added to Miller's, it was not long before both Dupuy and Pahuta were turning on as well.

Miller kept coming up to see us and we kept going down and seeing him, getting high together, sharing experiences, sharing new music, and sharing new smoking techniques like the hookah pipe that bubbled the harsh smoke through water to filter it.

When Miller was up visiting us, he would go around and meet friends from the year before. It wasn't long before he found other people who were getting high too. Drugs were starting to happen everywhere in little pockets. And because drug people had the benefit of an experience that others didn't have, they could recognize each other on sight, while the straight people couldn't. The first time Larry came up, he ran into another drug user by the name of Rex. They could tell just by looking at each other that they were "heads."

It wasn't long before Larry came up with some LSD. This was what I had heard about in the Life magazine article, and it was all over the press. It was a chemical compound that gave the same effects as marijuana, but to a much higher degree and for a longer time. We agreed to take it together and see what happened.

We settled on Friday morning. Ron and Mark were in class, while I was skipping mine. Larry brought out two little pills. We each swallowed one and sat down to see what would happen.

After about fifteen minutes, the first noticeable effects came. We felt ourselves getting high, not all at once, but gradually. We decided to get out of the house and walk around. It was daytime and the whole world was out there waiting to be explored.

The world was a different place. Colors not only looked more vivid like they do on marijuana, but they also looked different—skewed in how they affected our brains. They looked funnier, as in "strange." I saw a car painted a light shade of purple, and I started to laugh. "Look at that car," I said to Miller. "Does that driver have any idea how bizarre his car looks? How could he be seen in public in such a bizarrely-colored car?"

While marijuana let us see the difference between a straight person and a drug person, it was just an observation. LSD, on the other hand, not only drew a clear line between the stoner and the straight, but it also made the straight seem ridiculous. There was a mocking, judgmental spirit about LSD that was quite destructive. On LSD, straight people were despised in our eyes: they seemed so dumb, so out of it, so inferior.

Larry and I wandered up to the college. Once there, we got the idea of revisiting our old dorm: third floor, west wing. Walking down the hallway again with rooms on both sides, it seemed so cramped, so small, so confining. "How could we have lived here for a whole year?" we wondered aloud as we walked down the hall. It seemed so juvenile. We had to get out; it was suffocating.

We didn't want to see anybody we knew because it would be hard to carry on as normal people in front of them. It would be hard not to laugh at them because they were so ridiculous. To keep from meeting anybody, we went down the steep hill to the creek that flows through the undisturbed redwood forest by the side of the campus. There was a winding, one-lane gravel road that went through the thick forest along the stream. We walked along through the woods, grooving on the sights and sounds of nature.

After awhile, we turned around and started walking back along the road. Unexpectedly, around the next bend in front of us, a car appeared, rudely interrupting the pastoral feeling of our walk. We stepped out of the road. The car went by us and disappeared around the next bend. We stepped back into the road and continued walking. If you had been observing from a vantage point above us, nothing could have looked more normal: two men walking down a gravel road; a car comes, they step out of the road; the car goes by and they step back into the road; two men keep walking down a gravel road.

But to us, it was a weird and bizarre happening. The car wasn't supposed to be there. Our present existence was in one world and the car was from another world. The two worlds shouldn't be mixed like that. The car was out of place. It was like dreaming you're sleeping in bed with your wife and then you look over and it's your sixth grade teacher. She's from another world, even another time in your life. She doesn't fit into your present circumstances.

There is a whole school of painting based on this idea of the juxtaposition of differing realities in a single moment—the school of surrealism. One of its most famous paintings is a scene of a fireplace inside a house. Coming out of the inner wall of the fireplace is a railroad locomotive—coming right out of the wall! Surrealism is very much a part of the LSD experience.

The whole episode of the car suddenly appearing on our road, going by, and vanishing again, shook us. It was unexpected. It shouldn't have happened, but it had happened. And there was no way to be sure it wouldn't happen again. The security of our pastoral scene had been compromised; we couldn't enjoy it quite as much. We'd have to give up some of our attention to be alert for more cars suddenly intruding into our world.

Later, back at our house, evening was coming on and Mark and Ron were home. They were quite interested in what we were experiencing. We were still pretty high, though not as high as before, and were in their bedroom, grooving to the music on their stereo.

It was comical because it was as if we were these freak animals at the zoo, the bedroom being our cage. And they were the weird people that came to gawk at the animals.

Mark had a young friend over who was especially funny. He would appear in the doorway, drawn out of curiosity and fascination, and say something really silly like, "So I hear you two went for a walk today." Instead of answering, we'd just laugh. It was so silly because we could see right through it. He didn't care about our walk; he wanted to know about our high.

So this guy kept coming to the door, each time with a different approach, but each time we'd see through him and laugh at him.

Mark and his friend were baffled. They couldn't understand why we were laughing at them. They sensed that somehow they were being made the butt of a joke, but they couldn't figure it out.

STUTTERING

Later on, Mark's friend had gone, night had come, and the house settled down. I was still in Mark and Larry's bedroom, lounging on Mark's bed. Larry was off somewhere, and I was left to myself. I picked up a magazine and started reading it. Then for some reason I started reading it aloud.

I had a serious stuttering problem. It had been with me all my life but hadn't gotten bad until high school, where I became insecure and very self-conscious. This greatly aggravated my stuttering, turning it overnight from a minor malady to a major problem. Due to fear that I would stutter and be laughed at, I would "block"—my throat muscles would constrict so tightly I wouldn't be able to make a sound: frozen like a deer in the headlights. It was a vicious circle.

Past embarrassments of blocking and being unable to speak increased the fear that it would happen again. The fear tightened the muscles, making the blocking worse, setting the stage for the next round of embarrassment.

In certain classes, like Spanish and Speech, we did a lot of speaking in class, which was bad. But literature class was the worst, because we went around the room taking turns reading portions of the poem we were studying, out loud! In speaking, I could select my own words. If I thought I was going to block on a word, I could substitute another one for it. But in reading, I had to say exactly what was on the page. And some words were almost impossible not to block on, such as words that began with a soft sound like "easy" or "where." Waiting for my turn as we went around the room was like waiting for my execution.

To combat the problem and to face the fear, I joined the debating team, forcing myself to speak in public. People "admired my courage" but it didn't help.

It was during this time that I became an outspoken and militant atheist. Perhaps the intense humiliation I suffered from my stuttering hardened my heart into a fierce rejection of the God I claimed not to believe in.

When I left for college, I took the problem with me. Miller used to ridicule me some, but overall, it was not as bad as in high school; in college there was little need to speak in class. I was determined but unable to overcome it. For a while in both high school and college, I received speech therapy, but that didn't help either.

Even more than the problem of the stuttering itself was the mountain of fear that had grown up in my mind over it. This mountain was so large, it dominated my life: controlling where I went, what I did, and who I was.

But now, under the influence of LSD, with its mindset that mocked everything, this mountain of fear that I had struggled under for so long suddenly looked ridiculous too! Nothing seemed more absurd than to be dominated by fear over such a little thing as speaking. Upon seeing this truth, the bubble broke, the boil was lanced, fear was vanquished, and faith and triumph sprang up in its place.

I began to read aloud from the magazine. It was so easy! The words flowed effortlessly off my tongue. I jumped to another paragraph—the same thing. By this time, I was shouting, "I can read! Hey guys, I can read!" Right then I couldn't even *make* myself stutter. There was no word I could think of that I couldn't say. Even my great uncle's name, "Eslie, Eslie, Eslie, who lives in Etna, Etna,

Etna," did not bother me. I suppose the guys thought I was crazy, or hallucinating. I was on cloud nine, but not from the drugs.

That night broke the back of my stuttering problem, even to this day. Not that I speak that fluently. I still have extra pauses and stumbles when I talk, but the mountain of fear that dominated my life during high school is forever gone.

HIGHS AND LOWS

The trip was winding down. An LSD trip typically lasts twelve hours. The last four hours were a bummer. On the one hand, the high was lifting, getting progressively less intense. We were no longer up in the heights of experience, but were drifting back ever closer to earth. But on the other hand, we *were* still high; we couldn't go back to everyday life yet. It was a weird, intermediate state, like a suspended animation. All we could do was wait, and the time seemed to drag on interminably. Our bodies were tired. Our minds also were tired from the over stimulation of the high, yet still excited enough that sleep was impossible. Coming down was a bummer.

Then there were the aftereffects.

Though the LSD gave me an intense, pleasurable high, when it was gone it left me empty and depressed. The depression started in the long coming down experience. In the days following the high, it continued, as my mind struggled to integrate what I had experienced during the high with the rest of my life, trying to bring it all into some kind of coherent whole. That was hard to do. All my life I had assumed that what I experienced every day was reality. Through drugs, I had found a totally different world claiming to be the true reality. Which one was right?

Then there was the "culture shock" of returning to the humdrum world. The world I experienced during the high was so intense—colors were vivid, music deeply felt, food out of this world. All the senses had been stimulated in such pleasurable ways that it was hard to relate to ordinary life where everything now seemed drab, mundane, and lifeless.

But more than that, the LSD experience seemed to bring into question the entire foundation of my life. I began to question all my life goals. Why was I getting a degree in forestry? So I could go out and get a lifeless job laying out timber sales? And for what purpose? To get old, retire, and die, having accomplished what? A much better plan seemed to be to explore this exciting world of drugs rather than studying to become some sort of "paper shuffler," or even a forester.

So I followed the cry of the drug generation as articulated by our guru Timothy Leary: "Turn on, tune in, drop out." That's exactly what we did: after turning on and tuning into the world of drugs, we dropped out of the old world of study and careers in order to explore the new spiritual realms of getting high.

Not that any of us immediately quit school. We continued out of habit and momentum. But the focus of my interest, the driving force of my life, was no longer on why I was going to school, but on exploring the drug experience.

The second time I took LSD was the most intense. Larry was up again for the weekend. He brought with him a couple, Carl and Sue, and the four of us "dropped" together.

During this experience, I felt an incredible love for the world. It was a feeling like eastern mysticism teaches about: a feeling of love and oneness with all nature.

We decided to drive twenty miles north to the ocean at Patrick's Point State Park. Carl was driving his station wagon, with Miller and I in the back.

Sitting in the back seat watching the traffic go by on the freeway, I was intoxicated with this feeling of love and oneness. I wanted to merge with everything and be one with the universe. As a car pulled alongside us to pass, I felt an urge to merge with it and become one with it. If I had been driving, I might have done just that: swerved our car into theirs at sixty mph! Stories like this were not uncommon in the newspapers about this time. "Flower Children" would step out onto a freeway and face the oncoming traffic with their arms outstretched, dying instantly as they "merged" with an oncoming car.

This was as close as I ever came to experiencing the hideous portrayal of the marijuana smokers drinking Coke from smashed bottles and laughing as they impaled themselves on shards of the broken glass. In a way, if only I could have realized it, this was even more dangerous. If I had carried out this drug-induced impulse, it could have cost us all our lives. However, the movie was still false, because neither marijuana nor LSD affected people the way it showed. In fact, I've never experienced any psychedelic that numbed the body from pain while granting euphoria to the mind—only alcohol does that!

Patrick's Point was a wild and beautiful setting in the best tradition of the rugged North Coast. Moreover, it was a magnificent day. A freshening south wind was blowing—the forerunner of an approaching Pacific storm. The first of the storm clouds were streaming in slow motion across the sky, though the rain itself was not imminent. The breakers were rolling over the rocks in a kaleidoscope of never-ending motion.

If my life's goal was to have powerful experiences, then that day at the ocean would rank as one of the greatest days of my life. Everything in nature seemed to be animated; everything seemed to be alive; everything seemed to have a soul.

Out on the rocks being washed by the waves, short plants were growing. With their single stalks and bushy tops, they looked like limber, miniature palm trees—an extensive forest-in-miniature being drenched by powerful, successive tidal waves. And everywhere I looked among the waves and rocks was another world of drama, action, and beauty. And above the roar of the surf, the storm clouds streaked overhead.

The clouds themselves seemed to be making a sound. There was a sound in the very heavens! It was somewhere between a musical note and a vibration, like a hum. And just as the eastern religions describe it, the sound could best be articulated as "Ohm."

Coming up the trail from the ocean, even the plants seemed to be singing and swaying together in the breeze—the whole realm of nature was alive like the cartoons where the flowers sing and dance and possess personality. And I was in perfect harmony with it all.

It was a whole universe that I never dreamed existed back in my atheistic high school days. Then I only believed in the natural world I could see. But now I was "seeing" a whole new world. Not only was I seeing it, I was walking right in the midst of it.

Back home again that evening the wonders continued. I had never hallucinated much, though Miller seemed to do it a lot. This time, I was sitting in a chair in the living room smoking a cigarette and listening to rock music with the rain now coming down outside. I stared at the lit tip of my cigarette, fascinated at the glowing coal of fire that moved and changed as the cigarette burned down. As I was listening to the rhythmic beat of the music and staring at the burning coal, the coal became a belly dancer grinding her hips in a sensuous sway in time to the music. I watched spellbound as she continued her dance as long as the coal burned in that place on the cigarette. When that part turned to ash and the fire moved on down the cigarette, she disappeared.

Coming down from that high was again very hard—the time dragged on. I just wished with all that was in me I could get it over with. In the depression that followed, I came close to suicide. In fact, I came closer to committing suicide during my times of using LSD than at any other time in my life—close enough that I was actually considering it.

However, I never put two and two together. I never figured out the obvious—that it was the LSD that was responsible for my suicidal depression. The cost of my high was the depression that followed. To me, these drugs were our own wonderful discovery. If everybody would but turn on like we did, all the world's problems would be solved. There was no way *they* could be responsible for such depression.

The next time I took LSD was in Berkeley, down at Miller's place. We "dropped" on a rainy, winter afternoon and then walked to a nearby house where a friend of his lived in the attic. This guy was in a rock band and his group had come up to the attic to practice. They were all crammed in there with their amps and drums and microphones. And there was also a small group of "wannabees" like us, who had come to watch them practice and groove along with them.

This time I got an idea of what a bad trip can be like on LSD. A bad trip is when you get high all right but it's not a pleasurable experience. In fact, it can become like a bad dream, as negative things become amplified in your experience instead of positive ones, and you can't get back to normal to deal with them. You're stuck being high. That's why there were so many drug crisis clinics around in those days. Having a traumatic experience when on LSD, like a breakup with a boyfriend, being mugged in the park, or an auto accident with injuries, could become a terrible nightmare. With everything in the experience amplified, and no way of coming down, people could be driven to or over the brink of mental breakdown.

This trip was not that bad—not a crisis trip—but it did show me what could happen. I don't know if it was the cramped, claustrophobic atmosphere of the attic; the gloomy, rainy day; the problems the band was having; or some of the strange people there. But it was a bummer—no fun at all. One "groupie" spontaneously picked up a tambourine and started playing along with the band. But he wasn't hitting it at the right times. The drummer kept leaning over to him during the breaks between songs and saying, "Two and four! Hit it on beats *two* and *four*!" But the guy didn't seem to know what "beats two and four" meant.

Maybe also it was because we were at cross-purposes with the band. We wanted to groove along with the music—let it carry us away to faraway worlds in our minds. But the band was practicing—trying to get better. If somebody made a mistake, they stopped, talked it over, and then practiced that part again. No matter that we the listeners were left stranded in some faraway world, left to hobble home under our own power as they stopped and started and stopped and talked.

None of those things would have been that serious to a straight person, but the psychedelics magnify whatever experience is happening. Good experiences become much better, while bad experiences become awful. All the disunity and cross-purposes were magnified in our minds until we had to get up and leave. The whole thing had turned into a giant "bummer." Not long afterward, the hot water heater in the attic of that house exploded. Nobody was home at the time, but the house burned to the ground. *That* would have been a *real* bummer trip!

I only took LSD four times. It was too powerful, too unpredictable, and the lows it left me in after the highs were too devastating.

It would have been very hard to remain an atheist after taking LSD. It opened me up to a vast spiritual realm of unseen forces that I had never dreamed existed. It was exciting and stimulating, but also scary and overwhelming. Because in this spirit-realm, I found out as a human how insignificant and powerless I really was.

Though LSD ushered me into this realm of invisible forces and altered reality, it provided no road map or rules of conduct for this vast new "country." It didn't reveal who the Ruler of this spiritual realm was, or what He considered appropriate conduct for those who entered His realm. The responsibility of providing answers in this area is the prerogative of religion, and I wasn't religious, nor were the rest of us in the drug culture. My impression of Christianity was that it was concerned with rules of conduct:

1) **Be nice;**
2) **If it's fun, it's wrong; and,**
3) **Love your neighbor as yourself.**

I wasn't aware of Christianity saying *anything* about this new dimension we had found on drugs.

But the eastern religions... *they* were something else! You just had to look at a picture of some of those eastern gurus to see they had what we had—those guys were high! The state they reached through their religious exercises and meditation was the same state we reached through drugs.

There was one thing for sure: I now knew there had to be a God/god in charge of this spiritual realm somewhere. As far as *who* He was, I didn't have a clue. But of the fact there was some invisible Power out there somewhere, I had no doubt. Madalyn Murray, goodbye.

I found that the psychedelic drugs had some serious downsides. I mentioned the problem of depression that could lead to suicide. Also, there was the problem of how it interfered with thinking processes, a topic too complex to get into here. But more than those, the most pervasive drug-induced side effect was paranoia. What we were doing was illegal! We could be busted at any time. The fear was always with us. Policemen became our enemy. At times when I sat stoned in Miller's apartment, I would vividly experience in my imagination the act of getting busted. I could imagine the sirens wailing, the police banging on the door, barging into the apartment, turning on all the lights, the static crackle of their radios, the confrontation with our guilt....

And there were times we would be sitting stoned in Miller's apartment when a siren would start up in the distance. As the wailing got louder and closer we would sit transfixed, waiting for it to pull up to our curb and the police to rush in. Louder and louder it would wail, until suddenly it would scream by outside and begin to fade away down the street. "Hey man," Miller would say with a nervous laugh, "when they bust you, they never come with the sirens on."

"Yeah, ha-ha, that's right." The logic of his statement somehow broke the spell, and we would return to normal.

MUSIC

It may seem strange that I went from a triumphant summer fighting fires right into the drug scene. That's because we tend to think of drugs as something that "losers," hopeless, or depressed people do as an escape. I didn't use drugs to fill internal emptiness or soothe inner pain. I was seeking out experiences in life. The fire fighting and helicopter experiences had been exciting beyond measure. The drugs were just as exciting in a different way, and music was about to ring another bell. I thought by pursuing what was exciting and stimulating, I would find the answers to the unspoken questions inside.

We were still in the experimenting stage with drugs, but they had not yet taken over our lives. The normal rounds of classes and studying went on. The changes drugs were making would be radical and profound, but we hadn't experienced their full impact yet. The seeds of major change had been sown, but we were in a period of time while the seeds were growing toward their full maturity. Meantime, momentum carried our lives forward.

When the semester break came late in January and my full load of sixteen units ended, I embarked on a new semester just as ambitious, with five units of inorganic chemistry leading the way. I also continued taking a smattering of music courses, including chorale, choir, and elementary piano.

For some time, music had played an important part in my life. In my first college year, I started taking some music classes as general education units.

During my second year at Humboldt, while I was experimenting with drugs and continuing to take general education classes in music, I began having profound musical experiences. These gave me hope that at last I might have found something in life worth giving myself to.

They started in chorale, a class where college students and community singers met for one evening a week to sing together and practice for concerts that we put on throughout the year.

Music in general was starting to come alive for me. Once I came to chorale stoned and heard the music in a whole new way. I was sitting next to the altos, the lower of the two women's parts. Their singing was beautiful! Soft, melodious, and peaceful, it was like female deer singing in the forest.

But our altos didn't seem to have a clue to the beautiful music they were making. When we came to our mid-practice coffee break, instead of sitting in hushed and reverent silence at the beauty they had been creating, they got up and started talking and laughing and gossiping. The chorus of beauty from their lips was replaced by a cacophony of noise. I wanted to stand up and preach to them, to open their eyes to the beauty they were creating when they sang, and how they were throwing it away by chattering. But how could I do that without appearing a fool? It gave me a lot of appreciation for our director, Dr. Barlow, who was able to bring them back to order, to focus on the music, and let its loveliness flow from them once more.

Another time, we were doing a religious choral piece. One number within the piece had a tenor solo—a *Sanctus*. Dr. Barlow had given the tenor solo to a man from the community who had a clear, sweet tenor voice. The combination of his captivating voice and the effortlessness with which he sang the flowing melody was indescribably beautiful.

About this time Dr. Barlow released us for our break while he stayed behind to rehearse the solo with this man. After getting my cup of coffee I was drawn back to the door of the rehearsal room by the sound of his lovely voice.

It was beautiful! Captivating! It stirred me to the depth of my soul! While listening to it enraptured, something opened up inside me. Here was something in life that had value; here was something in life with true beauty; here was something that was worth everything I had!

Spontaneously, I decided to "give myself" to music. "Here in music is something precious enough to live my life for."

THE NIGHTMARE COMES TRUE

Miller continued to cultivate the relationships he had made with other drug users on campus. That way, when he came up to visit, he could sell some of the drugs he brought up, making his trips profitable as well.

One such fellow was Rex. Rex was a big, good-natured guy who played the harmonica and had even experimented with some of the harder drugs like heroin.

Rex lived off campus and had a roommate named Dutch, an unusual chap from the southern Central Valley. Once Dutch came over with Rex and smoked marijuana with us. We all shared a pipeful together: getting high, mellowing out, listening to music, talking, and grooving. But it didn't seem to affect Dutch the same way; he didn't get high like we did. In fact, it hardly seemed to faze him at all. We were sitting around mellowed out and he still wanted to smoke more. In fact he smoked another pipeful all by himself, sucking away on it like he was smoking a pipeful of tobacco.

Around the middle of March, Miller came up to see us again. He brought along his roommate Tom White this time. He also brought some LSD and about seven "lids" (ounces) of marijuana to sell and smoke. Right after arriving, he went over to Rex's place to sell him some. But nobody was home, so he scribbled a note on a scrap of paper and left it on the door, saying something like: "Rex, I got the stuff. I'm over at Hobbs' house, [signed] Miller." That was on Thursday afternoon. That evening we were all sitting around our house getting stoned.

Mark's high school-age cousins, the twin sisters from next

door, and a red haired boy who hung around with them used to come over and spend time with us. They were our "groupies." This was the same boy who kept coming into the bedroom trying to act cool that first time we had taken LSD. They knew we were using drugs and were interested in the scene, but hadn't used any themselves.

We were back in my small bedroom that night, sitting on the floor, grooving. The bedroom had an overhead light that shone like the sun blazing down at mid-day strength. I might have been working on one of my toothpick sculptures.

One of Mark's cousins came over and said she had to talk to him. He left us still grooving in the bedroom. Then he called Miller out and talked to him. It gradually filtered through my marijuana haze that there was some sort of crisis at hand.

Mark's aunt was the typical single parent trying to work and raise a family at the same time. She didn't have any idea what was going on at our house. She had a good friend in the Humboldt County Sheriff's Department. He had called her and told her that a big drug bust was going down that night. He was concerned because he thought her daughters might be involved and wanted to warn her to get them out beforehand. She confronted her girls who told her that we were smoking marijuana, which floored her. One slipped out for a moment to warn us that something was up.

We didn't know what to make of it. It was news filtered third hand and, in our stupefied state, it was like news from a foreign country. Still we gradually got the idea that maybe we were in trouble; maybe we should take some precautions, like hiding the stuff. But the idea of what to do with it was almost more than we could handle. Being stoned is no way to face a crisis. Do we send someone out carrying the stuff to get it out of here? Maybe the house is already being watched, and he'd be intercepted. Do we throw it over the back fence and hope we can retrieve it later? We might be throwing it right into their hands. After mulling through endless possibilities, Larry finally took it and put it in an old five gallon milk can we were using as a leg to a makeshift coffee table. The mood gradually grew more somber as the fear of what might be happening grew in our minds.

Our house was on the back of the lot, with the landlord's house on the street. To reach our house, you had to go between his house and the side fence, then through a gate into his backyard. After crossing the backyard, where his dog had free rein, you had to go through another gate, and *then* you were at the cement stoop in front of our front door, illuminated by an outside light.

The landlord's dog had been poisoned once and had almost died. As a result, it was afraid of people and set up a torrent of barking anytime someone approached the fence or came through the gate towards our house.

About an hour after we had received the strange warning, the dog started barking up a storm. Our front door had a big window right in the middle of it. A few minutes later, a man appeared in the light on our stoop and knocked on the door. When we answered, he asked if we knew where such-and-such a street address was, which we had never heard of.

It was very strange. In fact, the more we thought about it, the stranger it seemed. The person himself was peculiar to begin with, kind of a hard-bitten fellow. And why he would come back to our house hidden in a backyard to ask such a question after 10:00 p.m…? It didn't add up.

This incident really shook us because it was the first concrete evidence that something really was going on. It was the locomotive coming out of *our* fireplace! Up to this point, there had been a sense of unreality about the girls' warning. But this grim and unexpected intruder brought the reality home with a sudden, chilling fear.

We didn't know what to do. We had taken all the precautions we knew. We thought our house was probably surrounded and sealed off, or at least being watched. And we preferred the security of our lighted home, fragile as it had become, to the unknown terrors of the night. So nobody left. Instead, we all gathered in the living room, sitting quietly in a circle on the couch and chairs, smoking cigarettes, listening to music, but mostly just waiting.

Sometime later the dog began barking furiously again. We froze. It was as if we all knew—this was it! Again the same man appeared on our doorstep, then others behind him. Without bothering to knock, they opened the door that we hadn't even locked, and came in, quickly fanning out through the house. Some headed down the hall to my bedroom, others came into the living room where we were sitting frozen. Without a word, they went through the living room into the master bedroom. A couple of the last to enter wore policemen's uniforms, but most were in plain clothes. Nobody said a word.

It was the ultimate surrealistic scene. Here we were sitting in our own living room listening to music when a gang of grim men marches into our home unannounced, and without a word of explanation begin searching the house from top to bottom. Finally, White got up the nerve to speak to one of them, "I mean, like who are you guys and what are you doing in our house?"

"You know very well what we're doing here," the man snapped. He was right of course, but still, there is supposed to be a certain protocol for such occasions. They finally did flip their badge identifications to us.

They were going over the whole house with a fine-tooth comb. Almost immediately they found partially burned seeds and residue in our ashtrays. We hadn't even thought of that. But they were looking for more than residue. They were looking for the big stash. Search as they would, they couldn't find it.

Then they started taking us one at a time into the master bedroom to question us while the rest were kept in the living room. They were hoping to find someone they could scare into cooperating and spilling the beans. When it was my turn, my interrogator said things like, "Do you have any idea how much trouble you're in? What are your parents going to say when they find out what you've been doing? If you cooperate with us, we'll put in a good word to the judge for you. Otherwise...," his voice trailed off, "you might not be back on the street for a long time."

But this didn't work either. We were too scared to say anything.

Finally, they read us our rights and led us in handcuffs to their squad cars for the ride to the sheriff's department. It was an overpowering feeling of shame and humiliation to be taken from my own home in handcuffs. Now I could understand the humiliation those must have felt in cases I'd seen on TV where the police would arrest some high-profile person at his office and lead him away in handcuffs in sight of his underlings. It was as if life as I knew it had ended. I had blown it so badly that they had to forcibly evict me from my own home, leading me away like a wild animal in chains to be punished. I was glad for the covering of night that mercifully hid the humiliation from the gawking stares of the curious.

Once we left our house for the sheriff's office, we were separated from each other. The idea they wanted to get across was, "You'll never see your friends again until years later after you get out of prison." The idea was to break the power of the group. They wanted to sever our loyalty to each other by getting us to feel cut off and dependent only on ourselves. Then the weak ones would crack, cut a deal with the police, and testify against the rest.

So they separated and interrogated us individually, continuing to stress what trouble we were in, how our parents would react, what would happen in the court system... hoping to find one to cooperate. As we found out later, their case against us was very weak; they still hadn't been able to find our stash.

I spent a lot of time sitting in a chair out in the hall of the sheriff's department, which took me back to sitting on a chair in the hall in front of the principal's office in junior high school, when I got in trouble for running in a "gang."

When trauma comes to me, I habitually clam up. It could be called the "turtle defense;" I retreat into my shell until things get better outside. So I didn't say anything. I just sat in stony silence as they questioned me and told me frightening things that merely made me clam up more.

But down inside, I had learned enough to know that, though they were presently in total control, their power had limits. It could only be for a time. They had to allow me a phone call at some point. We did have the right to consult an attorney. We still lived in a free country with due process. The picture they were painting to scare us does exist in totalitarian states, where they can pluck you off the street and nobody hears from you for the next ten years, if ever. But this was the United States! We didn't live under that kind of system. And nothing they said or did could change that fact. In spite of my fear at what was happening, I could hold onto that truth. And truth, when you find it, never lets you down.

Later on, when they interrogated me again, they threw in my face that Miller had cooperated with them. They said he'd even signed a confession! I couldn't believe that. Miller was our leader! If *I* could hold out—the "obsequious one" as Miller used to call me—surely *he* could. I took it to be a sign of their desperation. But they showed me his signed statement! There it was in black and white. I was dumbfounded. How could this be?

They had started by getting Miller talking with them and then they offered him a deal: First off, his goose was cooked and they were going to send him up big time. However, if he cooperated with them by telling them where the stuff was and signing a statement, they would drop the charge on the LSD and only charge us with possession of the marijuana. Since LSD was a much more potent and dangerous drug, it seemed like a good idea to get it eliminated from the charges. So Miller cut the deal. He told them where the stuff was and signed a confession. It was only later we found out that possession of LSD under California law at that time was only a misdemeanor, while possession of marijuana was a felony! Since misdemeanor charges are usually dropped when there is a felony, in all probability only the felony marijuana charge would have been prosecuted. So in his ignorance, Miller cut a deal that gave them everything they wanted, while not gaining us a single thing!

The police had tried and tried to get the lid off that five gallon milk can. When they were unable to, they assumed it was welded or rusted shut and looked elsewhere. After getting Miller to cooperate, they took him back to the house to show them where the stuff was located. Once they knew for sure the drugs were in the milk can, they took a hammer to the lid and pounded it off.

With the signed statement from Miller, our leader, they were able to extract confessions from the rest of the group except for me. I didn't understand it. I didn't know what had happened to Miller. But my heels were dug in and I wasn't going to yield, no matter what.

That ended the interrogation phase. From the police's point of view, it had been a highly successful night. They had arrested the perps, gotten the drugs, and had signed confessions from all but one. Their job was finished and they turned us over to the jailers for booking and locking up.

I was totally ignorant about the nitty-gritty of how the criminal justice system works. I had no idea that the interrogation part was over and that this next phase of fingerprinting, mug shots, and booking information was just mundane paperwork. I thought it was all part of the same process of trying to wrest information from me, so I didn't cooperate any more with these guys than I had before. I refused to answer even the routine booking questions such as name, address, date of birth, and so on. I was frozen in fear and not coming out my shell for anything. On top of this, they had taken away my glasses and, since I'm blind as a bat without them, this added to my disorientation.

I must have greatly frustrated them. This was part of the routine they went through every day, and here I was messing up their system. Finally, they gave up trying to book me and sent me down to get a shower, jail clothes, and a cell. As a guard escorted me from the booking cage down the corridor, he suddenly grabbed my arm and twisted it behind my back up to my neck. Yelling at me in anger, he ran me forward down the hall, and then pitched me headlong, falling to my hands and knees.

I think he was probably just venting his anger and frustration at my fouling up their system. But such an angry and aggressive display only heightened my sense of danger and trauma and caused me to retreat ever deeper into my shell.

After being clothed in jail garb, another guard escorted me to my cell. But this one was different. He talked to me in a gentle and kind manner. He explained that they were only trying to get information from me for their records, not evidence to use against me in court. He was so non-threatening and informative that my fear melted and my resistance ceased.

Seeing the change in me he asked if I wanted to go back and complete the process. I said, "Sure." So I went back, got fingerprinted, my mug shot taken, and gave them the booking information.

After that, they let me have a couple of phone calls. The first call was to my parents. It was about 3:00 a.m. my time, which made it 6:00 a.m. in Ohio where they lived. In spite of the trauma of the night, I could still sense the poignancy of the moment from my parent's point of view—getting a phone call in the wee hours of the morning from their good middle-class son in college across the country saying that he was calling from jail after being arrested on a felony drug charge.

My mother answered the phone. "Hi, Mom," I said, gamely, I'll bet you can't guess where I'm calling from."

Parents often have more poise and resiliency than teenagers give them credit for. After I told her the circumstances involved, instead of fainting, wringing her hands, having a nervous breakdown, lecturing or condemning me, she went right to work trying to contact people nearby who could help.

They also allowed me a local phone call. I remembered an incident in my soil science class a few months back. We had a graduate student teaching the lab. Once he was telling us about a young attorney friend he had, who had said, "Hey, if any of your students ever need legal help, just have 'em give me a call." For some reason, I had written down his name and number. It was still in my wallet! So I called him. I must have gotten him out of bed too, but he seemed to understand, seeing all that had happened to us and from where I was calling. I told him about my lab instructor who had mentioned his name. He said he didn't usually handle criminal cases, but he had a law partner who did. He would talk to him that morning as soon as he got to the office and see what he could do.

The guards were ready to put me in a cell again. As they were taking me back down the cell block, another guard called out to the one escorting me. After a consultation, he led me back to the booking area and into the elevator where we went up to the next floor. This, I found out later, was the felony area, where the worst offenders were kept. They took me deep into the felony block, and put me into an individual, padded cell. They must have thought I was crazy, or psycho, because I had refused to cooperate with them, although since that one guard had spoken nice to me, I had been as docile as a lamb.

Then I was finally alone in my padded cell and had a chance to think. The nightmare had come true, leaving a trauma on my soul that I would never entirely forget. I had made my stand against society, asserting my will and wisdom against society's conclusion that drugs were dangerous. Now, society had struck back through its agents—the police. If only I could have seen that society was not just trying to protect *itself* from the harm of these drugs, but it was also trying to protect *me* from my own bad decisions. But instead, I was as firmly committed to the cause of drugs as ever, and saw myself as a martyr for the cause.

COURT

After a few fitful hours of sleep, the lights came on at 6:00 a.m. Though I was exhausted, this made continued sleep impossible. At 7:00, a jailor brought a tray with a breakfast of hot oatmeal covered with watery, reconstituted milk, black coffee, and a piece of bread that had been dried out instead of toasted. I wolfed it down anyway and felt better with some food in my stomach. At 9:00, a guard took the five of us along with the other assorted "night's catch" of criminals down to court for arraignment.

The spectator section of the courtroom was crowded. We had heard our arrests being trumpeted on the local radio news while still being processed into jail. Now we found ourselves being stared at by a packed courtroom of spectators, as if to uncover our secret—why had we done such a thing? The Bay Area drug craze had finally spread to remote Humboldt County.

Appearing in court was an intimidating experience. There we were in our ill-fitting, blue denim, jail-issue clothes with "flip-flops" on our bare feet in the midst of a sea of suits and wingtips to answer felony charges of criminal wrongdoing. If it's true that "clothes make the man," then we were not men at all, but rather some sub-species. The clothes alone made me feel powerless to put up any kind of fight against this well-organized system.

It was not a user-friendly place. I glanced around the room at the faces, hoping to find some reason for hope. I knew I'd blown it, but this was my life on the line; this was serious stuff and I needed help. There was the uniformed bailiff, busy about the details of his work, oblivious to the human drama unfolding before him. There were the bored court workers, one stifling a yawn, idly waiting for the judge to come in—no help there. At a table in front of the spectator section was the D.A., preparing to launch into his case against us. He was the focus of fear, not hope. Behind him was the crowd of curious reporters and courtroom gawkers. My heart felt bleak. Nowhere was there a single face that offered any encouragement or might have suggested, "Relax, I'm on your side."

Suddenly, in the midst of the sea of faces, at the very back of the courtroom, I saw a familiar, friendly face, shining like an angel of mercy. It was Dr. Cranston, professor of physics at Humboldt.

My mother had indeed been busy. She had been on the phone seeing if there was any church like ours—Unitarian Universalist—in the local area. She found there was no actual church, but there was a church fellowship, a group of people who met together without a pastor. The contact person she had been given for this fellowship was Fred Cranston. She had reached him and asked for his help. And here he was, radiating good cheer. I had no idea how he came to be in the crowd, but as soon as I saw him I knew he was there for us. My spirits lifted for the first time since the nightmare began an eternity ago.

We all stood for the judge to enter, and court was in session. When our case came up, I was surprised to find more people there for us. The partner of the attorney I had called and an attorney accompanying Fred Cranston were present. Our arraignment was postponed until the question of legal representation could be sorted out.

Mark's aunt had been busy also. Our bail had been set at $10,000 apiece, a hefty sum back then, when you could buy a house for less than $20,000. She signed over her own home as collateral to a local bail bondsman for a $30,000 bond to bail the three of us she knew out of jail. Soon we were free and on our way home. I've always been amazed at that act of trust and self-sacrifice, especially for a single mother just getting by. I'll never forget the help we received right when we needed it most.

We were the front page story in the local newspaper that night, as well as being on the local TV evening news. We even rated a mention in the San Francisco Chronicle on the second page of the A section, the "drug bust" page. It was scary but in a strange way exhilarating, being suddenly in the limelight—after a lifetime in obscurity—and hearing our names bandied about. To some, we were heroes of the new order, to others, we were public enemies numbers one through five.

Under Fred Cranston's recommendation, we didn't use either of the attorneys who had showed up in court, but retained Brian Rohan, a noted San Francisco counter-culture attorney. Rohan represented various '60s Bay Area celebrities such as Ken Kesey, the

EUREKA, CALIFORNIA, FRIDAY EVENING, MARCH 17, 1967 10c Per Copy 24 Pages Today

Arcata Marijuana Raid; Five Seized With Drugs

College Students Held As Suspects

Five men, including three Humboldt State College students, were arrested in a surprise midnight raid last night by sheriff's officers and Chief Jim Gibson of the Arcata police department and booked at Humboldt County jail on charges of possession of marijuana.

Seized were some two pounds of marijuana, two capsules of LSD and two LSD pills, along with an East Indian or Turkish water pipe, three ordinary tobacco pipes and several ashtrays, all of which contained traces of marijuana seeds, the officers said.

Booked and slated for Grand Jury indictment on the felony counts are HSC students David Andrew Hobbs, 19, of Kent, Ohio; Ronald J. Dupuy, 19, of Alhambra; Mark Douglas Pahuta, 19, of Hollywood, along with non-student Lawrence G. Miller, 20, of Berkeley and Terry M. White, 19, student at a bay area Junior College.

Deputies who had spent two months cracking the case with the cooperation of the Arcata police, said White and Miller arrived here from Berkeley last Tuesday night with the drugs and that the five had been using them since then in a house rented by the three Humboldt State college students in the Sunset Addition just north of Arcata.

Officers said the men were "higher than kites" when they struck at exactly midnight.

Three plain clothes sheriff's detectives, Chief Gibson, and four uniformed deputies staged the raid, with the uniformed officers transporting the prisoners to jail after the arrests.

Officers indicated much of the case centered around Miller, whom they said had been known to them throughout the investigation only as "Bal-man."

THE MARIJUANA and LSD were hidden throughout the house, broken into two and three ounce packages except for one larger one which had not yet been reduced.

Sheriff Gene Cox, who announced the successful conclusion of the case this morning, said the marijuana was purchased in the Bay Area for $80, and would have a value of more than $200 "on the Eureka market".

The raiding officers said the five offered no resistance, but that Hobbs was "visibly shaken" and refused to talk or to give his name to the jailor when booked.

The entire operation took from its launching at 8:30 p.m. yesterday until 6 o'clock this morning. Sheriff Cox, who was ill at home with the flu at the time, said today to "give the credit to the boys."

Sheriff Gene Cox contemplates some two pounds of marijuana, a quantity of LSD pills and other narcotics paraphernalia, including the long flexible-stemmed "hookah", or water pipe used in Turkey and India seized in a midnight raid on a house just north of Arcata today. Arcata police assisted in the two-months-long investigations which led to the arrest of five men last night.

Shively Boy Killed In Viet Action

A Shively youth, George Cook, 20, was killed in an encounter between Viet Cong and U.S. Army forces near Saigon Tuesday, according to reports received by the family.

He is the son of Mr. and Mrs. Clifford C. Cook and the nephew of Mr. and Mrs. Clinton Cook, all of Shively. Word of his death was reported to the family Wednesday by Sgt. Raymond Cope, unit advisor of the National Guard. Arrangements are now being made to return the body to the parents.

Cook was graduated from Fortuna High School in 1964 and for a time attended a barber college in the Bay Area. He entered the Army and was sent to Vietnam in December, 1966. He served as a machine gunner.

o Siberia

Monday to visit an American industrial design exhibition in Moscow's Sokolniki Park—the scene of his famous 1959 icebox debate with Khrushchev.

Nixon, then vice president, staged a battle of words with the balding then-Soviet Premier on a wide range of policy and national accomplishments.

Nixon returned to Moscow in 1965, when both were no longer in office, and rang the doorbell at Khrushchev's Moscow apartment. Nobody answered.

Shelter Cove Road Closure

All access to Shelter Cove and the southern county area

Dodd Cries 'Liar

WASHINGTON (UPI) —Sen. Thomas J. Dodd, D-Conn., denied pointblank charges of financial trickery today and termed his principal accuser a liar.

With his wife watching from the audience, the silver-thatched senator testified in his own defense before the Senate Ethics Committee which is looking into allegations he used nearly $150,000 in testimonial funds for his personal debts.

When Dodd concluded his testimony, Chairman John Stennis, D-Miss., announced that the hearings were completed, and the committee would begin writing a report on their fellow senator.

Dodd asserted he made no secret of his intent to use the money to pay off long-standing personal bills and debts.

"I didn't take the money under false pretenses," he declared.

At another point, the senator told his investigators "my conscience is clear."

Of the fund-raising affairs, Dodd said: "I believe in my soul that no one was flim- that he dug himself into a financial hole in running for election in 1956 and blamed his plight on "the unfriendly Democratic party organization in Connecticut."

As he concluded nearly three hours of testimony, Dodd emphatically declared: "No one can look me in the eye and say I did wrong."

"I never held myself out as a halo wearer," he asserted. "But I tell you, I haven't been trimming the government."

Dodd told the Senate Ethics Committee that he could not really separate his personal and political obligations.

"Almost everything I did since 1956 until this moment was intertwined with politics," he testified.

Dodd also:

—Claimed he never knew h was collecting twice for ai fares in speaking appearances He said "there was not an attempt to defraud."

—Vehemently denied tha $8,000 he received from the International Latex Corp. was a payoff for his help trying to get an ambassadorship for board chairman A.N. Spanel.

Dodd said that he was in desperate financial straits in 1957 after his 1956 campaign. He said that, except "one-half of a billboard," he has received no campaign help from the Connecticut Democratic organization "Because the organization was unfriendly to me then, as it is now."

"I think that is where my difficulty, principally, lies," the Senator added.

U.S. Jets Smash Key Power Plants

SAIGON (UPI)—U.S. Navy ... In the main Saigon Sea

Grateful Dead, and the Jefferson Airplane. He charged our parents $1,500 each to handle the case, in addition to the $1,000 fee they each had to pay the bail bondsman for use of his money. Rohan quickly got Miller and White released on their own recognizance, and we were all free.

"Bo" as we called him, was confident that he could get us off since a search warrant had not be obtained and thus the police lacked "probable cause" to arrest us. It's funny that in our modern day, a person's actual guilt or innocence is of little consequence. We loudly, even shrilly protested our innocence—not because we hadn't done something illegal, but because they hadn't caught us the right way!

The very same day, Friday, I had a midterm in my economics class. I got bailed out just in time to take it. I couldn't have done very well on it, and nothing was said by the professor about me being one of the students busted. But he knew, and I think showed me kindness. I ended up getting a "Sympathy A" in the class.

At the preliminary hearing where the evidence comes out, we found there had been a secret informant who had tipped off the police that we had the drugs. It turned out to be Rex's roommate Dutch! To hear him tell it on the stand, he had become greatly concerned by seeing his roommate getting involved in drugs and was only trying to protect him. He had come over and smoked marijuana with us to gain our confidence. Later Dutch filed a disability claim against the county, claiming that the drugs he had used in his undercover work had permanently scrambled his brain!

The case was bound over to superior court, where Judge Wilkinson presided. The judge was blind and read everything in Braille. Even in those days, before all the federal disability acts and common access laws, he seemed to do just fine, and all the necessary adjustments had been made in the courtroom to accommodate his disability. He seemed to be truly impartial and dedicated.

Our attorney argued our cases: the police never had probable cause to enter our house and search it without a warrant. Therefore, none of the evidence gathered from the search or the confessions could be used against us. The case should be dismissed. The judge took it under advisement and promised a ruling within sixty days. We were already into May by this time.

AFTERMATH

Our case had generated widespread publicity. The drug and hippie explosion had already gone off in the Bay Area and the ripple effects were spreading. And everywhere they spread, they generated big news. My aunt heard about us in her mountain cabin over 300 miles away on the other side of the Sierras.

Then, one day I received a letter from the Forest Service in Seiad. It was from Zack. He wrote:

Dear David:

It has come to my attention that a certain David Hobbs from Arcata, California, has recently been arrested on felony charges of drug possession. Are you that David Hobbs? If you are, please be advised that federal law prohibits anyone from working for the government who is either charged with or has been convicted of a felony. Therefore, we would not be able to hire you back this summer as long as these charges are pending.

Sincerely,
Zack Walton

I had to write him back that I was indeed the man, and that, while I was confident of beating the charges, it probably would not be resolved before summer.

"So there goes my summer job," I said to myself. I was really in a quandary as to what to do. We weren't going to keep the house over the summer, so I not only didn't have a job, but I didn't have any place to stay, and no car for transportation.

Fred Cranston had taken a strong interest in us and began to invite us over to his home where we met his wife, Bonnie, and his children. His oldest was a daughter our age named Carol. Next were sons, Rick and Rod, both in high school and "baby" daughter Claudia in middle school.

They had a home close to the campus on the edge of civilization. Above the house was the redwood forest. Below the house were the rooftops of Arcata and the college.

I really appreciated Fred and Bonnie practically adopting us into their home. It was therapeutic to be in a family again.

But what soon captivated us more than the house, the view, or the family was the daughter! Both Miller and I seemed to discover Carol about the same time.

Carol was short but spirited: a vivacious girl with short hair, a husky laugh, and penetrating eyes.

Then began a brief but very intense competition for her favor. She seemed to like both of us. When she was with Larry, she got along famously with him. When she was with me, we got along like we were made for each other. It was a battle for her time and attention until she decided which of her two suitors suited her best.

It was nip and tuck. When she was with me, I was sure I had won, until she spent time with Larry. Seeing her with him, I was deathly afraid I had lost, until she spent time with me again. Thus it went back and forth, balancing and tipping.

I'll never forget the sinking feeling I had when I realized I really had lost, that Larry's "magic" to attract her was stronger than mine. I hadn't had any girlfriends in high school, and Carol was my first serious attempt in college. Losing was hard, but life went on. Larry and I continued as friends.

SUMMER IN BERKELEY, 1967

June 1967

School was winding down. The door with the Forest Service had closed. There was no place for me in Arcata. Also, the seeds that drug use had planted during the school year were reaching maturity. The time had come to head into this drug lifestyle full bore, follow it out, and see where it took us. Ours was a generation that was going somewhere, riding the waves of psychedelics, rock music, and counter-culturalism. And I wanted to be part of it.

Therefore, it was only natural when Miller invited me to spend the summer with him in Berkeley that I would accept. Besides, it was always a relief to get out of Humboldt County and be free of the dreaded Sheriff's Department. Down in the Bay Area was a spirit of freedom—an openness to our lifestyle and us.

In Berkeley and the Bay Area, the drug craze was going full blast. The Beatles were just coming out with their psychedelic blockbuster "Sgt. Pepper's Lonely Hearts Club Band." The Beatles, Rolling Stones, Grateful Dead, Country Joe and the Fish, Jefferson Airplane, Bob Dylan, Big Brother and the Holding Company constituted a veritable explosion of rock musicians and groups that were bursting onto the scene. From all over the world, young "people in motion" were streaming to San Francisco's Haight Ashbury District in the most powerful social and cultural upheaval of our generation.

And we were right in the middle of it—almost at ground zero—and yet like the flea on the astronaut who went to the moon, we were mostly oblivious to what was going on. Only once during the summer did we drive across the Bay Bridge into San Francisco and through the Haight Ashbury and Golden Gate Park. It was wide open! There were hippies everywhere! Yet we just drove through and came home. Another time we went to a park in Berkeley to attend an open-air concert. Yeah things were happening, but for the most part, we stayed home in our upstairs apartment in a converted house on Derby Street, smoking marijuana, visiting Miller's friends, watching TV, listening to music, trying to get enough money to pay the rent, buy food, and score dope.

Originally, we didn't plan to goof off all summer. We both intended to get jobs and practice music in the evenings and on weekends. We were already planning to start our own rock band—Larry, Pahuta, and me. For awhile Larry and I went job hunting in the industrial area of Berkeley. I also signed up with the state department of employment. We spent perhaps a week making "cold calls" on businesses, filling out job applications and seeking openings.

But job hunting is a hard business, prone to discouragement. It didn't take us long to wear down and give up. In fact, in retrospect, it almost seems like the whole job hunting episode was merely a subconscious "bone" of compliance to throw to our middle class upbringing. Once it "failed" us, we didn't look back.

After our job hunting fizzled, we quickly settled into a routine of doing nothing. Our lives came to revolve around eating and sleeping, smoking weed, listening to music, and watching TV.

Living without income was a new challenge for me. It was an obstacle, but not insurmountable. It showed us how much we could do without. We had to have money for rent and utilities. But we didn't have any other bills. Miller had an old red Hillman that barely ran, but got us where we needed to go. The only other things we needed were food, cigarettes, Coca-Cola, and a baggie of marijuana every few days.

We never got to be in serious need. We always came up with money from somewhere. Miller's parents sometimes sent him some. I remembered a childhood savings account I had back in Ohio. It had been started for my "college education," but was still less than $200, and here I was *in college*! In fact, in my two years of going to college, I hadn't even remembered it. I was able to cash it out by mail. Sometimes when things were tight, we would gather all our Coke bottles together and take them down for a refund.

Eventually we might have taken to hustling and the petty crime that is part and parcel of big city life. And we probably would have started selling dope. But we were not that deeply in need yet, and I was still intimidated by the bustle and danger of the big city.

We quickly fell into the rut of sleeping late and squandering the day with trivial pursuits. When evening came we would settle in, smoke dope, listen to music, or watch TV. No matter what else, the climax of our day was watching the "Tonight Show" at 11:30. We would rarely leave the house except to walk down to the supermarket at the corner of Derby and Telegraph.

Up to this point, drugs had been a peripheral part of my life—something recreational to be worked around schoolwork. But now they became the central focus—everything else revolved around them.

But as the marijuana became more central to my existence, in a strange paradox it seemed to supply less of the desired effects that I smoked it for. Instead of receiving heightened experiences, instead of lifting me to new worlds to explore, it just made me tired and sleepy. Night after night my pattern came to be smoking pot and then going to bed shortly after. For awhile, I could groove along with music, but soon I'd get so tired I couldn't stay awake. Finally, I would just crawl off to bed.

So if the summer was finally an opportunity to fully explore the realm of drugs and getting high, it was a dud. Instead of getting more intense, the experiences had actually leveled off and were getting more predictable, even "normal."

Without realizing it, I was reaching a crossroads that most drug users come to. The effect of the drugs had lessened; they no longer delivered the experiences they first did. I too faced the choice: quit using them; keep using them with lesser results; or go on to stronger, more dangerous drugs in pursuit of that elusive high.

LEGAL SURPRISE

It was a typical day late in June. White happened to be up visiting us from Los Angeles. Miller's friend Steinitz was over hanging out with us. He was very Jewish, a student at the university who lived in a studio apartment, had few friends, and liked to come over and spend time with us. He might do a little pot, but that was about as far as he would go in adopting our "freer" lifestyle.

Miller was off taking drum lessons, practicing to be drummer in our rock band.

Our drug supply was at a low point—all we had left was a baggie of stems and seeds, which make the harshest smoke and have the least psychedelic effect of any part of the plant. Miller was planning to buy more on his way home from drum lessons.

Just the day before, we had received a welcome phone call from Bo. He told us that Judge Wilkinson had finally issued his ruling in our case. He ruled that there were insufficient legal grounds for the police search of our house and our subsequent arrest. Therefore, the evidence and the confessions were inadmissible in court. He was dismissing the charges against us. We were free men!

I felt elated! It was wonderful to be free from that cloud of fear and uncertainty that had hung over our lives for months. It was also sweet revenge against the sheriff's department and the anguish they had inflicted on us! I wanted to go out and buy a "sympathy card" and send it to Detective Ames, the hard-bitten "Dragnet" type who had led the charge against us, as a way of rubbing his face in his defeat and taking the opportunity to gloat over our vindication. But I discovered they all had unlisted addresses and phone numbers, and I didn't want to send it to him at work, so I scrubbed the idea.

It was 11:00 a.m. the next day, and there was a muffled knock at our street level front door. White got up to answer it, first looking out the window to see if there was a police car parked out front, which there wasn't. Then he went down the long staircase to see who it was.

He was downstairs a long time. I wasn't paying much attention, still being somewhat stoned from our morning joint smoked before Miller left. When White finally came back up there was a man in casual clothes behind him. I looked up as he said apologetically, "It's the police; they want Miller."

I couldn't believe it. Then more men appeared and began to fan out through our apartment again. "This can't be happening," I thought. "IT'S OVER! DON'T THEY KNOW IT'S OVER?"

They asked me for my ID. When they found out who I was, they were surprised but said I was also one of those they wanted. When they ID'd White, he was also on their list, though he was supposed to be in Southern California, and I was supposed to be in Ohio.

Once again, they began searching our apartment, looking everywhere for drugs. Only these police officers were professional: they were polite; they were trained; and they were thorough.

We sat there helplessly watching them systematically search the living room area, trying not to look at the drawer in the desk where the plastic baggie of seeds and stems was, the only drugs we had at the time. The lead officer was the one searching in this area, as others searched the kitchen and bedrooms. He finally came to the desk. He started pulling open the drawers one by one and looking inside, working his way from top to bottom. He opened the drawer with the baggie, looked right at it, then flipped it shut and went on to the next one.

We couldn't believe it! We expected him to seize it and hold it up triumphantly: "Bingo! Busted! Book'em!" Instead, he went right on without batting an eye.

We could never figure out this oversight. It seemed impossible that he didn't see it. We thought he might have chosen to ignore it, because it was such a small amount, not worth burdening the courts over. Maybe in such a big city, they had already given up on the small-time users and cared only for the suppliers and dealers.

Whatever the reason, we were soon cleared of having any drugs on the premises. This brought them back to the reason they had come in the first place: they had warrants for our arrest from Humboldt County!

"But," we protested, "we were just cleared on charges from there, and we certainly haven't been back since. How could there be fresh charges?"

They couldn't explain it. They only knew they had warrants for our arrest and were taking us in.

They checked out poor Steinitz too, running his driver's license through their records back at the station to see if there were any warrants out for him. When he proved clean, they let him go, warning him sternly about the danger of criminal association. After letting him go, they stood by the upstairs window watching him leave our apartment and start down the street. He walked nonchalantly down the sidewalk for about twenty feet, and then suddenly took off running for his life.

"Look at him go!" they laughed together in amusement as he tore off down the street like his clothes were on fire.

They called on their radio and had the uniformed officers with the squad car drive up from around the block where they had been hiding to take us to the station. So much for our system of police detection! Again, we left under arrest, bewildered by this turn of events. However, by this time I was feeling glad I hadn't sent that sympathy card to Detective Ames at the Humboldt Co. Sheriff's Department!

For all that was going on that summer in Berkeley, the jail was surprisingly empty. We were put into a large cellblock by ourselves.

We did get to make a phone call, however, and called Bo's office to find out what was going on. "Not to worry," he said, "I should have warned you they might pull a trick like this."

"But how could they do this? We were just cleared!" Our sense of justice was again outraged.

"They simply rearrested you on the same charges."

"But isn't that double jeopardy? Forbidden by the constitution?" Memories from high school civics class came flooding back.

Bo explained that the prohibition against double jeopardy only applied to cases where the defendants go to trial and are acquitted by the jury. Then they can never be charged with the same crime again, even if new evidence surfaced later. But if something else happened to the charges before the case went to a jury—like with us where the judge threw them out—the D.A. could always re-file them, claiming new evidence or whatever.

We were suddenly struck by our vulnerability to the judicial system, if not to convict, then to harass. "But what protection do we have against over-zealous prosecution then?"

Bo hedged, "Well, eventually you could sue the prosecutor for malicious prosecution, but we're probably not to that point yet."

"You mean we have to go through this all over again?"

"I'm afraid so. You know your case is a highly visible one, the first college drug bust in Humboldt County and all that. The D.A. needs to look good on this one."

"Well that's real encouraging!"

"Don't worry about it. Just hang tight. Humboldt County will come down and pick you up and take you back. Then you'll appear in court again for arraignment. This time, I'll try to get you all released on your own recognizance."

He got angry, "This was all so unnecessary! They knew I could get you back there any time they wanted. All they had to do was call. They're playing hardball!"

Hardball was right. I found out later they even sent a deputy to my folks' home in Ohio to arrest me, and deputies in Southern California went to White's, Pahuta's, and Dupuy's houses to arrest them. But of the five, White and I were the only two they caught.

We were more than a little struck by Bo's first offhand remark, "I should have warned you they might do this." Because of his neglect to warn us, we came within a hair's breadth of having a second felony drug charge lodged against us in Berkeley. *This,* we thought, was undoubtedly their diabolical reasoning for springing a surprise arrest on us instead of just informing Bo and having him tell us to appear for re-arraignment in Humboldt County. They were hoping to catch us with dope again. But for the inexplicable behavior of the arresting Berkeley police officer, their plan would have succeeded! That part was easy to understand. But why didn't Bo, knowing all these things, take a moment to warn us? That part was hard to fathom. "Oh well, another drug charge against us would only have meant more business for *him*!" we thought darkly.

This whole thing had happened on Friday again. We spent Friday night in the Berkeley jail.

The Humboldt Sheriff's Department had a deputy with a private pilot's license. The next day, he rented a small plane, flew down to the Oakland airport, picked us up, and flew us back to Eureka. It must have been quite an expense for them, but we got a nice plane ride out of it. I guess they were glad they didn't have to fly me back from Ohio!

We got an unintentional admission that they didn't consider us dangerous criminals. The deputy didn't even bother handcuffing us for the flight. He sat in the front seat, and we sat behind him the whole time with nothing in between, but he didn't seem concerned.

Meanwhile, Miller, warned by Steinitz, was spending an incredibly paranoid weekend in Berkeley! Afraid to go back to our apartment, he hid out in friends' apartments, traveling from one to another only at night with his face covered. He had been right about one thing, however: in neither bust had they come with lights and sirens on!

Because it was the weekend, we had to spend Saturday night and all day Sunday in the Humboldt County Jail.

When we finally got released on Monday, the Cranstons again took us in. But we had to pay our own way back to Berkeley.

After that, life returned to normal. White went home, and Miller came out of hiding. We were all free on our own recognizance. The case plodded through the courts.

But our level of paranoia increased markedly. Whereas before we had felt reasonably secure in Berkeley and only on our guard while visiting Humboldt County, now we had seen that the long arm of the law could reach us as easily in Berkeley as anywhere else. As a result, we began to experience panic attacks.

When a series of unexplained circumstances happened, like a suspicious car parked on a side street near our house... or an unexplained noise out the back window of our apartment... or a knock on our door by a stranger . . . suddenly Miller would LEAP to his feet, sure that we were about to be busted.

"The cops are here! The cops are here!"

Then we would both run wildly about the apartment. "Flush the dope! Flush the dope!" he would hiss. We might have a brand new lid of finely chopped leaves—it didn't matter. Down the toilet it went with a gurgling flush. Then, in a moment of incredible tension, he would go to the door and see who it was.

"Hi, I'm soliciting for the March of Dimes," the stranger would say, "would you care to contribute?"

Miller would growl, "No thank you, we gave at the office."

Then, the door safely shut, "Oh no, I can't believe it, a whole lid of prime stuff flushed for the March of Dimes!"

It's funny to look back on now. But we flushed a lot of stuff that summer in sudden panic attacks, all to no avail. They never came for us again. The ancient proverb says, "The wicked flee when no one pursues them." We sure were living proof of that proverb.

WORK

Sometime toward the end of August, the State Employment Department called about a job painting some apartments. The apartment complex was owned by a young Japanese couple. The difference between their world and mine was like night and day. They were young, industrious, and serious-minded—working hard to get ahead in life. The apartments they wanted painted were clean, sterile, and bright. I was a drug-using hippie, long hair, old clothes, driving Miller's "beater" car, living in a hippie pad with wicker pads for carpet, hanging strings of beads for doors, old movie posters on the walls.... It was a real culture shock.

I didn't know much about painting, but I tried to remember back to the times at the Forest Service when I had painted for good old Fred Clark. I knew you had to make sure not to leave any "holidays" (missed spots), you had to cover things so they didn't get spattered, and if it was latex paint–which it never was with Fred–you could clean it up with water.

But after only a few days of working at the apartments, Fred Cranston called with word that there were job openings with the concessionaires up at Sequoia National Park. His daughter Carol had just gotten on as a secretary for the personnel manager who was hiring.

It sounded good: way up in the mountains, a resort-like existence. The guy Fred talked to said if we could get there, he would hire us. Fred even bought me a bus ticket. His second son, Rod, went with me to get a job also. Larry was going to go too, but had some things to do first, and would drive up in a couple of days.

I was drawn there partly because I hadn't totally given up on Carol. After all, she and Larry had been apart for the summer. Maybe things had changed. But I only saw her once when I first arrived since she was working in the administration building down the road while I was a busboy in the restaurant, and, of course, I didn't have a car. Then Larry came up, supposedly to work. But instead, he found Carol, their relationship reignited, and before I knew it, she took off with him for parts unknown.

I was alone and unhappy. The work was hard and unrelenting. We lived in cabins in the woods without electricity. And the pay, after deductions for room and board, was $.70/hour. The waitresses were supposed to give us 20% of their tips, but there was nobody keeping track. At the most, that provided a small amount of spending money. I ended up working nine straight days and leaving. They mailed my check later. For the nine days of work, I received $44!

A HOUSE IN THE COUNTRY

After a series of bus rides, I ended up back at our apartment in Berkeley. Miller was there! He'd been running around the state with Carol. He was packing up and closing the apartment, so my timing was perfect. He had decided to go back to Humboldt–it wasn't hard to guess why. But other than Carol, we also had the rock band to start. Pahuta had come up several times during the summer to practice with us, and Miller had been taking drum lessons. We closed down the apartment, loaded our stuff, and headed north to Arcata, where we stayed temporarily at the Cranston's. Fred was upset at Larry for "kidnapping" his daughter, but they soon smoothed things over. Larry and Carol were in love after all, and that made everything right.

We couldn't find any place to rent, but Fred, through his contacts, heard about an economics professor who was taking a sabbatical and looking for someone to rent his house. Though he was not keen on renting it to three single guys—who'd just been busted for drugs at that! —Fred vouched for us and persuaded him. The house was in the woods a few miles north of the tiny fishing town of Trinidad, fifteen miles north of Arcata.

We were soon joined by Pahuta and, to our surprise Mark brought his cousin Perry with him. Perry was a drummer and wanted to play in our band. We couldn't believe our good fortune! This would free Miller to go back to rhythm guitar while Mark played lead guitar, and I played electric bass.

The setting was beautiful and perfect. We were out of the sight and the earshot of all men. We were all together in one place so we could practice together to our heart's content. The only thing we needed was a lead singer. Beatles look out; here we come!

DRUG BUST FINALE

The biggest item of unfinished business was the unresolved drug charge. Bo's philosophy was to stall as long as possible until people just wanted to get rid of it. Finally, after numerous delays, we did have a preliminary hearing again back in municipal court.

The charges had been dismissed because the search was ruled illegal. The only way for them to legally enter our house without a search warrant was if there was probable cause to believe that a felony was being committed in the house right at that moment.

So this time Detective Ames "just happened to remember" that instead of coming right into the house, he actually had stopped to look in the windows first, at which time he had smelled marijuana smoke coming through the open louvered windows—as if we would have windows open when the temperature was in the fifties! The story was patently false, but he was playing the game. They knew we were guilty. From the judge's previous ruling, they also knew what they needed to convict. So he changed his story just enough to make it work.

At the time, of course, we were outraged that he would do such a thing. It's amazing how we could get so outraged at them for their faults while ignoring our own!

In an attempt to buttress their case, they brought out the note Miller had left on Rex's door, which said "I've got the stuff. I'm over at Hobbs' house." But it only referred to having "the stuff" at "Hobbs' house," without specifying what "the stuff" was.

You could tell the judge didn't fully believe him. After all, he knew how the system worked. On the other hand, he had a dilemma. He knew we were guilty, and ours was a high profile case—the first from the college—and a message needed to be sent. I can almost see the wheels turning in the judge's mind. How to find a solution? Meditatively he sifts through the different factors in the case: the officer, the drugs, the college, the community, the note.... The note! Wait a minute. A mini-brainstorm goes off in his head....

So we're called back in to hear the verdict: The case against Pahuta, White, and Dupuy is dismissed! Larry Miller and David Hobbs are bound over to superior court and held to answer.

They needed to nail someone to make a statement. So why not pick the two guiltiest ones—Larry Miller who brought up the drugs, and David Hobbs who opened his house for Miller to use. It was the perfect compromise. It sent a message to the cops that sloppy police work could not just be covered up by lying on the stand. After all, they could have hung us good if they had sent their informant Dutch in to make a buy from us. On the other hand, it sent a strong message that drug use wasn't going to be tolerated in our community either. Especially to be condemned were those importing drugs into our community and those who welcomed them. It was the perfect compromise.

Only it wasn't my house! I hadn't rented it! I hadn't found it! I'd just moved in, and at the last moment at that. I felt like jumping up and screaming, "Wait a minute! You can't hang this on me!" Just like in the movies. But the decision had been made. It was my name on Miller's note and that was all that mattered.

That left us with a mixed bag of emotions. Pahuta, Dupuy, and White were ecstatic to be finally out from under the charges for good. But their ecstasy had to be tempered by sympathy for us.

For us, the drama moved back to superior court and Judge Wilkinson. I wanted to go to battle over the fact it wasn't my house and that I shouldn't be singled out, but Bo correctly saw that as being a side issue. He realized that they needed to convict somebody of something, and until they did they wouldn't rest. So he spent some time talking with the D.A. and came back with a proposal.

"Here's the thing, guys. We can keep fighting it in court, maybe get it thrown out again, maybe eventually sue them for malicious prosecution if they keep arresting you. However, that's going to take time and money." We were aware of the burden our families were going through paying his fees. "On the other hand, they just want to get something to show for the case. I've talked to the D.A. and he's willing to let you guys plead to a misdemeanor charge of knowingly being in a place where marijuana was being smoked. You'd have no felony conviction, your records could be expunged later, and though you could receive up to six months in jail, he's agreed not to ask for it. We'll ask for probation, and he said he won't contest it. So what do you think?"

Here was an ethical dilemma. We'd been telling ourselves and others that "we were innocent" and "going to get off" for so long, that to face the prospect of actually being found guilty, even of a misdemeanor, was hard. On the other hand, to keep fighting seemed futile. It didn't seem "fair" that we were being singled out for such intensive prosecution, but there wasn't any good way out. The long arm of the law had wrapped around us at last.

So we plead guilty in superior court and were sent to the

probation department to see if we were suitable candidates for probation.

One of the probation officers was pretty hard-nosed. He flat out told us that no one guilty of a marijuana violation had ever made it through probation before, and he didn't expect us to be the first. He acted like he'd just as soon see us sent up now, so he wouldn't have to waste any more time on us.

But to our great relief we were sentenced to two years probation.

It was so good to have it finally over and done with. We had already quit using drugs when we returned to Humboldt County, so at last we knew we were clear with the law.

We were not assigned to the hard-nosed probation officer, but to another man who, in his spare time, was a Baptist preacher. He had a quiet strength and kindness, and did his job with competence. He seemed to cautiously trust us. He was the kind of man I didn't want to let down.

He never spoke to us about religion. I wondered how he could keep from it, since according to his beliefs; we were doomed to hell unless he or some other preacher could get us saved.

When he found out we were still all living together—all the old gang—he was surprised and worried, especially when our location seemed so ideal for using drugs. Usually the authorities try to break up criminal groups such as ours, in the hope we would get involved with a better peer group. But we told him we were going straight and wanted to be together because of our rock band, and in the end, he allowed us to continue. Maybe he had a gut feeling that it was going to be all right, which it was. We'd had more than enough trouble from our scrapes with the law. It was time to straighten up and fly right.

COLLEGE YEAR #3
THE GREAT MUSIC YEAR

September 1967. The Ruprecht's house was in a beautiful setting. Hidden one quarter of a mile back from the highway, it stood on top of a little rise, with pasture fields stretching down to the old road, beyond which was the rugged coast. When the surf was up, you could hear the waves pounding on the rocky shore. In the afternoons, the fog would often roll in over the trees.

The house itself was somewhat ramshackle, but the Ruprechts were in the process of fixing it up. There were two bedrooms in the house that Larry and Perry got, while Mark and I slept in part of the garage that had been remodeled into a kid's bedroom.

The order of business for the year was to launch our rock band, something we had been working toward since before the drug bust. We might be done with the drugs, but we were still very much immersed in the counter-culture, with no confidence in the traditional life path of college, job, wife, home in the suburbs, children, and retirement. A rock band was the perfect alternative: it gave us something to do; it was creative; and when we hit the big time like Country Joe and the Fish, there would be more than enough money, fame and groupies to go around. Larry, Mark, and I already had good chemistry about living and playing music together. The addition of Mark's cousin, Perry, though filling the drummer slot, also added a whole new dimension to the equation.

Perry traveled a different path. For instance, Mark, Larry, and I pooled our money and ate together. But Perry wouldn't join us. He was into health food, and was always criticizing us about our food.

Perry did things that might make nutritional sense, but no culinary sense. If we were fixing potatoes, for instance, he would take our potato peelings, berate us good naturedly for "throwing away the best part," and then fix the peelings for himself by frying them in a skillet with a little oil, perhaps scrambling in an egg as they neared completion. That would be his supper—fried potato peelings with egg and some lettuce leaves with vinegar and oil dressing on them! "But Perry," we said once, "how does it taste?"

"It doesn't have to taste good," he smiled sheepishly, "it's good *for* you!"

But the crowning experience with Perry and food came on the one disgusting day we found a rat floating belly-up in the drinking water storage tank behind the house. We were all grossed out. After removing the rat, we resolved never to drink the tap water again. The three of us started living on Cokes. But only a few days later we found a pitcher of Kool-Aid in the refrigerator. "Perry!" Miller exclaimed, "you're drinking the rat-water!"

"But I'm not drinking the *water*," he maintained stoutly, "it's *Kool-Aid*!" We could only shake our heads in disbelief.

Though humorous at the time, we didn't realize it was a foreshadowing of things to come.

PROFOUND MUSICAL EXPERIENCES

I continued to have profound experiences with music. These had started the year before at the music department. They were so moving they altered the course of my life. Because of them, I had resolved to give my life to music.

These musical experiences transcended my drug experience. Marijuana and LSD did help tune me in to music. But while some of the experiences did happen while stoned, they were by no means limited to that. Once we quit using drugs in the fall of 1968, the experiences continued.

The previous summer in our Berkeley apartment, I had been high, listening to "Turn, Turn, Turn" on a newly released album by the Byrds. The words to the song are actually from the Bible, from the third chapter of the Book of Ecclesiastes. It was said to have been a favorite passage of John F. Kennedy, too. The refrain goes:

To everything turn, turn, turn; there is a season turn, turn, turn
And a time to every purpose under heaven

The verses are a combination of opposite concepts such as:

A time to be born, a time to die
A time to kill, a time to heal
A time to love, a time to hate
A time of war and a time of peace

The words are powerful and the Byrds' musical arrangement is compelling, but the *tour de force* comes after the singing when the twelve-string guitar launches into its lead solo. The guitar follows the song's melody but exceeds it, rising higher instead of coming back down, playing off the melody and embellishing it.

In listening to it, I became totally absorbed in it for the first time, thrilling as it soared to the heights. As it came back down toward the grand finale, I became aware of the rest of the instruments moving along underneath. They were both approaching the finish but from different directions. Suddenly, I realized that the lead guitar was going to get there first. They weren't going to meet together at the finish! But then, in a flash of inspiration, at the very last moment, the lead guitar threw in an extra flourish that delayed him just long enough to meet the rest of the instruments rushing up, miraculously all coming together at the very last note! Then they stopped! For one breathless moment, there was the power of that unison rest, that ringing silence as the glory and beauty of what had just happened reverberated through my soul. Then out of the silence rose the voices again, the drummer fired a rim shot, and they were off into the next verse.

That one moment had been an incredible experience for me. I had gotten so absorbed in the guitar's lead solo that I was able to recognize in advance the approaching musical problem with the timing of the ending. Thus I was in a perfect position to receive the sublime musical solution that exploded on my soul in a joyful wave of wonder.

Less ecstatic but also moving was another experience I had at the Ruprecht's. Miller loved jazz, and Mark liked it too, though I had never gotten into it much. One warm, fall afternoon, Mark and I were in our big bedroom. I lay down to take a nap while he put on a jazz album. Just after I dozed off, a song came on called "A Star Fell on Alabama." Because I was in the lightest stage of sleep, the song bypassed my conscious mind and spoke directly to my subconscious. It spoke of the unfathomable sadness of slavery and affliction in the Black Experience. It was at once incredibly sad yet hauntingly beautiful. It spoke of bitter experiences and suffering but in such a wistful and tender way. As the song was ending, I awoke, my heart stirred by this sublime communication. I felt that in my sleep, through this song, I had learned more about the Black Experience than in all the civil rights rallies and marches in which I had been involved during high school and my first year of college.

A NEW MAJOR

I came to Humboldt to major in forestry. Ever since my first semester, I had been turning away from that as I realized I was not interested in the nitty-gritty of plant identification or forest pathogens. Last year I had changed my major to the more general "natural resources." But the continuing influence of music on my life kept me moving in its direction. Though I had decided last year to "give my life to music," it still wasn't clear what that meant. But it seems like when you “give your life” to something you are making it the focus of your existence. At any rate, at the beginning of the year, I decided to at least minor in music.

But as music played an ever more important part in my life, midway through the year I decided to forget natural resources completely and make music my major. Nothing else moved me so powerfully or looked so rich with potential.

OUTSIDE LOOKING IN

Having the ocean practically in our backyard was a great opportunity, and I spent many hours down on the beach.

The coastline was rocky and deserted. There was one small sandy beach where the stream below our house emptied out.

The solitude of the beach and surrounding ocean was consummate. It was a world apart where humans seldom intruded, a world of waves and sand and sea gulls and the ubiquitous mussels that covered every rock. The trees and brush on the exposed rocky bluffs were stunted and sculptured by the storms that whistled in off the ocean, offering mute testimony to the power of the forces of nature.

One evening coming back from the beach, I had a strange experience. I was walking up the first little hill on our lane from the old road. There in the distance through the border of trees and across the pasture was our house. It was dusk, and I could see lights on in various rooms through the uncurtained windows. There was a light in our bedroom as well. Inside, I knew Pahuta would be studying or listening to music. Smoke was rising from the chimney. It was a serene, pastoral setting.

Then something came over me and I began to imagine *me* being in that room also—that I was here on the outside looking in on my own life. But more than that, it was like I was some kind of predatory animal, like a panther or big cat, looking in on my unsuspecting life. How vulnerable it seemed! The person inside didn't have a clue that I was out here, waiting and watching, looking for an opportunity to strike. It was a new form of paranoia that I had never experienced before. It was like a split personality, where one part of me was possessed with the other part's enemy.

It sent a chill up my spine. Finally, I shook off the feeling and went up to the house. But after that, there would come times when I would be *in* the house, and I would remember that feeling and shudder. I would think, "Here I am, seemingly safe inside, while outside something is waiting and watching from the darkness, biding its time until in an unsuspecting moment it can attack suddenly from the shadows."

Even though we had been off drugs since the start of the school year, I still had flashbacks of being high again, and even had dreams where I was high and floating out of my body. And now this! Had drugs opened up my soul to some dark and sinister realm?

I wasn't always paranoid. But there were times it would come over me. Once when I went home to Ohio, after we all went to bed and the house was quiet, a sudden feeling of fear gripped me. I felt like there was a hideous, crazed, slathering "thing" out there that could enter our house at will, glide upstairs unhindered, come down the hall, break through my bedroom door and fall upon me. It was a feeling of unreasoning fear close to panic. I had no protection against this thing! The fear was so real that I actually got out my old .22 caliber rifle, dug out some ammunition, loaded it, and leaned it against the wall at the head of my bed. Meanwhile, I locked the bedroom door, leaned a chair under the doorknob and slid a heavy wooden trunk against it. I hoped that would slow it down long enough so I could grab the rifle and get off a quick shot!

Fortunately such fears, though intense, always vanished with the morning light. As I left drugs further and further behind, the fears gradually ceased.

MAJOR SHIFTS

I lived frugally, my only bills being my share of the rent, utilities, and the food we ate. Most years, working for the Forest Service during the summer was enough to get me by.

But this year I had not worked in the summer. I had no money saved up. So my folks not only had to pay for my legal costs, but the whole burden of my out-of-state tuition and all of my living and schooling costs fell on them this year. I'm surprised they didn't make me come home, but they believed in higher education, and they still believed in me. They sent me some money to live on, but it wasn't a lot. Miller and Pahuta were in the same boat. We had all strained our parents' finances with our drug shenanigans. As a result, we had to be careful about the money we spent for everything, including the food we ate. We developed a lot of meals from hamburger meat. For breakfast, we had a steady diet of oatmeal.

Winter set in and it got cold. In the Ruprecht's remodeling of the house, they yet to upgrade the heating system. There was only one gas wall heater in the kitchen. Other than that, we had the fireplace and electric space heaters. We couldn't afford the electric heaters, so our bedroom in the garage went mostly unheated.

Over the course of the winter, the cold and poverty and primitive conditions wore on us. I got tired of living in an unheated room and a cold house. On the plus side, my music classes were going well, I was learning a lot about music theory and my piano playing was improving rapidly. On the other hand, we were having some real problems with the drums. Perry proved to be more of a "classically trained" drummer than a rock and roll drummer. He could do a lot of drumming exercises, but had a hard time imitating what the drummers were doing on the songs we were trying to copy. Overall, he didn't seem to have much of an ear for music.

Also, when we would get into a song and begin to move with it, Perry had a tendency to "put his head down and run." He would get self-absorbed with his drumming and block us out of his hearing completely, all the time getting louder and faster. Soon the song would collapse in confusion. Sometimes we would realize the thing was falling apart, look at each other and stop. Perry, however, would go thundering on alone for a few bars before he even noticed that the rest of us had quit playing.

An even weaker point than drumming was our lack of a lead singer. We put the word out, hoping for someone to audition for us.

But I was tired of always being cold. Pahuta had an electric blanket to sleep under; I had to crawl under the covers in a forty-degree garage. My feet especially suffered. We burned a lot of wood in the fireplace, but it was not an efficient way to heat the house.

One morning toward the end of February, I got dressed and went outside as usual to go over to the house for breakfast. Most mornings, unless it was raining, it would be in the cold thirties; often there would be frost on the ground. But this morning it was unexpectedly mild. The jet stream had shifted; spring was here.

It sometimes happened like that. The jet stream would blow a certain way for a month or more, establishing a long weather pattern. Then overnight it would shift and usher in a brand new pattern. That's what happened here. When I went to bed it was winter; when I woke up it was spring.

But the change in the season brought other changes. The Ruprechts were coming home early! They had decided not to be gone the whole year; they would be back by the end of April. We would have to get a new place to stay.

That looked like it might spell the end of our dream for the rock band. We were close, close enough that there had been talk of setting up a gig in a local bar. One of Carol's girlfriends had a contact there. But it never quite happened.

Perry couldn't overcome his drumming problems; there were barriers he couldn't cross no matter how hard he tried. But we couldn't replace him because he was living with us and because he was Mark's cousin. He also suffered from low self-esteem to boot!

And though we did get a couple of singers to come out and audition, whatever they found in us they didn't like; we never heard from them again.

But in the end, the thing that finished the band more than anything else was the growing seriousness of the relationship between Larry and Carol. He was spending more time in town with her and less time with us. They were intimate and his interest in the band was waning. He had always been the driving force behind it. Mark and I were committed but Larry was always the leader.

Before we knew it, we were splitting up. Larry and I found an upstairs flat in an elderly lady's home on the outskirts of Eureka. Mark and Perry went to stay with Mark's aunt in Arcata.

It was an isolated and difficult time for me. I spent my twenty-first birthday, which I had looked forward to for years, holed up at home, unable to go anywhere, because I had no transportation other than Miller, who was gone.

In this unhappy situation one event stands out. The California presidential primary was fast approaching, and the Democratic candidates were stumping the state.

All through the winter, the pressure against the Vietnam War had been growing. First came the famous Tet Offensive in January.

Out of the Fire

We watched the war every night on the network news in our living room. Gradually, David Brinkley became skeptical. But the real change came when Walter Cronkite of CBS began turning against it. With Cronkite's growing disenchantment, I could sense the mood of the nation beginning to shift. There had always been the shrill anti-war protestors, the campus radicals, and the hippies. But the defection of Cronkite signaled a shift in the vast middle class majority. This was exciting; we could sense we were winning the heart of the nation to our side.

And then came that fateful day when President Johnson delivered the speech taking him out of the presidential race entirely. We were jubilant with victory; we felt the counterculture had won!

That threw the whole Democratic nomination open. Johnson supported Humphrey, his clone. Many were for George McGovern, who was tapping into the hippies and intellectual/left vote. Me, I was excited about Bobby Kennedy. I loved his energy and youthful enthusiasm.

Because California is so large and populous, it was extremely unlikely that any national candidate would come up to the far North Coast to see us. The population of huge Humboldt County could be swallowed up in just one of Los Angeles' bedroom communities. So it was quite surprising to hear that my man Bobby Kennedy was coming up on a campaign swing. He would be flying into our "international" airport, greeting the common people, and then motoring into Eureka to meet the movers and shakers.

I determined to go out to the airport and see him. Miller, who supported McGovern, wouldn't come, but let me borrow his car.

Out at the airport, there were several hundred people gathered outside the cyclone fence on the edge of the tarmac. Bobby was very late, but at last his plane landed and taxied to a stop. We were all straining for a look at him. We eagerly scanned every person who came out of the plane to see if it was him. Thirty or forty people straggled out over a period of five to ten minutes. Some were quite young and good looking, but none appeared to be Bobby because nobody paid them any attention. Finally, after a pause, Bobby suddenly appeared, and we all knew it was him and burst into spontaneous cheering and applause.

His speech was boilerplate campaign rhetoric—some words spoken in appreciation of our local area and some references to local issues to show that "we were in his heart and mind"; then some comments on the national issues that were a part of his campaign: his opposition to the Vietnam War, support of civil rights, and poverty issues; then some stirring statements and promises about what could be accomplished with him in the White House. It was a good, upbeat speech, and it got me excited.

After the speech he came over to the four-foot cyclone fence behind which we were standing and started going down the line of hands reaching over the fence and shaking them. At this point, I was torn. One part of me wanted to run over and join the crowd and stick my hand over the fence for him to shake, to reach out and touch this man I had come to believe in. But another part of me wanted to hold back, to remain aloof, to not "make a fool of myself," to remain the detached, unemotional intellectual.

As he came down the fence and others hungrily surged forward, I still held back, torn by these crosscurrents, unable to break free of my inhibitions and "go for it." Then the moment was past and he was down the line. Soon he was caught up in the swirl of dignitaries and news people and off to the waiting cars to be taken to town.

Only a few days later, on Election Day, I was home in our upstairs flat watching the election returns on TV. Bobby was winning California and McGovern finally conceded. I watched Bobby make his victory speech. It was a great moment: Johnson was history; the war protesters were winning; Bobby was the rising star—history was unfolding right before my eyes!

Then it happened. He had just finished his speech and left the podium in a happy crowd of people, while the network cut away for commentary on his speech–when tragedy struck. Something had happened but I couldn't tell what. The network flashed back to the ballroom camera still focused on the podium where people were screaming and running around. A man seized the microphone and tried to calm the crowd. He announced that police and paramedics had been summoned. "Everything's been done that can be done; please calm down. The medics are on their way." But on their way where? And for what?

Somebody finally said that Bobby had been shot.

After that, it was like the awful tragedy of Dallas revisited. Then it was his brother, John, who had been shot. I was a sophomore in high school at the time. I was in study hall and the school authorities immediately began broadcasting the radio coverage live over the public address system into our rooms. At first, we didn't know what was going on. Then we realized there was some kind of incident involving the president. We all sat in stunned silence as the tragic details unfolded. We found out he was wounded; he was on his way to the hospital; he was being operated on. Though each new bit of information was more ominous, they always left reason to hope; until the tragic announcement came—"President Kennedy is dead!"

Alone in the upstairs flat, stunned and disbelieving, I watched the same drama play out again: the same unrelenting progression of events, each holding out some hope, yet each worse than the last.

"Could it be happening again?" I thought grimly. "Does it have to end the same way?" With heartbreaking inevitability, the same announcement was made. Bobby Kennedy was no more.

First John Kennedy had been shot. Then Martin Luther King Jr. had been shot. Now Bobby Kennedy was shot. The antiwar movement was winning, but youthful idealism was bleeding in the streets. The radicals had taken over the antiwar movement, the Black Panthers were taking over the civil rights movement, and hard-core drugs were taking over the hippie movement. The idealistic 60s were ending. History was marching on. For me too life was marching on. The school year was over, the band was finished, my legal troubles were behind me, and I had been accepted back at Seiad for another summer with the Forest Service!

THE SECOND FIRE YEAR

June 1968

It was a measure of trust that the Forest Service, especially Zack Walton and Tom Beers, had allowed me to return. Drugs were unknown and scary; and just as they had taken a chance on hiring me the first time... they were taking a chance again. I'll always be grateful to Zack and Tom for their faith in me.

"Say, did you hear what happened to Dave Dreyfus?" It was the first questions Tom asked me. Dave had been our pilot during my first summer.

"No, what?"

"Well just this spring, Dave and the president of his company were checking out a new helicopter. The sales rep was taking them for a test ride. As he was landing at a helispot to show them how it could handle, he clipped some brush with the tail rotor, which threw them out of control. Though only a few feet off the ground, the violence of the crash and the ensuing fire killed them all."

I was aghast. I was stunned. How could it be? Someone so young, so full of life, with whom we had spent the summer, and suddenly he was gone? And then I remembered Dave's anguished cry that afternoon on the Indian Ridge Fire when our blue plywood board had gone through the main rotors. "You #%&*@$'s are trying to kill me!" he had screamed. I had passed it off at the time, because obviously neither Tom nor I were trying to kill him. But now he was dead. Could death itself have been stalking him all along? And though it had failed on the Indian Ridge Fire, this attempt had been all too successful? If so, how did that work? Was death a being, like the "Grim Reaper," who had the power to stalk people? Then how did he pick whom to stalk? Was there any protection from him, anyplace Dave could have turned for help? Or was it all one giant coincidence—freak occurrences over which we had no control? When your time is up, it's up! Is that what we were talking about? I couldn't buy the coincidence theory, but if the stalking theory were true, it raised more questions than it answered. Life suddenly got more complicated. It was no longer enough to choose *whom* I wanted to be like; I also had to consider *where* that person might end up.

The parallelism was sobering. On the Indian Ridge Fire, Dave and two other people—Tom and I—had a serious incident with the helicopter when the plywood board went through the rotor blades. But we all lived. A year and a half later, Dave and two other people had been in an incident in their helicopter when they clipped brush with the tail rotor. This time everyone died. Dave could have died just as easily in either situation, but Tom and I were spared while the president and the sales rep were killed. Why them and not us?

I'll never forget Dave and his boyish enthusiasm. He loved life; he was always fun to be around. But none of that mattered any more—*none of that had been enough to save him.* He never found any Power beyond himself that could have protected him. Now it was over.

Some things had changed in my absence. Fred Clark was still there, but Wilbur had found a position as a city fireman in Ashland, Oregon. In his place, a young guy by the name of Freddy Solaegui had been hired.

My position as Tom's assistant had been taken by a fine featured, friendly guy by the name of Jimmy Gould. Jimmy was even smaller than Tom, and fastidious in dress. Since he had my financed position on the helitack crew, I would have to go to the slash crew. But when the fire danger was high enough to require increased manning, I would go on the helitack crew as the third man, the one who would usually drive our truck.

The year in drugs had taken its toll. Though fortunate in being rehired, I had lost my old position, having to start further down the ladder. But worse than that, in personality and character, I found I was less confident, less able to think boldly and clearly, and less able to take decisive action. I was more withdrawn, more tentative, and more fearful—all qualities usually associated with cowardice. And, of course, as far as physical fitness went... well let's just say I wasn't. In every way I was less of an asset to my employer and to myself.

And there was still another change: we had a new helicopter!

Helicopter technology was rapidly changing, spurred on by the war in Vietnam. This year, we were chosen to try out a helicopter brand new to the Forest Service—a Bell model 206A called the "Jet Ranger." It had a light, turbine-powered engine that made its empty weight nearly 400 pounds lighter than our old two-passenger one. So it could carry four passengers instead of two. Its horsepower had been increased by almost fifty, and could cruise almost twice as fast, all the way up to 135 mph. It was superior in every way to the little two-passenger Bells and Hillers we had been using, and we were one of the first districts in all of California to try it out.

1967 had been a bust of a fire year, so I hadn't missed much. But the spring of 1968 was dry, and the summer started out with the fire danger increasing rapidly. I had to start out working with Frank Fazakas on the slash crew. But because of the rapidly increasing fire danger, they soon financed another position on the helitack crew. Then I was back working at the station again like before.

THE NEW HELICOPTER

1968 seemed to get off to an even faster start than1966. Within the first couple of weeks, we had a hot fire in Happy Camp, unusual for so early in the season. Not long after that, we had another thunderstorm upriver in the Horse Creek area, the same locale as my first lightning fire.

The fire season was already in full swing when the helicopter arrived, even though it arrived early, in the middle of June. It was a real beauty, sleek and streamlined. The whole thing was powered by a turbine engine that only weighed a hundred pounds! The Jet Ranger was new to the helicopter world, having entered commercial service only the year before.

Because the helicopter was so new, there had not yet been a retardant tank developed (like the L.A. Tank) to fasten between the skids for retardant dropping on fires. Instead, a man by the name of Sims had developed a fiberglass, cup-shaped "bucket" that could be hung from the helicopter's cargo hook. This "Sims Bucket" revolutionized water dropping from helicopters.

The whole operation could be accomplished by the pilot alone, in seconds instead of the several minutes it used to take to fill the L.A. Tank. The bucket's biggest drawback was that it required a large source of water close to the fire. On the Klamath National Forest, these were few and far between. If there was no water source close to the fire to dip from, the bucket was useless.

This and other problems meant we didn't use the Sims Bucket

much that year. It wasn't until the following year that we began to iron out some of the wrinkles.

However, with the greater speed, double passenger load, and greatly increased cargo-carrying capacity of the new helicopter, we still had a lot to be excited about and happy that we were chosen to try it out for the Forest Service.

Our pilot, Fernando, was a swarthy, mustachioed, swashbuckling type with the good looks and mischievous eyes of Clark Gable.

AN INTERRUPTED LUNCH

One day late in June, lunchtime had rolled around. Though it was hot, the fire danger was still *Moderate*, so normal days off were in order. Jimmy Gould and Freddy were off duty. The tanker crew was out working slash with Frank Fazakas, and Tom Beers had gone home for lunch. Fred Clark and I were the only ones on the compound, though Fernando was around somewhere lounging in the shade.

Lunch had been eaten, and Fred was asleep, stretched out on one of the narrow wooden benches in the dining room. I was sitting at a table nearby reading. Outside, the heat waves were shimmering over the compound. It was one of those hot, lethargic moments when time seems to stand still.

Suddenly, the fire alarm went off, rudely shattering the somnolence of the hour. Fred leaped up and ran for the tanker, while I sprinted for the heliport. Fernando materialized out of nowhere and we ran together to the helicopter. I thought maybe we should wait for Tom to be fetched from home, but instead, we jumped in and Fernando cranked it up. Before I knew it, we were airborne, making a right, looping, 180-degree turn over Seiad and heading upriver, carrying the empty Sims Bucket underneath.

Since I was the only Forest Service official on board, I thought I should handle the radio communications, but it didn't work out that way. Maybe my headset wasn't working, but the pilot did it all, and I was "just along for the ride."

We didn't follow the Klamath River east, but angled away from it in a northeasterly direction. When we crossed the first ridge out of Seiad Valley, I saw straight ahead, five to ten miles away, a great cloud of smoke boiling up from the far side of another ridge.

When we arrived at the fire, I had no idea where we were. The fire was by a big river, but I couldn't figure out what river it was. As far as I knew, there weren't any big rivers in this direction. From the way we had come, I thought it might be Horse Creek, which flowed out of the north and into the Klamath. But there was too much water in it for Horse Creek. In all this time, Fernando never said a word to me. He dropped off the Sims Bucket, then me, on a grassy sand bar by this unknown river and flew away.

I didn't know what to do or what he was going to do. I wondered if he would come back and need my help hooking up the Sims Bucket to make water drops. Or maybe he was going to come back and pick me up to help ferry men or equipment, or build a helispot on top of the ridge. Or maybe I should take my shovel and hike up the hill and start fighting the fire that was already on its way to becoming a major fire. I had no radio or bearings. I was completely disoriented and confused.

After a period of indecision, I noticed a main highway along the other side of this unknown river. Through the trees along the highway I saw tankers and other Forest Service vehicles coming up the river to the fire. This furthered my confusion. I knew there was a road along Horse Creek, but not a major highway like over there. Where in the world was I? I waited awhile longer but the helicopter didn't return. From time to time, I saw him flying around high above on the fire, but I was outside the loop.

It seemed like I should be doing something, but I wasn't sure what. Here we had a developing campaign fire right on our own district, and I was doing nothing. Finally, I took my shovel in hand and started up the side of the mountain to the fire somewhere above. But a little ways up, I stopped, torn by indecision again. It seemed so ridiculous, one person with no communications hiking up to a major fire somewhere "up there" to do what? Stop it with my shovel? In the meantime, what if I was needed on the helicopter; shouldn't that be my first priority?

I was finally convinced by this last argument, and began to walk upstream along an old dirt road toward where the main activity seemed to be. I came to where the road had been severed by a washout. On the other side, were Forest Service tankers and trucks and Glen Robinson, Walt's brother, the FCO of the Oak Knoll District. I crossed the washout, went up and stood there, intending to ask him where I should go, but he was busy on the radio. I caught the drift that he was acting as line boss for the fire. He was calling in smoke jumpers to jump on top of the ridge far above us near the head of the fire. He kept repeating instructions where to jump and what to do once they got on the ground. He was on the radio almost continually, and ignored me for so long I was embarrassed to still be standing there.

Finally, I got up enough courage to break in and ask if he knew where the helicopter was operating, and he waved me further up the road. About one quarter of a mile up the road, I found Jimmy Gould and the Forest's other helitack crew operating out of a makeshift heliport.

After greeting Jimmy and the others, I took him aside and asked, "Jimmy, where in the &*%~ are we anyway!?" I was totally frustrated. "What's this river here?"

"Why it's the Klamath River. What else could it be?"

"The Klamath River? The Klamath River?" My wheels were spinning. "I thought maybe it was Horse Creek," I said weakly.

"Well we are right by Horse Creek. It's only half a mile up the road. But this is the Klamath River."

I was thinking hard, my mind reeling, trying to make it all fit, "But we left the Klamath river... flew away from it... flew in a straight line... never turned back... now we're on it again...." It wasn't until later studying a map that I realized the Klamath River makes a big loop south to Hamburg and then north again to Horse Creek. I never noticed it driving along the river road. The pilot had merely taken the shortest direct route over the hills instead of following the river around the loop.

My first day's experience on that fire seemed to epitomize the impotent state where drugs had brought me. Though I had been off them nearly a year, I still had trouble functioning at times. Being so out of it instead of a main participant was a miserable place to be. Others by their actions were helping to *write* history, determining how big this fire would ultimately get: 50 acres? 500 acres? Or 5000 acres? But I, even though the first to arrive, was playing no part. It was a feeling like being dead, but coming back in spirit to watch the rest of the world go on without you, and realizing you were not even missed!

After finally getting plugged back into what was happening, I joined the firefighting effort that raged all afternoon. The fire, which was named the "Sambo Fire" because it originated in Sambo Gulch, was on steep terrain rising out of the river—on the dry, southern exposure where it burned hot and fast. The only access by road was one corner at the very bottom, where I ended up with the helicopters.

Because of the steep terrain and lack of roads, helicopters were sorely needed, and we ended up with a couple more in addition to our own. We were so busy loading and unloading that I never got off the heliport to see any of the fire itself. There were two incidents from the fire however that made lasting impressions on me.

The first was an incident concerning John Brannon, the head of our timber department. John was intense and hard working. Still in his 30s, he was on the fast track to becoming District Ranger; from there, it was no telling how far he would rise in the Forest Service. He seemed motivated by a grim obsession to succeed that caused him to push himself and others as well. He was friendly enough, though lacking in warmth.

On the first day of the fire, John was toiling up the steep fire line in the hot sun with a crew from another district, heading toward the top of the ridge. The other fire crew was cutting up a little, goofing off and horsing around as they made their grueling way up the slope. It was too much for John. He blew up at them, shouting that this was a FIRE! It wasn't supposed to be FUN! This was WORK! The part especially about "it wasn't supposed to be fun" stuck out to me. It seemed too intense even for one's own personal philosophy, much less one you try to impose on others. John seemed to be a guy destined to go far in life, but he sure wasn't enjoying the trip.

The second incident involved Brad, the pilot of our second helicopter from the Callahan District, a young fellow in his 20s.

Most of the pilots took off from the heliport slowly, applying power until they had lifted into a hover position, and then gingerly tilting their craft to get some forward motion, edging off the pad and away into the sky.

But Brad was different. He would pull pitch, push the stick forward, and power out of the heliport without hesitation. He was the quickest out and the first back. But he wasn't a showoff or a hot-dogger; he was just a workhorse.

One time in particular we were standing there watching him power out in such a resolute manner, when one of the other crew members said admiringly, "There goes Brad again. Man that guy is always 'balls to the wall.' He's 'redlining' it all the time!"

Running at redline meant that the machine was producing all it was capable of producing—it was running at 100%. There is an awesome beauty to a great athlete or machine running at maximum power, putting forth everything it was designed to produce, reflecting to the fullest the skill and creative genius of its designer.

But running at redline called for the greatest skill on the part of the pilot as well. This was sweaty palms flying. All the gauges must be monitored constantly so the red line is not exceeded. Safety margins are cut to the minimum—there is no room for error. Running the helicopter at redline required a pilot who was willing to push himself to the limit as well.

And a crewman was saying that this pilot ran that way all the time; he had a lifestyle built around giving his all.

This made a deep impression on me. Here was a way of living that was inspiring. Here was a model, something to strive for. Here was a way of life that had glory and virtue.

AN UNEXPECTED CHANGE

By the middle of August things were looking grim. The forest had dried out to dangerous levels. The fire danger was steadily creeping toward the *Very High* range. It only needed a hot dry wind to push it into *Extreme* again. And it could be a month or more before the weather changed. We appeared destined to repeat the fire season of 1966 or even surpass it. We hadn't had any big fires on the forest yet, but it seemed only a matter of time. The fire fighting organization was on the ragged edge.

The only reason we weren't having a lot of thunderstorms was because of the dryness of the atmosphere. So when we heard of a change in the weather bringing in moisture and clouds with a cold front, I expected the worst. The cold front came through, bringing clouds and cooler air and even some light rain showers, but scarcely a rumble of thunder. Then another system came through, bringing even more clouds, still cooler weather, and some—dare I say it? —real rain! Yes, it rained in August and not just sprinkles. It rained over an inch in most places, more in the higher elevations. And then still another system with more rain.

Far above us, the jet stream, that fast-flowing river of air in the upper atmosphere, had looped far down from the north and was bringing a flood of cool, moist air from the Gulf of Alaska. The whole fire season changed overnight. The fire danger fell back into the *Moderate* zone, then into *Low*. Frank Fazakas' slash crew, long dormant, its members at the station with the tanker, was suddenly revived and sent back into the woods to ready the cut-blocks for burning in the slash season.

For the last two weeks of August and into the first week of September, the weather continued cool and unsettled. By Labor Day, when the jet stream finally shifted to a more seasonal pattern, the fire season's back had been broken.

ROLLING LOG

Since the fire season was finished, the Forest Service switched gears early and began to prepare for slash burning that normally doesn't start till October. The slash from the cut-blocks logged during the summer needed to be burned before the winter rains fell.

Slash burning is tricky. Conditions must be dry enough for the slash to burn, but not so dry as to let the fire escape into the forest.

Out of the Fire

Usually the first blocks to be burned are the ones highest in elevation, where the air is cooler and the moisture level higher.

So it was in early September we got word that our neighbor district to the south, the Scott Valley District, was going to be burning a slash block up in the mountains near our border.

Meanwhile, we also got the unexpected news that Tom Beers was leaving. He had done such a good job establishing the helitack crew and making helicopter fire fighting work, he was being promoted to Assistant FCO on the Ukonom District.

A going-away party for Tom was planned at his house, only a long block away from the ranger station. Most of the summer help had gone back to school. I was still there, as was Tim who had replaced Freddy as TTO. So there were a couple of us to party with Tom. Zack came over, but didn't drink and excused himself early. He was nervous because this was the night Scott Valley was going to burn the slash block.

They would start it in the evening so the heavy burning would happen overnight, as a further precaution against the fire's possible escape. Because of the earliness of the season, the fire fighting organization seemed quite worried about it, and Zack was going to stay close to the radio all night. Since the block was close to our district, if anything went wrong, we were sure to be called.

The party was dull. There were just the three of us sitting around talking as we drank ourselves toward oblivion. Along about 11:00 p.m., I was quite drunk, as were the others, sitting around telling "there-I-was-surrounded-by-fire-on-every-side" war stories. Then Zack reappeared, only this time to tell us there was trouble.

Even with all their precautions, the slash fire had jumped the line. They wanted us to send our tanker and also our 3,000 gallon mother tanker. They were also calling the inmate crews from the conservation camp and others.

Tim was as drunk as I was, and in no condition to drive. Zack left to call Fred to drive the tanker. Jack Byers would follow with the mother tanker.

We returned to the bunkhouse, got our gear, and tried to sober up with a combination of hot coffee and cool night air, neither of which helped. Then Fred arrived and we started up Walker Creek along the miles of twisting logging roads that would take us over the mountains to the fire. I was sitting in the passenger's side of the bouncing cab of the tanker with Tim in the middle, hoping I wouldn't get sick from the rough ride and all the beer I'd consumed. The ride itself remains a daze in my mind; the trees and cut-banks of the logging road swam by in a continuous blur in our headlights.

We arrived at the fire sometime after midnight, and were directed to a landing near the bottom of the slash block, where the fire had jumped the line into the brush below. The fire was not spreading quickly, though it was burning well. A chainsaw crew had already cut a fire line through the waist-high Manzanita and buck brush that was so thick as to be almost impenetrable.

It was easy to see why the fire had escaped: though the ground was sloping, no trench had been dug to catch rolling, burning material coming down from the fire above. Instead, a cat had scraped a line the width of its blade along the bottom of the block on the same contour as the slope. Such a line would be sufficient to stop the fire from creeping out of the block, but offered no protection from rolling material. The result was that burning material, especially pine cones, had broken loose, rolled down into the brush below, and started fires now burning merrily outside the block.

We were disgusted by this lack of professionalism, but not sure how high up the ladder it went. The district's own worry beforehand and the alerting of the other districts seemed to show that they knew the block was ill prepared for burning. The fact that they burned it anyway without fixing the problems, indicated serious errors in judgment.

Our immediate job was to run a hose lay along the new fire line through the brush. We spent some time doing this: laying out the hose, putting on laterals, charging them all with water, and hosing down the fire close to the line—"holding the line" we call it—while letting the rest of the fire burn itself out.

Along about 3:00 a.m., we had things pretty well under control in our little sector. I was working the tanker with Fred, while Tim ran the nozzles. We were out of water, and there was still no sign of Jack Byers or the mother tanker. But some Scott Valley men had directed us to a marshy area only a mile from the fire where we were able to refill our tanker. Now, the tanker was full, our hose line was all laid out, and Tim was down at the fire, spraying water.

"Let's get some coffee started," Fred said, indicating that the emergency, as far as he was concerned, was over. We had a large blackened coffee pot in a tanker compartment for just such a time. I filled it with water from a canteen, poured a generous amount of coffee grounds on top of the water, and put it on the warming fire we had started.

While the water was heating up, Fred and I went to check on the fire. It was burning well, but stable, and seemed in no danger of jumping the new line. We found Tim manning the hose. He wanted to talk to Fred about something, so I took the hose and casually sprayed down a couple of hotspots near the line while he and Fred talked below me. There was no wind; the air was cool, damp and invigorating. I took some refreshing draughts deep into my lungs, feeling pretty good, the alcohol all but gone from my system. The sky was still dark, but I could sense the promise of approaching dawn. Everything was calm and right.

Then I heard an ominous sound.

The most frightening sounds in life are not always the loudest. The smallest sounds—like the cocking of the hammer on a loaded gun—can contain the most fearful message of impending doom.

Not loud, yet disturbingly out of place, it immediately caused my head to jerk up and look intently into the fire burning above me. There was a huge burning log, waist high and 100 ft. long, lying across the slope above us. Only thirty feet away, it had been burning in place unnoticed, while whatever was holding it quietly burned through. The sound that caught my attention was the log breaking free of its mooring. With nothing to hold it any longer, it was rising from its bed of coals and starting to roll down the hill toward us.

In an instant of panic, I realized our predicament. The log was too long and too near to run around. We were standing with fire above us and impenetrable brush below us, on the fire line that angled between the two down the hill: the same path that the log was sure to take. We were trapped like rats on a doomed ship! The only possibility of escape was to get down the fire line quickly and try to get beyond the end of the log before it caught up with us.

I whirled around and charged down the fire line, flinging the fire hose unheedingly into the air. Tim and Fred right below me were still unaware of the danger. In a few steps I was storming between them, shouting wildly. Tim said later all he remembered was the fire hose spraying crazily and me running through their midst shouting "Log! Log!"I can still recall the startled look on their faces as I shot full speed through them. Then I was off down the hill.

The fire line, though it was the only escape route, at this point was running almost directly up and down the hill. Since the longer the log rolled, the faster it would go, there would come a time when it had to overtake us if we were still underneath it. The fire line did angle ever so slightly across the slope, but the angle was so slight I was sure the log would overtake me before I could get far enough down the line to get out from under it. I saw a better chance of escape, in the brief instant that I was flying down the line, by heading directly across the slope through the fire. Though still a slim chance, running would be easier where the brush was partially burned, and it would afford a quicker way of getting beyond the end of the log than by following the slight angle of the fire line.

It's amazing how fast you can think when your life depends on it. Coming to a point where the line turned even more straight down hill, I leapt with a bound into the fire that at this point had mostly burned down to beds of coals and half-burned brush. My goal was to go straight across the slope, but I had only taken one step off the line when I was immediately tripped by an unburned stob of brush and plunged headlong. This turned my panic into hysteria. I tucked my head and somersaulted forward to get the maximum distance out of my fall. As I came up from the roll, I was vaguely aware of hot coals going down the back of my neck. Desperately, on hands and knees, like a wild animal, I clawed my way through the brush, trying to get past the end of the log before it came through. It had picked up speed and was coming down the mountain like a freight train, flattening the brush with a snapping, cracking, wicked "swooshing" sound that curdled my blood.

Then it was past. To this day I have no idea how close it came.

But the next instant I heard a scream in the direction of the fire line. It was Fred! It was the most awful scream I have ever heard, like the scream of the damned as hell opens its mouth under him—the scream of terror at the moment of doom when there is no escape. I knew the log had gotten him.

Tim and Fred had followed me down the line, going straight where I had veered into the fire, trying instead to outrun the log down the line. Before it caught up to Tim, it smashed into a big rock and broke in half. The upper section of the log was stopped by a small tree in the brush field, while the lower section bounced off the rock back into the fire, missing Tim and thundering down the final precipitous slope into the bottom of the ravine.

Fred however, following on Tim's heels, had tripped on a stob of brush that the chainsaws had left sticking out of the ground. He had fallen headlong in front of the rampaging log, his last scream wrenched from the depth of his soul as he met his certain doom under its crushing weight.

I was the first to reach him, though I was burned and bleeding and without my glasses. Surprisingly, I found him still alive, trying vainly to sit up, and brushing ineffectually at bits of flame from the burning coals the log left on his clothes. He was in shock of course, and disjointed. People from the landing above who had heard his scream were yelling down to us, trying to find out what happened. I yelled back to them to send help. I brushed the burning coals off Fred's clothes, saw that he was not in any immediate danger, and headed up the line to get assistance.

It would be hard to exaggerate the problem I had just getting out of there in the dark without my glasses. I am extremely nearsighted, which means that everything blurs together and overlaps in my vision. I had nothing but the uncertain glow of the fire and my sense of feel to help me work my way back up the hill to the landing. The light from the fire tended to be a glare in my eyes, instead of illuminating the path for my feet. Near the top, the fire had pretty much been extinguished close to the line, so it was hard to tell when I was in the fire and when I was on the line.

Finally I met some people coming down to help. I explained that a log had rolled over Fred and that he was in bad shape. Someone pulled out a first aid kit and bandaged the worst gash on my hands from fighting through the brush, and helped me the rest of the way to the landing. The rest of my injuries seemed to be scratches on the face and hands that didn't require any immediate medical attention. However, the back of my neck burned like fire from the hot coals down my shirt.

The part that follows is the hardest to tell because it exposes the frailty of the human condition. We are used to hearing about human laxity before tragedy strikes. But tragedy, when it strikes, is supposed to galvanize the human spirit—to break it out of the apathy in which it habitually languishes and to unite it with others to tackle the tragedy together. Indeed, this is often seen as one of the hidden benefits of tragedy: it causes people to rise above themselves. "It brings out the best in people," we often hear.

When that does happen, it is wonderful. Selfless sacrifice in the face of tragedy gives a great lift to the human spirit, which helps to offset the effects of the tragedy. But that's not always what happens! The saddest times are when just the opposite occurs—when tragedy causes hidden fault lines in human character and relationships to break out in the open and be suddenly manifest to all. Tragedy can either bring out the best or expose the worst in mankind.

Fred's accident unfortunately was closer to the latter than the former. While his life within his crushed body hung in the balance, there followed an hour or more of such confusion and disorganization that after awhile I just went off by myself rather than witness it. Without glasses I was useless anyway, and it was too painful and frustrating to look upon.

There were six people in charge, but really there was no one in charge. For every problem there seemed to be six different solutions. Just to bring Fred up the hill to the landing brought out many conflicting opinions. Everybody became an instant expert on emergency medical care. Some thought he shouldn't be moved at all, but we should wait for an ambulance crew, which would have taken two hours to get there, then another two hours to get him to the hospital! Those that did want to bring him out couldn't agree on how to do it. Some wanted to do a blanket carry. Others wanted to use a stretcher to keep his back straight. But what kind of stretcher and where to get it? One person was sure there was one at the top of the hill with such and such a tanker crew.

Someone else said, "No that's a basket stretcher. You don't want to use that because you couldn't immobilize the back. We need a plank stretcher."

"But where can we get that?"

"Let's call on the radio and see if we can locate one." And on and on it went: diverse, swirling currents of opinion and activity with no one able to exert sufficient authority to take charge. One person was searching for blankets, another was driving around to the different crews on the fire line looking for a stretcher, another was making "calling all stations" calls on the radio trying to track down a plank stretcher, another was trying to relay instructions to the ambulance crew through Frank Grove in Yreka on how to get up to the fire. Others were down with Fred still lying where he had fallen, watching his vital signs fade and saying, "It doesn't matter *how* we get him out, but we've got to do it *now*."

And I, nearly blind in the darkness, in shock and emotionally traumatized, was alone in the eye of the storm with everything swirling around me. I was utterly powerless to do anything to help Fred—or keep him from dying. Not knowing God, I didn't even have the option of prayer, which would have been a personal comfort, and might have been able to do more than all the other frantic activity combined to pull Fred through.

When they finally came up with a stretcher, they discovered they still had no blankets to cushion his body. The man who had been chasing down blankets for the blanket carry had disappeared. So the blanket search started again. Others were trying—mostly unsuccessfully—to get people to give up their jackets.

It seemed to take an hour to get him the fifty yards up to the landing where the vehicles were. Then there was the question of whether to wait for the ambulance or start down the mountain with Fred in a vehicle. If so, which vehicle? Every question that came up seemed to bring a swirl of conflicting opinions, which stopped all progress dead in its tracks. Finally, it was decided to take him down in the back of the fire prevention officer's pickup. Then they had to figure out how to make Fred a bed in the back of the pickup to cushion him from the jarring of the rough logging roads, which meant finding more blankets, etc.

I had to convince them to take me too, as I wanted my burns checked out and to get my hand re-bandaged. But it turned out I couldn't ride in the cab of the truck because the fire prevention officer had his large dog with him. It had to sit in the front seat because they didn't want it in back with Fred, and he didn't want to leave it behind because he was afraid it might run away. To be arguing over the fate of this dog, which shouldn't even have been there, while Fred's life ebbed away was almost more than I could bear. So I climbed into the pickup's bed with Fred and a couple of others to watch him, and at long last we started down the logging roads toward civilization.

We were up in the mountains around 6,000 feet in elevation. The ambulance was supposed to meet us where the logging road hit the highway along the Scott River, at about the 2,000 foot level, leaving us a long, winding, downhill trip.

It was a wrenching experience. Fred was in bad shape: his legs were broken, his hip was broken, his pelvis was broken, his ribs were broken. He was delirious and kept mumbling that he was dying or was going to die. Breathing was difficult for him with his broken ribs, and every breath was labored. And I, traumatized and in shock myself, was stuck back there with him in the morning chill, while the dog had a nice pleasant ride in the cab!

We were driving slowly so as not to bounce Fred around. But going ten to fifteen mph down the twisting dirt roads with the dark trees silhouetting the sky made the trip seem to go on forever. Fred's moaning continued monotonously, punctuated occasionally by sudden, loud, eerie pronouncements that he was going to die.

After experiencing this for awhile, I decided that I never wanted to go to war. Fred had gotten broken up by accident while we were fighting a common enemy. But in war, people did this to other people on purpose! The thought filled me with horror. I couldn't comprehend the idea; it seemed too terrible.

The first filtering of morning light was coming through the trees when we finally reached the highway and met up with the ambulance at a small, river resort. They quickly put Fred in the back and me up front for the forty-five-minute ride to the hospital in Yreka. One attendant drove and the other was back with Fred.

The guy driving the Forest Service pickup we had been in, for some reason, insisted on "leading" us back to town, which meant we had to eat his dust on the long, gravel portions of the road. Without my glasses on, the clouds of dust swam in front of my eyes like fog, making it look as if we were driving blind.

We finally reached paved road and sped towards Ft. Jones, the home of the Scott Valley Ranger District. As we slowed down to go through town the attendant in the back said matter-of-factly to the driver, "Better speed up as much as you can; we're about to lose him." The driver turned his red lights on and hit the gas. But mercifully, he kept his siren off. It was about 6:00 a.m. and the roads were completely deserted. There weren't any signal lights or stop signs to worry about, and my nerves were frayed enough without the unsettling wail of a siren.

We pulled into the Yreka Hospital as the sun was rising, and they rushed him into emergency. Later in the morning, after they had stabilized him, they whisked him over the Siskiyous to the major hospital in Medford, Oregon, where he spent hours in surgery getting his pieces put back together again.

Fred had come within a hair's breadth of dying from shock on the way to the hospital, but whatever Power had spared him from death by the log and during the long delay getting him back to civilization was not about to let him go now.

They checked me over, found that the burns on my neck were only first degree, cleaned and re-bandaged my hand, and sent me off to the forest headquarters building to wait for someone from Seiad to pick me up.

As I was resting in a side room, I heard some of the fire control men talking next door. They were commenting on how well the burn had gone. "If it hadn't been for the tragic accident," they said, "it would have been a success all around."

Back at Seiad, I put my spare pair of glasses on and could finally see the scratches and welts covering my face.

Tim and I took his car for the two-hour drive to Medford to see Fred before I returned to the coast. He was glad to see us. He was all bound up in traction, but was in pretty good spirits. He was out of danger, but they didn't know how well he would recover.

Then I returned to college and life returned to normal--on the surface. But the horror of what happened went so deep that every night for months, I couldn't go to sleep until I relived the whole experience in my mind: the sudden discovery of the rolling log, the desperate flight down the mountain, the "swoosh" of the log flattening the brush behind me, the headlong fall and desperate clawing through the brush to escape, Fred's scream and the log's exit down the mountainside. Then at last, I could go to sleep.

Though not realizing it at the time, I was seeing the need for God as I never had before. The failures of man, even man's organizations, were so obvious: from the failure of the district to adequately prepare the block, to the total lack of organization, leadership, and even common sense that nearly cost Fred his life as he lay crushed in the dark on the fire line. People weren't willing to give up their coats, the fire prevention man wasn't willing to give up his dog, and many others weren't even willing to give up their opinions in order to save a life. How reassuring it would have been to be able to petition and receive comfort from the God who cares and has the power to intervene. But my theology didn't allow for that, and so I was left with my own inability to help, and the thin gruel of comfort that came from the bungling efforts of man. Yes I had left atheism behind, but I was still a long ways from connecting with the God I so desperately needed!

THE SENIOR YEAR

September 1968

When I left Seiad to return to college after my first season, we had just come through the trauma of the Indian Ridge Fire. I had almost been in one helicopter accident, and had witnessed another. The fire had been explosive, consuming 12,000 acres in two days, trapping and almost killing men in the process.

Going from this dangerous fire back to Arcata had been like going to a different planet: a happy world of college students and activity, friends and reunions, so different from the world of smoke and ashes; sweat, struggle, and danger from which I had just stepped.

Once again, the same remarkable transition was repeated. I stepped out of the world of the recent terror of the rolling log, Fred's scream, the heart-stopping closeness of my own escape, the eternity of haggling over what to do, and the long ride down the dark mountainside in the back of the pickup, listening to Fred's terrible moans and pronouncements of his impending death. From that, after a half-day's bus ride, I stepped back into the friendly, bustling world of Arcata, and getting ready for another college year. Except for me, the dichotomy of the two worlds was complete. I was the only one in either world who knew about the other, and the only bridge between them.

This time, there was none of the triumphalism I had felt after the first fire year. This time, there was the soberness from the trauma I had experienced and the memory of Fred's terrible scream. There was also loneliness in not being able to share these experiences. People were full of the summer worlds they had just come from, and there wasn't much room left for mine. But at least we were all together in the college world that for the next nine months we would share.

Miller and Carol had continued their romance during the summer, and were planning to live together on their way to getting married. So Mark Pahuta and I decided to look for housing for the two of us. As usual, at this late date, there was nothing in Arcata near the school.

We finally found an upstairs flat in a run-down section of Eureka, eight miles away across the Bay. It was on Cedar Street, a street dominated by older homes lived in by older people, all of which were decaying together. Right across the street on the corner was a dilapidated building with a worn sign "Deliverance Temple" that I took to be a Jewish synagogue.

I needed transportation to school ten miles away. At Fred Cranston's suggestion, I bought an old '48 Dodge from a "friend" of his for $100. But almost immediately, it developed valve problems. By winter, it wouldn't even start, and I was back to scrounging rides any way I could.

MUSICAL ECSTASY

Once again I was singing in the Chorale, and a Christmas performance in the college gymnasium was planned. This was to be a major event, with full orchestra, the College Chorale, the Choir, and even the high school chorus group.

This time, in addition to the mandatory "Hallelujah Chorus" and some other pieces, we were singing a modern piece called "Something Like a Star," a poem by Robert Frost set to music by a modern composer. The gist of the poem was that there are stars in the heavens that are eternally unchanged and constant, no matter what kind of convolutions life goes through down here on earth. And when life gets hard, even impossible, then:

We may choose something like a star
To stay our minds on and be stayed.

The climax of the piece was a long, richly textured chord on the word, "choose," where the song swelled and soared into the heavenlies. The tenor part leading up to this chord was a simple descending line of four notes on "we-ee may-ay" then the "choose," but when combined with the other parts leading to their own climatic notes, the line gathered incredible power as each part's four notes resulted in four rich polyphonic chords building to the grand climatic chord on "choose."

As we were singing the song in the concert, I got totally caught up in the message of the song and the power of the music—the idea that, in spite of all the turmoil and problems in my own life and in man's affairs on the earth, there was another realm in the heavens above that was beyond the turmoil, a realm that glided effortlessly along according to an order fixed in eternity past. Men's kingdoms may collapse overnight, or my car may break down and leave me scrounging for rides and hitch-hiking in the rain, but the constellations are still revolving through the heavens in their places, the North Star is still in the north, the sun still rises in the east. I think it was this vision of a world of stability and predictability compared to my own world of uncertainty and powerlessness that suddenly came alive to me in the song.

My car problem was still unresolved, my girl problem was no closer to a solution, and my life's-work-and-career problem was still like so much muddy water. In spite of my best efforts, life's answers were as elusive as ever. Yet high above, there was another world where stars wheeled silently and majestically through the heavens. This song was saying it was possible for those in this world to fix their minds on things in that one, and by so doing, to receive some of that surety and serenity down here on earth—a noble thought indeed!

When we started into that climatic line, my spirit soared with the music, completely engulfed by its power. Screaming "Yes!" to the lyric with all my being, I entered the music flowing like a rushing river. It was an irresistible force! I had never been gripped by something as powerful and unstoppable in my life as in the progression of those four notes to the climax.

When we hit that impossible chord on "choose," it was as if the mighty wave of music had crashed upon the shore and exploded into a thousand droplets of individual voices in a thunder of sound as we poured out our beings, all rushing upward in an incredibly rich rainbow of voices to the very heavenlies.

Then, without breaking stride, the music dropped away from the soaring climax to the almost whispered conclusion, "something like a star, to stay our minds on and be stayed, to stay our minds on and be stayed." I left deeply moved. I felt I had touched the eternal.

PAHUTA, TV, AND BILLY GRAHAM

Miller and Carol had found half a duplex to rent on the western edge of Arcata, down on the coastal plain. They learned that the renters in the other half were moving out. We talked to the landlord and were able to rent it. This left me within bicycling distance of the college *and* we were living right next door to Miller.

Living with Miller had been one thing. We were so different that in a way we fit together. He was the leader, I was the follower. He was the initiator, I was the responder. He was the Type A personality, I was the Type B.

But with Pahuta, we were both Type B personalities. We were so much alike that it was hilarious. We were both like Garfield's owner, Jon, in the comic strip: dull, stay-at-home couch potatoes, without female friends or social lives.

Because Mark had the car, we did everything together: went to the grocery store, the Laundromat, the movies.... It was like we were married. But it was strictly a "marriage-of-convenience." I used to joke that now I knew what it would be like to live in a loveless marriage: perfunctorily shopping together, cooking together, eating together, watching TV together, a living-together-but-sleeping-in-different-bedrooms kind of marriage.

Our social life was so boring that for the first time in my life I learned what it meant to sit down in front of the TV and spend hours there, glued to the set out of boredom instead of interest; and because of the monotony, to get completely sucked into the little tricks that are used to keep you watching: "Stay tuned right after 'Mr. Ed' and see Flipper fight off the whale poachers!" Oh yeah, I gotta see that. I learned what it was like to finally wrench myself free after a marathon TV session and feel empty and cheated, like several hours of my life had been sucked out with absolutely nothing to show for it.

This was back when TV was being called a "vast wasteland," before the onset of the current mind-numbing violence, endless sexual preoccupation, foul language, and gutter humor that so fills TV today. At present, we refer to those earlier times as TV's "good old days." But it was not really better, just not as far advanced on the scale of decay. Out of the many hours spent watching TV that year, I can't remember a single show I watched.

But there was something else we watched that I do remember:

the Billy Graham Crusades. They would run an hour every night for a week at a time. I don't know why we watched them; neither one of us was religious. Nor did we agree with his premise: that all of us were sinners who needed salvation that was only available through Jesus Christ. We would argue and mock. But the next night there we'd be, tuning in again, listening to the music, waiting for the moment when The Man himself would come out and preach to us.

I think there was something about his boldness and the simplicity of his message. There was also something fascinating about his rugged good looks and the conviction of his preaching. Just watching him, I felt like here was an honest man who believed what he was saying so much that it energized his entire life. Here was a straight shooter to whom what he believed, what he preached, and what he lived were all one and the same thing.

He always addressed issues close to home like drugs and emptiness and finding meaning in life. His answer to life's problems was so simple! Invite Jesus Christ to come into your life. Not having found many answers myself, I was naturally interested in listening to someone who had.

My life was certainly empty enough. Finishing my fourth year of college, I had no more idea of what I was to do with myself than the man in the moon, except for the vague commitment I had made earlier to "Give myself to music." I had decided to add a political science major to my curriculum that year, and was taking a full load of political science courses in addition to all my music courses for a total of nineteen units—thinking perhaps that all that work would somehow produce meaning and satisfaction. Yet there was still a listlessness in my spirit: a boredom, a lack of motivation and direction. Yeah, Billy had put his finger on my problem all right, but I wasn't ready to embrace this Christ who was his answer to everything. But how I longed for his enthusiasm, confidence, and clear direction in *my* life!

I had an automatic respect for those like Billy Graham, whom I took to be men of God. Another one was my first probation officer, who was a Baptist preacher on the side. He seemed so honest, so straightforward—a truly good man.

It's funny, but even in my atheistic days in high school, I had a certain respect for the holy. I used to do janitorial work in our Unitarian-Universalist Church in Kent. For a couple of years, my older brother Howard and I cleaned the whole church every week. I can remember when it fell to me to clean the sanctuary. Vacuuming the carpet was no big deal, nor was cleaning the platform where the minister and choir sat. But I always approached the pulpit with a certain amount of trepidation and reverence. The pulpit was somehow my contact point between the mundane things of the earth and "the holy"—the unseen, the eternal, the realm of God Himself. It was the only contact point I knew of in a church and a culture that had pretty much cast God aside. Yet even in such a church—where belief in God was a dying flicker, and in such a person as myself—a hard, evangelistic atheist—I approached the pulpit with fear; I dusted its polished surface reverently. Here was a point of contact with "the holy."

PROBLEMS

Our diet was terrible. We didn't have much money so our meals were simple and cheap. Sometimes we would make a meal out of just eggs, scrambling up a whole dozen and sharing them between us—that would be dinner! Other times dinner would be pancakes. Since that was all there was, we fancied them up by adding strawberries, and smothering the whole thing with whipping cream and syrup. The whipping cream had such a high butterfat content that when I used it in my coffee, it left an oily film on top. One habit we had gotten into with Miller was cooking up a pork roast every now and then. Also, we liked to French fry our own potatoes in a skillet filled with oil. Along with this high fat diet, our exercise was nil, except for riding my bicycle to school.

In the spring, I developed little bumps on my feet, then some on my fingers. When they didn't go away, I went to the campus health center. After a series of tests, the doctor discovered I had dangerously high cholesterol. That plus my smoking was going to ruin my arteries. Alarmed, the doctor put me on a strict low-fat diet and began giving me medication to lower my cholesterol. I asked how long I would have to continue the medication and diet.

"Indefinitely, you seem to be at risk for high cholesterol."

I don't think I can adequately describe the feelings of an almost twenty-two-year-old who's never had any health problems and in the prime of life who's just been told that he has a problem that will follow him to the grave, mandating medication for the rest of his life. Also, he'll have to take out of his diet, forever, the things he craves most: French fries, burgers, eggs. It was like the whole world caved in on me. "I'm not ready for this. I'm not ready to be old and decrepit, careful about everything I eat, taking daily medication, constantly monitoring my cholesterol." It was a heavy blow.

I was shaken by another problem about this time that created additional insecurities. Behind our duplex was another one built at right angles, off the alley. Just beyond the back wall of my bedroom was the front yard of this duplex. None of the duplexes had real yards, people just parked in the gravel in front of their building.

It wouldn't have been so bad, but these guys were partying college students. Late at night, after I was asleep, they would come roaring down the alley, locking up the brakes in the gravel and sliding into a spot sometimes as close as six feet from my bed. I had a fear that some night they would miscalculate and slide right through my bedroom wall! Many nights, I would be awakened from a light sleep to the approaching sound of a roaring engine down the alley followed by tires sliding on gravel, then the slam of car doors almost in my ears, and loud boisterous voices as they went inside, only to have the experience repeated a half hour later.

The previous fall, after the rolling log incident, I had to relive the whole experience and escape the log every night before I could go to sleep—for months. Now I noticed I had to have another fantasy before I could go to sleep: I had to fantasize some kind of confrontation or fight in which I shot somebody with a gun. Even though it was only a creation of my mind, every night it had to happen before I could go to sleep. The details could vary, but it couldn't end until I shot somebody. It was probably suppressed aggression against those guys scaring me with their cars.

Meanwhile, I was still working in music and doing some writing on the side. About this time, I wrote a play that was later published in the *Toyon*, the college's literary publication. It centered on a man of extreme aggressiveness and his battles with the world and his wife, patterned after the movie *Who's Afraid of Virginia Woolf?*—full of strife and personal conflict.

Laziness, lack of motivation and direction, fear and insecurity, internalized violence and aggression. No wonder I was drawn to Billy Graham and his messages; my life was a mess!

A NEW BIRD AND A NEW BOSS

June 1969

The Seiad Ranger Station was all abuzz with talk of change. The Forest had made the decision to reduce the number of ranger districts from eight to six. The Seiad District would be merged into the Oak Knoll District by the end of the year, although the old ranger station would be kept as a work center with a foreman and tanker crew. Everybody else would be reassigned.

Fred Clark was back! He had spent a large part of the winter in the hospital, but amazingly, the tough old bird was able to return to work in the summer, held together, he said, "with steel pins and duct tape." Though it was a remarkable recovery, he was still a far cry from the old Fred. He was taken off the station foreman job, and was used for other kinds of less strenuous work.

Another thing was different—Fred started going to church! He never talked about it to us, but every Sunday he would attend the local community church near Horse Creek.

Even acknowledging his more gentle side, Fred was still a hard old cuss. But after that night, though broken in body, he seemed quieter and humbler in temperament.

FRED CLARK AT AGE 86, 37 YEARS AFTER THE ROLLING LOG

But while Fred was back, John Brannon, the head forester, was not. During the winter, John suffered a severe stroke. He was paralyzed, confined to a wheelchair! I remembered his words the year before on the Sambo Fire: "This isn't supposed to be FUN! This is WORK!" Now all that drive and bright future were cut off. Not yet forty years old, he had driven himself to the point of self-destruction.

But the changes didn't stop there. 1969 also brought major changes to our helitack crew. Tom Beers had gone to the Ukonom as assistant fire control officer. Meanwhile, the Ukonom station foreman, a fellow named Jim Kuphaldt, became our new helitack foreman. Jim had been a smoke jumper at the regional fire control center at Redding before coming to Ukonom. He had a broad fire experience background, though still in his 20s, like Tom.

Jim was a muscular six feet tall with a characteristic heavy mustache that drooped around either side of his mouth. He was handsome in a rugged way, friendly, a natural leader though soft spoken, and possessed a good sense of humor. On the one hand, he was pure local boy from Scott Valley, country raised, a local football hero from Ft. Jones who married his high school sweetheart—simple, beer drinking, unsophisticated and unpretentious.

And yet, there was another side to Jim. Jim was a thinker. He listened, he read, he considered—he was a student of life. In many ways, he was ahead of the times; like he was the first person I ever knew who recycled aluminum cans. These deeper qualities were sometimes obscured by his public persona. In a crowd, he always seemed to be the center of conversation, telling jokes and endless funny stories from his smoke jumping days. With him around, there was always something happening.

But underneath all that, He was a man of integrity, a loyal friend, and possessor of a truly gentle spirit. He had, in fact, a heroic combination of manly courage and gentleness.

In addition to a new foreman, this year we again had a new helicopter. While our Jet Ranger last year had been successful, in a way it was just an improved version of what we had been using before. This year, we were getting a machine that would revolutionize helicopter fire fighting—the Bell 205.

The Bell 205 was a technological advance spurred by the war in Vietnam. It was turbine powered, with an engine that weighed only 150 pounds but could deliver over 1,000 horsepower to the rotor system. Whereas the little Bells and Hillers could carry three people, and last year's Jet Ranger could carry five, this "Huey" could carry fifteen. Whereas the Jet Ranger could dip fifty to seventy-five gallons of water out of a lake to drop on a fire, the Huey could dip 300-350 gallons.

There were only two Hueys being used experimentally in the region, and we were chosen to be one of those crews. It would mean a bigger helitack crew. There would be four of us full-time all summer, with two more in times of high fire danger.

And then came the biggest change of all, one that was to have the deepest impact on all of our lives. In order to use the helicopter's greater assets most effectively, it was decided to move us from Seiad to the Forest Headquarters in Yreka, making us more centrally located to the whole forest. But there was no place to put us in Yreka, either at the headquarters building, or at the downtown warehouse/shop compound.

So in a strange pairing, we were housed at the Yreka, California Division of Forestry (CDF) headquarters, an unusual combining of federal and state organizations that were usually kept separate. But the CDF headquarters on the outskirts of town had an open field, ideal for a heliport, and there was room in their bunkhouse for the four of us, so a deal was struck. There was even talk of using us on state fires.

ON TO YREKA

We left Seiad in a state of ferment over the coming reorganization that would cause all the regulars to be relocated. But we had other things on our minds. We had a date in Yreka with a big bird.

Yreka is the largest city in Siskiyou County, a county that is larger than Connecticut and Rhode Island combined. Yreka is the county seat of the third largest county in the third largest state in the nation. But no matter how good you tried to make it sound, Yreka still didn't amount to much. Even after the fifty-mile drive from Seiad, you're still hardly anywhere: just a few thousand inhabitants strung out along a two-mile strip of old highway 99 through a desert valley of sage brush and dead grass.

However, once the initial disappointment dies away, Yreka does have some redeeming features. At 3,000 feet elevation, it's not as hot as towns like Seiad, down on the river. And the lack of trees gives it a feeling of openness, unlike the steep and cramped canyons of the Klamath. It has the dry climate and the clear air of the high desert and water for irrigation from the rivers flowing off Mt. Shasta.

About a mile south of town, near the fairgrounds, is the California Division of Forestry (CDF) base where we would be staying, complete with fully staffed kitchen.

Past the bunkhouse and warehouse was an open field that was given to us for our heliport. A military-type pad had even been placed there, made out of plates of interlocking heavy metal mesh.

When the helicopter arrived, we were surprised to find the lead pilot to be Tom Pfeiffer, whom I first met on the Indian Ridge Fire in 1966.

Tom was thirty-five going on fifty. He was a pipe-smoking, likeable, laid-back guy, settled in life, absolutely imperturbable. The other pilot was a guy by the name of John Worley. In his 20s, he was more the typical pilot: bachelor, womanizer, party animal. To John, piloting a helicopter was his ticket to the fast life: the bucks, the bars, the booze, and the babes.

Having a helicopter so much bigger brought many changes to our operation. For instance, Jim could ride shotgun in the co-pilot's seat at all times and still have room for thirteen passengers in the back. But in the midst of many other changes, the change that was to prove most momentous was one I hardly noticed at the time: the change in the initial attack plan for the helicopter.

The first year, with our little 47G Bell, our initial attack plan had been to take the L.A. Tank and immediately set up a pumping and water dropping operation. We had perfected this plan to a science and had worked it with great effectiveness all through the summer until the Indian Ridge Fire overwhelmed us.

Now we had a man-moving machine that became the centerpiece for a forest-wide attack plan. The plan was to take off from Yreka toward the fire, filling up with fire fighters at the closest ranger station, and taking a full crew of thirteen fire fighters directly to the fire. This could triple the initial-attack manpower, arriving early at the scene when the fire was smallest and most easily controlled.

What I didn't realize at the time was that on fires on our forest, my job in effect was being changed from helitack crewman to a member of a "Fire Fighting Swat Team." Instead of staying with the helicopter in the support mode, I would be fighting the fires directly. I didn't have the foggiest notion of what I was getting into.

BLOWUP!

One hot, dry afternoon, the phone rang. The next thing we knew Jim came running out of the CDF back office, shouting to us where we were sitting in the shade of the helicopter. "Crank her up, Tom, we're heading for Ukonom!"

For the first time, we were being ordered out according to our new dispatch plan. We loaded up tools for thirteen men and took off for the Scott Valley Ranger Station where we picked up additional firefighters to fill the helicopter. The thirteen of us would hit the fire *en masse* as a kind of shock troop, joining the local district's tanker crew, hoping to knock the fire down fast.

We could see the column of smoke as soon as we got out of Scott Valley, when we were still thirty miles away. This was not going to be a little lightning fire! When we arrived at the scene, we found it to be in a logging operation straddling a major ridge. The weather was hot, the humidity was low, the wind was blowing, and the fire danger was in the *very high* range.

We had a hard time landing because the logging roads were so dusty that the big helicopter's powerful rotor wash stirred up a blinding cloud of dust every time we got close to the ground. After several aborted attempts, Tom brought us in in a kind of a suicide landing, picking the least dusty spot he could find and coming in fast and plopping down hard before the dust was stirred up enough to blind us. After dropping us off, he left the same way, pulling power and fairly jumping the helicopter into the sky.

So it happened that suddenly we found ourselves miles from

home, standing on a dusty logging road in the middle of nowhere, gripping a fire tool, smoke all around with the sound of the helicopter fading off into the distance.

Logging fires are the most dangerous, dreaded, and destructive of all timber fires. Because of the difficulty of logging in steep terrain, the loggers use a method called "clear cutting": cutting down everything within the cut-block. They take out the good tree trunks by hooking them to an overhead cable and dragging them out, leaving behind a thick layer of limbs, tops and refuse called "slash" that bakes tinder dry in the hot sun. The blocks will be burned in the fall after the fire danger is lessened. But in the meantime, if a fire ever gets started in the acres of this tinder-dry slash, look out! They burn with a ferociousness that is almost unbelievable.

Nevertheless, the situation that first greeted us at the fire seemed benign enough. Being so near the top of the ridge, the terrain was not steep, but rolling. Though the fire was burning in the dry slash, the loggers had been able to get a cat in and bulldoze a fire line through the middle of the block, separating the burning slash from the unburned. Then they had pushed everything inside the line into the fire to be burned up, which was happening with great heat and intensity, but little danger.

Thus the loggers had stopped the fire themselves. Our job was to string a hose lay along this cat line from the road to the end of the block with laterals every few hundred feet. While a mother tanker at the road fed us water, we could spray down the fuels on both sides of the line while the fire burned itself out, which could take 24 hours.

This was "piece-of-cake" kind of work. We didn't even need our hand tools. Quickly, we spread out and started stringing hose all along the fire line.

In one place where I was stringing hose, the fire was too hot to even walk by on the fire line. I had to detour through the slash in the cut-block. Doing this made me realize how potentially dangerous the situation was. The slash was so thick as to be almost impassable. We had to clamber over cull logs with thick branches still on them, and fight our way through the mass of slash that seemed to average about six feet high.

I was with one of the extras who had been added to our crew in Yreka. Political appointments, they had no fire fighting or helicopter experience, nor did they have the capabilities picking up the necessary skills quickly. They wanted to learn, but even on this fairly tame fire, they were hopelessly out of their element, and were apt to hinder rather than help us. I had attached myself to one of them named George and was pretty much "babysitting" him to get him through the fire.

Out of the Fire

George and I scrambled through the slash past the hot spot, got our hose strung out, turned it on, and found there was no water. So we went back to investigate.

Just after we clambered through the slash again around the hot spot, we heard a strange sound like rushing wind. It came from over the ridge to the west of us, a loud sound like "whoosh." Suddenly a huge cloud of black smoke obscured the afternoon sun.

Unknown to us was another part of the fire over the ridge on our flank. I had seen smoke coming up from over there earlier but hadn't given it much thought. We had been sent to this part of the fire, so I assumed it was the most critical.

But now this hidden fire over the ridge was "blowing up," leaping from the ground into the branches of the trees and crowning, burning the trees from top to bottom simultaneously like giant torches. The cloud of smoke and burning embers from the blowup ascended to the heavens as from a giant furnace.

At first, we were awed by this demonstration of power but not overly concerned. But moments later, as the cloud rose higher; the wind over the ridge caught it and pushed it toward us, laying it down over the unburned side of the cut-block in a huge black cloud. Out of this cloud came burning embers falling on us like an evil rain. Instantly, I knew that our line and the rest of the slash block were lost, and we would be too if we didn't get out of there fast.

We were in the worst spot imaginable, right in the middle of the block. The cat line was too hot to run along, and we didn't have time to clamber back through the slash around the hot spot. We didn't dare go in the other direction towards the road as that would have been right into the teeth of the crowning fire. There didn't seem to be any escape route for us; we were trapped!

It's in moments like these that thoughts tumble through your mind faster than you can sort them out, and you either get the right ones and act on them or you leave in a body bag. Or maybe you either have a guardian angel looking out for you or you don't! Anyhow, in this critical instant of decision, I looked in the only other direction there was, straight into the slash-block itself. Normally, that would have been the worst choice, but as Providence had arranged it, we happened to be standing right in the middle of an old cat trail, where a bulldozer at one time had made its way through the cut-block, clearing a path through the slash one bulldozer blade wide. It ran straight down into a little ravine and up the other side to the road.

With burning embers raining all around us, I screamed at George, "RUN FOR IT!"

We raced at top speed down the cleared path to the bottom of the ravine and started up the other side that led to the road at a point past the blowup. Halfway up the other side the slash thinned out considerably. Winded by this time and out from under the hail of burning embers, I stopped to catch my breath, and turned around to look at where we had just come from. I was staggered by the sight! The entire slash block down to the ravine was going up in flames at once! Where we had been only thirty seconds before was a solid mass of flames! The suddenness of it was incredible; the closeness of our escape made an imprint of horror on my soul.

LAKE OF FIRE

That fire in Ukonom shook me, though I wouldn't have admitted it. I had seen plenty of fires before. In fact, I'd seen just enough to think I'd seen them all. But it was as if I had been living in a bubble called "It Can't Happen To Me." Now that bubble had suddenly burst, and I'd seen the frightening reality of fire's power and unpredictability "up close and personal." It left me shaken inside. This time it was me it was after!

The fire call came again, on another hot, dry afternoon, this time to the Salmon River District–a district at that time perhaps devoid of a single mile of paved road–located on the Salmon River between Etna and Ukonom. Like the fire in the Ukonom District, this too started in a logging operation, by cables hot from friction coming in contact with a punky stump.

There was a logging road through the middle of the blocks, with one cut-block above and one below, offset like squares of a checkerboard. Like the Ukonom fire, once it got going in the tinder dry logging slash, it burned with an unstoppable fierceness.

Again, we picked up fire fighters at Ft. Jones. Again as soon as we got out of Scott Valley, we could see the massive column of smoke rising in the sky. By the time we arrived at the fire, most of the lower block was involved, and the heat had swept the fire up into the forest above the block.

It was one of the most awesome things I'd ever seen. It could only be appreciated from our vantage point in the air above the fire. It was a physical lake of fire, frightening in its power and its extent. The forest trees were 100 or more feet high, and from the ground to well above the tops of the trees was a solid mass of flame. It was not like there were trees burning in the forest; rather the entire forest was burning at once! The size of this sea of fire was perhaps twenty-five acres, and over 100 feet high. Being all flame, it was mostly transparent; I could see the dark shapes of logs on the ground at the bottom of the lake of fire. Everything was burning at once!

I didn't want the helicopter to land; I didn't want to get out; I was not mentally ready to face this voracious beast. I'd had enough scary fire down on the Ukonom, and this was even worse!

But the world doesn't always turn on what we want or don't want. As sure as fate, once more we found a wide spot on the logging road; once more we piled out with our tools and canteens; once more the helicopter roared away in a cloud of dust; once more we were left with the fire.

They sent us above the road to build line up the side of the lake of fire, between it and the other block, which had not yet caught fire. Because the fire was so hot, we had to build the line at a safe distance and then backfire from the line towards the fire. This way the line would be burned out, and the draft from the main fire would suck in the backfire and the whole thing would safely burn up. (This always sounded so good in theory!)

But this was only a flanking action. There was no way we could stop the head of the fire that was moving rapidly uphill, consuming everything in its path, pushed by the torrid draft from the fire below. The best we could hope for by our indirect attack was to keep it from spreading sideways, and most importantly, keep it out of the other cut-block. So we started building fire line uphill from the road, burning it out as we went along.

I was not comfortable with this arrangement. We had the lake of fire on one side, a tinderbox slash block on the other, and more unchecked fire below us! Just like at Ukonom, we were in danger of being outflanked by the fire we weren't fighting. The main slash block where the fire had started was below the road. Though most of its explosive power had gone up over the road into the huge crown fire, yet it was also making lateral progress, sneaking across the lower block under us. Though this part of the fire was spreading slowly, it was still burning very intensely in the tinder-dry slash.

Desperately short of equipment and manpower at this early stage of the fire, the fire boss had sent Callahan's helicopter to make water drops on this spreading fire in the lower block, hoping to slow its advance until more crews or a cat arrived to build line below the road.

However, it seemed like a lost cause. Their little helicopter with its small Sims Bucket would come in and drop fifty gallons of water at a time on the advancing flames. But even before the helicopter was out of sight, the greedy flames had evaporated the water and were creeping forward again. And it took ten minutes before the helicopter got back with another load. Our big helicopter was nowhere to be seen.

I couldn't focus on the job of building line. My mind was too concerned about what was happening elsewhere. I had a lump of fear in my throat and a sense of dread in my heart. I volunteered to be a lookout and went to the top of the little ridge that separated us from the unburned block to our left. I wanted to know what was happening and be able to run for it.

We had been warned to be careful, to be on the lookout for the fire underneath us and to maintain an escape route at all times. Pretty soon, I could see that the fire below the road had worked itself around that same little ridge and had started sending sparks into the dry, piled slash in the unburned block beside us. If this block got going, it could trap us with no escape route, leaving us completely surrounded by fire.

When I saw that the fire had moved below the unburned block and was sending a steady barrage of sparks into it, I reported back to the crew boss that all was lost and we should get out. Already the sparks were igniting some smoldering fires in the unburned slash. Some of the more zealous crewmen ran out into the slash block trying to put these out, but the whole thing was a powder keg waiting to go off.

Then the fire underneath the road hit a huge pile of dried slash. Before we knew it, flames were arcing across the road in a solid sheet, like a blowtorch aimed at the unburned block. The cry went up our useless fire line to pull out, and in a few minutes we all got safely down to the road. But even on the road, we were not out of danger. The way we came in was blocked by this sheet of flames blowing up from below and extending over the road as it reached ravenously for the doomed slash block above. Our only escape was to make a run for it under the licking flames. One at a time we grabbed a lungful of air, put our heads down, and dashed along the cut-bank under the flames until we all got out safely.

Out of immediate danger, we continued walking along the road to the far side of the second cut-block. The fire was now firmly established in this block, building in intensity just like the first one.

After taking a breather at the far edge of the block, the decision was made to begin building fire line up through the forest about 100 feet back from the edge of the block. The strategy was basically the same as before: build a line up the hill in a flanking action to stop the fire's lateral movement, hoping to pinch it off at the top of the ridge. More hand crews had arrived in the meantime from other districts, including some from the Seiad and the Oak Knoll districts, so there were many of us building line, working our way uphill.

The men I was with were mostly from the Oak Knoll crew under the leadership of a guy by the name of Jim Allen. We were not the first crew up the hill, but were following behind them, turning their "scratch line" into a good fire line.

All went well for awhile. It was cooler in the shade of the dense forest; the dirt was soft and easy to dig, and the fire was nowhere to be seen. But somewhere off in the block, the fire was coming, and it wasn't likely to stop on its own! It was just a matter of time before it reached the end of the block and found us.

And find us it did! We had just reached a point opposite the top of the block when the fire suddenly came roaring towards us in a wall of flames. The wind generated by the fire was like a hurricane, blowing the flames right at us. They hit the forest at the edge of the block like a crashing wave hitting the rocky shore. The first row of trees burst into flames with a roar. The whole crew up and down the line cried out, turned tail, and ran. To me, it was the Ukonom fire all over again, and I was running for my life. We were a long way up the mountain, but I tell you the truth, I was determined not to stop until I hit the Salmon River somewhere far below. I had been on edge ever since I first saw this fire from the air. Now my lever had been pushed to "total panic."

I was flying down the mountain for all I was worth when I heard Jim Allen and others behind me shouting "Wait! Stop!"

It was with great difficulty that I managed to stop, partly because of the fear driving me and partly because my downhill momentum was about to launch me into space! But when I finally did stop and turn around, I saw Jim motioning me and several others back. I realized that most of the crew had only retreated 100 feet from the line, and were waiting for the fire to die down. They had made a strategic retreat; I was headed for the river!

I didn't have enough knowledge yet of fire behavior and fire strategy. We were not really in danger there, even though the fire had come rushing at us as if to vaporize us. Those wiser than I knew that the power of the fire was only being sustained by the bone-dry piles of slash in the block. Once out of the block, the fire lost intensity.

But in the slash block and directly up the slope from the slash block, the fire was unstoppable. We had only gotten one blast of the hurricane force wind coming at us. The steady, stronger wind was blowing up the slope into the forest above the block, blowing almost hard enough to strip needles from the tree branches, carrying its hot gases into the unburned forest, drying everything out and preheating it almost to the point of ignition. Then the fire would make a sudden run up the hill through the forest--50, 100, even 200 yards at a time--almost like gasoline igniting. As this patch of forest burned fiercely, the wind it generated would preheat another patch up the slope and so on—nothing could stop its run up the hill until it hit the ridge.

But we were off to the side of the block, out of that fiery draft. Try as it might, though the fire could sweep up to the edge of the forest and slightly into it, once away from the heat-generating slash, it stalled. Green pine trees, even the needles, though filled with pitch, won't burn until they're dried out. However, I didn't understand all this at the time. I couldn't understand why we weren't in that much danger. But since nobody else was running away, I turned around and came back, overruling the fear within.

We waited till the fiery blast died down, just like waiting for a wave to retreat from the beach. Then we moved back in. But the wave had pushed the fire close to our fire line, making it too hot to work. So we pulled back another fifty feet into the woods and began another line. The line below us was all right. It was just this one spot at the top of the block.

Suddenly, another fire surge came as the wind shifted again, fanning the flames and pushing them at us with the same gale-like force. Another row of trees exploded into fire, sending flames shooting into the sky. Again, we turned tail and ran, but not as far this time. We were getting the hang of it.

Once past the top of the block things got easier. It became more like any other fire that you flank up the hill and hope to catch at the top.

Our crew never did get all the way to the top, but eventually, the first crews did. Once at the top, where holding the fire was so critical, they immediately built a helispot to ferry in additional men. With the extra men and the help of the air tankers, they were able to stop the fire at the top of the ridge, though it slopped over in some places. To those of us down the hill, the word filtered back to hold the line where we were. So we spread out along the line about two-thirds of the way up, finished burning it out, then sat down and rested.

It had turned into early evening and sack lunches and rations were sent up the line for supper. Then darkness came and people relaxed a little more. What with resting and the cooling of night, my insatiable thirst gradually subsided as my body's water replenishment caught up with what had been sweated out. As darkness deepened, people clumped together at hot spots near the fire line, heated water in empty ration cans and mixed in powdered coffee from the rations. Others stretched out on the ground if they could find any spot flat enough and tried to catch a little sleep. Nobody knew when we would be relieved, probably not till morning.

The fire was slowly burning itself out. With no new fuel, and no wind to whip the flames or blow sparks across the line, it was tame enough. We had to be there just in case any of these factors changed.

The appearance of peace and tranquility could be deceptive, however, as events later in the evening proved. Along about 10:00

p.m., as I was stretched out dozing on a flat part of the fire line by some glowing coals, I awoke to a creaking, cracking, popping sound: a snag had burned in two and was starting to fall—tons of smoldering wood thundering to earth! I jumped up, startled, momentarily disoriented. There was a terrific crash up the hill, sparks flew into the air, the fire blazed up where the tree had fallen, and a few dislodged rocks clattered down the hill. Then, only moments later, the quiet tranquility returned. Only a patch of brighter flames in the darkness confirmed that the frightening event had in fact happened.

Falling snags are a constant danger in fire fighting as well as rolling rocks. In timber fires, more people are killed every year by falling and rolling material than are ever killed by the fire itself. In fact, I've never been on a fire where anyone was burned to death. But I have been on fires where people were killed by falling things and by aircraft accidents.

Falling snags are especially dangerous because they are so heavy. They come crashing down so fast and provide little or even no warning. I was on a fire during the night once where a snag fell nearby with no warning whatsoever. There was no popping or splitting sound as it started to fall. The very first noise came when it hit the ground with a thunderous crash. In a case like that, you figure if you can hear it, it must have missed you because you're still alive! I've also heard them fall when the only sound was the snag hitting a few tree branches on the way down. That's unnerving too, because the few soft pops or swishes in the canopy above don't give anywhere near an accurate clue that tons of tree are hurtling toward the earth, or where they're likely to hit.

Rocks can be very dangerous also, whether dislodged by the fire or by a fire fighter somewhere up above. Either way, they can come bouncing down the fire line or through the woods like a deadly missile seeking prey. If you dislodge a rock and it starts to roll downhill, forest etiquette demands that you scream out at the top of your voice, "Rock!" to alert anyone who might be below. If you are the one below and you hear the sound of someone yelling "Rock!" up above, you immediately seek shelter behind a tree or boulder. If you're caught in the open, you tense up and crouch, scanning the hill above, looking for the rock. Even if it happens to be coming at you, you should have the opportunity to make one leap, so make it a good one! Night, however, when such dangers can't be seen, greatly adds to the danger.

We were finally relieved at daybreak and were trucked to the fire camp that had been established on the rocky flood plain of the Salmon River. We found the heliport and Jim told us to find a spot and sack out for awhile. This meant picking up a Government Issue paper sleeping bag and trying to find a spot shady and soft enough to get some sleep.

Night shift on a fire is rough because of the difficulty of sleeping during the day. With the sun beating down mercilessly as it was in the narrow, rocky, river canyon, even in the shade—if you can find any—it gets too hot to sleep by noon. You take off every bit of clothing you can, but you still lie there soaking in your own sweat, with buzzing flies forever landing on you and tickling you. Most people who have night shift end up taking catnaps out on the line if they can, because of the impossibility of getting good sleep during the day in fire camp.

So we got some breakfast and sacked out till about noon, when it got too hot to sleep, then got up, had lunch, and rejoined the helicopter.

THE GRAPESTEAK

I was spooked; I was skittish; I was intimidated by the raw power of fire we kept experiencing. Deep inside my spirit was overwhelmed.

It hadn't been long before we discovered The Grapesteak, a pizza place in Yreka that had just opened with a beer bar, jukebox, and great pizzas. Almost every night we were in town we would head there, banish the memory of the barrack's supper with a piping hot beef and bell pepper pizza, and take turns buying pitchers of beer until we were sloshed. The pop songs of those years, 1969-70, were fixed indelibly on my brain by the jukebox night after night.

I remember the nights in The Grapesteak so well because its cool, dark, sense-satisfying atmosphere stood in such stark contrast to the hot, bright, terrifying, and exhausting fires that seemed to follow one after another.

Each one seemed to come on a day with the sun burning down and the temperature pushing 100. Once more, there would be the fire call, the rush to the helicopter, the hurried flight, and the column of smoke surging into the heavens that could be seen for miles. Then the flames, the heat, the fear, the sweat, the hard work, and the raging thirst. After the first day on the fire line, we would be back with the helicopter, ferrying men and supplies. Then, another few days of listless boredom during mop-up, and we would be flying home to the welcoming dark coolness of The Grapesteak–the pizza, the beer, and the music–with only the memory of the terror left rattling around in the dark recesses of our minds. This fear was sometimes subtly played upon by the lyrics of such jukebox favorites as Creedence Clearwater Revival's "Bad Moon Rising:"

**I see a bad moon arising. I see trouble on the way.
I see earthquakes and lightnin'. I see bad times today.
Don't go around tonight, well, it's bound to take your life,
There's a bad moon on the rise.**

It was a stark and unyielding summer because of its overwhelming revelation of the power of fire. It was a revelation that most people never have, like the hell of war. Those who do experience it might only do so once or twice. This summer, it seemed like we experienced it with every fire.

GOOSENEST INFERNO

Relentlessly, the fire call came again, this time to the Goosenest. It was another in an endless string of hot, dry afternoons. On our way there, I kept hoping for a "piece-of-cake" fire. It seemed like every fire on the Forest had been a major confrontation requiring maximum effort. Weren't we due for a "just-for-fun" fire? However, as we approached the Goosenest and saw the white convection column rising into the sky, my hopes evaporated as quickly as the morning mist in the hot afternoon sun.

The Goosenest is, on the average, the least steep of the districts on the Forest. It has some mountains, but much of it is rolling, high desert covered with grass, sagebrush, and juniper. This fire was on such terrain. Intermingled with the sagebrush and junipers were groves of pine trees, none of them over fifty feet high. The fire was burning briskly in the open brush and dead grass as the north wind fanned it, but it had especially gotten established in a dense grove of pine trees, from which flames and smoke were pouring out.

There was no problem finding a place to land the helicopter; the terrain was level and there were many grassy openings in the brush. As we made our approach, we saw a Forest Service tanker from the district parked on a dirt road nearby, its hoses snaking off through the brush toward the back of the fire. We disembarked with our hand tools and the helicopter flew away. Because there was no ranger station at which to pick up additional men between us and the fire, it was just our small crew that jumped out.

We were on the west side of the fire, which was being driven south by the wind. We couldn't see the district people already there; they seemed to be in the brush behind the fire, working to secure its rear. So where we were, it was just us and the fire.

The two basic approaches to all fire fighting are the direct attack and the indirect attack. I took one look at that grove with flames crackling inside and smoke pouring out the top of it and said to myself, "There is no way I am going in there after that fire." Instead, we began scratching a line through the grass in the clearing where we had landed and the tanker was parked.

The sod was thick, the soil was dust, and it didn't seem like we were accomplishing much. We didn't have anything into which to tie our line, so we couldn't burn it out. But I was too intimidated by the power of the fire to do anything else.

As we were working away in the clearing, suddenly, "whoosh," the fire started crowning in the pine trees in the grove. The flames were leaping 50 to100 feet into the air, taking with them showers of sparks and clouds of black, resinous smoke.

What I thought was a grove of pine trees turned out to be more of a thicket. Trees and brush grew so densely together that just making your way through it would have been hard. If I needed any confirmation of my decision not to go into the grove after the fire, the crown fire that was erupting from within the thicket was it. It was definitely a dangerous situation, and we continued building our "sod" line safely out in the clearing.

Soon afterward, we heard a drone in the sky that signaled an approaching air tanker. "Now that's what we need—air support!" We needed a power greater than ourselves to quench this wild beast. Soon the air tanker was making a practice run over the fire.

I had seen many fires in rough terrain and tall timber where the air tankers were at a disadvantage, having to stay far above the fire in order not to get trapped in a canyon they couldn't fly out of. At last, here was the ideal situation for an air tanker to operate. The terrain was level and the pilot could get as low as he wanted. The trees were not high enough to dissipate the drop before it reached the ground, and the smoke wasn't obscuring the target.

I had never seen the total amount of damage an air tanker could do to a fire until that day. He came in low, thundering through the smoke right over the writhing ball of flames leaping from the pine thicket. Just at the right moment he dropped his full load of 3,000 gallons. It was awesome! The red retardant smashed into the red flames; there was a tremendous cloud of white steam... then just smoldering ruins. With one mighty bomb blast of retardant, he had squashed the fire like stepping on a bug!

However, that didn't change our strategy! We continued pecking away at the grass out in the clearing at least 100 feet from the smoking, steaming thicket.

Soon after, Vern Lewis, the veteran Goosenest FCO arrived in his pickup and calmly surveyed the scene. It must have struck him as incongruous: our hacking up sod out in the clearing. Our line had become worthless but we hadn't realized it yet. What were we going to do when our line was complete?" Were we going to start another fire to burn out the fuel between our line and the ruins of the wildfire? But there we were, working busily away under his inscrutable gaze.

Finally, he walked over to us and said, "You know, when you get a chance, you might want to go into the thicket and build your line right against the fire, now that it's pretty well knocked down."

My philosophy is: always agree with instructions when first given to you. That way you make the person giving them feel good, like they've accomplished something, while giving yourself time to decide whether you really want to follow them or not. So I was quick to nod my head and agree, "Yeah sure, that makes sense. As soon as we finish up here, we'll get right in there."

But inside I felt strong resistance to even the suggestion. Even though we could look in there and see that the fire had been totally knocked down, the hair-raising experiences I had had that year at Ukonom and Sawyers Bar, and remembering the raging of this fire such a short time ago, I was thoroughly intimidated.

We never did go in there. Soon another, more aggressive crew came along, burst into the thicket and jumped on what was left. I held back, expecting to see the fire rekindle itself and become again the monster it had been so recently. Then the helicopter came and picked us up and for us the fire was over. We left it to the tanker crews to finish up.

Because of the Forest's quick response, the level terrain, and the easy access by both air and ground, the fire was quickly suppressed. It had been hot; it had been dangerous; but before it had gotten big enough to take off and run, the air tanker had drowned it. If only there was some easy way to drown the fear and intimidation that at times seemed to paralyze me.

THE MUSIC CAREER

September 1969

When I returned to Arcata in the fall, for the first time since starting college, I returned to the same situation I had left—the same duplex and the same roommate. The band idea was dead, but my interest in music remained as strong as ever. As I got deeper into it, I kept casting about for what shape my music career was to take. Music had already proven many times that it was able to profoundly stir me, and I had made a commitment to "give myself to music." But just what form was this commitment to take?

The questions I didn't ask but should have were these: "Was music itself some sort of living entity with a heart, mind, and soul that I could give myself in service to? Was it a being that I could have some sort of relationship with? Or was there another entity behind it, some Power that created it and was using it in my life?" I might be completely in awe of a majestic mountain, but the mountain is an inert object. How could I serve it and how could it care what I did? Such thinking doesn't go deep enough. Better thinking would be, "How did this mountain get here? Who made it and why?" Likewise, I should have been asking, "Who created music and why was it given the power to affect me the way it does?" Music had stirred me deeply enough to awaken in me a desire to respond—to give something back, even to the point of wanting to give back the most precious thing I had, my life. But who was I really dealing with? Giving myself to music would be a lot like giving myself to a majestic mountain—a noble idea but somehow missing the point. If I had been able to think along those lines my journey might have ended much sooner than it did. In the absence of such higher thinking, I muddled along on a lower level.

In an apparent paradox, I was never a good performer; so I couldn't produce the thing I loved. The area I gravitated to instead was composing. Here was an opportunity to create. I had already taken some creative writing classes. I don't know where the idea first came to be a writer/composer/creator, but it seemed to be buried deep inside. Nothing has ever quite been able to dislodge it.

Music seemed like an excellent medium. It moved me so deeply at times; maybe I could use it to move others. As I was taking classes in different kinds and periods of music, one of my assignments was to write a Gregorian chant. These chants are among the oldest written music of Western Civilization. Minor in mode, they rise and fall melodically with a free flowing rhythm that causes the mind to think of ancient monasteries and medieval cathedrals.

I came up with a credible melodic flow for my chant, complete with crescendo of hope and dying away to resignation at the end that seemed to fit the age. For words, I decided to use some Latin lyrics from a choral piece we were singing at the time from an old Catholic mass. The lines I used could be translated:

Lord, in thee have I put my trust.
Let me never be confounded.

Though I was still an agnostic at best, and the words had no relevance to my life, still I was struck by the force and emotion of the statement. The more I heard it played, the more I could hear the heart's cry of the writer of the words. Here was someone who had committed himself to the God in which he believed. Now he—obviously in some kind of desperate trouble—was pleading to this same God not to let him down, not only in the present trouble, but throughout eternity: "Let me never be confounded."

My father, always a music aficionado, liked the piece, and wanted his church choir to perform it with me conducting when I was home for Christmas. So there I was, an unbeliever in my home church full of other unbelievers, conducting a song that was a cry of dependence and supplication to the God we denied.

The song is fairly short, but after the words are repeated a couple of times, the song stops and there is a sudden unison "NO!" thundered out on a high note. This is answered by a soft "no" on a low note. Then the last line is repeated, starting high and descending with each syllable, "Non con-fun-dar" then a leap to "in" where the high note is sustained for three beats. Then a moment of dramatic silence as the memory of the high note lingers. Then the choir comes in at almost a whisper level, "ae-ter-er-num," which is Latin for "eternity."

It was as if the song was witnessing to us of the glories and mysteries of a faith we didn't have: a faith that in my case I never had, while in the Unitarian Universalist church's case, a faith that over the years had been abandoned.

Of course, I wasn't making such deep reflections at the time. But I did know that in this song I had touched something of great value: I had quite by accident communicated a message that evoked deep emotion. I felt like I was onto something, but didn't know where to go from there. The powerful part of the piece had come out of its religious message, but I didn't have any understanding in that area.

I talked to Dr. Barlow, the Chorale director. He seemed to have faith, and he had already helped me with the words. I asked him how I could find more powerful words like that to write music to.

Dr. Barlow suggested exploring the book of Psalms in the Bible. He said in the psalms there was a lot of similar material; people crying out to God for help, praying, etc.

There it was: the door to lead me deeper into the search for who I was dealing with behind the music. But I missed the cue. I never followed up on his suggestion, and once more wandered off down my crooked road.

SUDDEN TRANSITION

June 1970

Soon it was time for another fire season.

Just like the school year had been a carbon copy of the year before, this summer with the Forest Service was also just like the previous summer. Once more we began the summer at Seiad, and then moved to Yreka and the CDF barracks when the helicopter came. We had the same helicopter; Jim Kuphaldt was still foreman: our crew, the helicopter company, and one of the pilots (Tom Pfeiffer) were all the same. Little did any of us realize at this time of comfortable sameness the major changes that were lurking down the road for all of us. This was the calm before the storm.

LIFE LESSON FROM A RIDGE

While still in Seiad, there was a lightning storm, and I was sent out in charge of a three-man crew to a smoke on top of a ridge above Hamburg. We parked above the fire where a logging road crossed the ridge and hiked down the ridge with our fire tools and lightning packs.

The storm had come late in the afternoon, but the hike was easy and this time we got to the fire before sundown.

It wasn't much of a fire. A dead snag was burning, and there was smoldering in the surrounding duff. We put a line around it and chopped the burning parts out of the snag, not wanting to have to deal with cutting the whole tree down.

The fire was very close to the ridge top, a favorite place for lightning to strike. On closer examination, however, we saw that the lightning hadn't struck the dead snag at all, but a smaller live fir tree next to it. The duff around the live tree had caught fire and eventually burned over to the snag that caught fire and put off enough smoke to alert the lookout. "Well so much for the theory that lightning targets snags," I thought.

After a quick hit on the fire, we dug in for the night, completing the mop-up the next morning. Then we hiked back up the ridge to the pickup and headed for home.

This was such a run-of-the-mill lightning fire that I wouldn't even have remembered it, let alone reported on it, if it wasn't for an additional incident, which I relate below.

This time I was the one chosen to revisit the fire a few days later to make sure it was out. Though after the fire we had hiked back up the ridge to return to the pickup, this time Nicholas, our new station foreman, concocted the idea of having me hike out from the fire by following the ridge down to where it hit the highway near the river. In his mind, that would be easier than hiking back up the ridge to the logging road.

Whether it would have been easier to walk the shorter distance uphill to the logging road, or the longer distance downhill to the highway was debatable. But the real difference was that now a second, and even a third person was required—a second person to drop me off above the fire on the ridge, then drive the pickup down to the highway by the River where I would come out. Now a third person had to drive out and pick up the second person and take him back to the ranger station, unless he wanted to wait three hours for me to emerge from the woods. No way did it make sense. However, if it hadn't been for this irrational plan, I wouldn't have the following story to report:

After confirming the fire was cold, I set out walking down the ridge toward the river far below. This was high adventure, just the forest and me, trying to get from point A to point B by a way never traveled before. It was also a great day for a hike, and a beautiful view of the Klamath River Valley presented itself when I could glimpse it through the trees.

Ridges are the best places to walk. There is less brush and undergrowth; you don't have to walk side hill; you have the best view; and it's the least steep way to get somewhere. Plus, it's almost impossible to get lost! Though there may be no trail, you do have something to follow. And by following a ridgeline, you know you will get somewhere and not go around in circles.

So I was enjoying myself coming down the ridge. For experiences like this I had left Ohio and come west. For experiences like this I had joined the Forest Service, the "guardians of the forest."

The ridge fluctuated in steepness. Some places were almost flat while others dropped off sharply. Also, in some places the top was very pronounced, while at others it was rounded.

In one place especially it got very flat, like a field. It was hard to tell where the exact ridge top was located. Then it began dropping off at a steeper angle, like a level field of trees at an ever increasing tilt. But it was going down everywhere equally, and just where the middle of the ridge was in that broad expanse I couldn't say.

As I continued following it down, I tried to stay in the middle of this broad expanse. When it grew hard to tell where the middle was, I zigzagged back and forth looking for the ridge top to reappear. As long as I was on the ridge top, I was O.K. But if that ever got away from me, I was lost and alone in the wilderness.

By now I was getting freaked out by what was proving harder than I had anticipated. I hurried up a little from my leisurely pace. The slope leveled off again, but remained as broad as ever.

At last, on one of my *zags* to the left, I spied a slight peak of ridge, a little higher than the ground on either side. I positioned myself on top of it and followed it. It rewarded me by gradually getting more and more pronounced. I was definitely on the ridge top now!

Out of the Fire

The ridge was dropping rapidly again, though the trees were thick and I couldn't determine what kind of progress I was making toward getting to the bottom.

Then, unexpectedly, I came out of the trees at a rock outcropping—the ridge had become a rocky bluff! I looked out from the bluff and was shocked—this ridge was taking me straight down into a brushy canyon! Then I looked off to my right. There towering above me but separated by another canyon was the main ridge!

Somehow during that time on the mountain when it all looked the same and the real ridge was indiscernible, I had wandered a little too far to the left. When a ridge finally did take shape out of the featureless terrain, it had been a spur ridge, a false ridge! This false ridge had taken me far from where I wanted to go and now had brought me to a dead end–a rocky bluff that would be difficult to climb down and maybe impossible to climb back up. And even if I got past the rocks, below awaited a brushy canyon far from my destination. Who wanted to fight through that?

But now between me and the main ridge a deep chasm had opened that looked as foreboding as continuing in the present way.

What was I to do? How, for all my good intentions and diligence, had I gotten here, so far off course? And how could I get back to the main ridge that was my ticket out of here?

I finally realized that the only way out was to retrace my steps, returning the same way I had come and finding the place where I first got off course. At that point, I could make the slight correction that would put me back on the right ridge, and soon I would be the one on the main ridge looking down across the chasm to this spur ridge, and pitying anyone unfortunate enough to be on it!

Armed with a plan, I hiked back up the ridge, not all the way to where it was totally featureless, but until I thought I could just make out the slightly higher main ridge from the one I was coming up. Then I went straight to it and started back down. Sure enough, it too became more prominent until it was impossible to miss. And lo and behold, there I was on the main ridge, looking across the chasm to the spur ridge I had gotten stuck on, that was taking me nowhere but into trouble. The rest was a piece of cake, another mile or two and I was back at the waiting pickup.

It wasn't until later that I realized how much like real life this incident had been. Life sometimes happens just that way—times without clear landmarks to show us the way. At such times, even with the best intentions and carefulness, we can get off on what looks like the right way, but is actually a false way leading towards trouble. It's only when we reach one of life's overlooks that we realize we have strayed from the true path and are heading towards *rocky outcroppings* and *brushy canyons*. But by this time, we have gotten so far away from the right path that we can't simply go straight to it. We must swallow our pride and with patience retrace our footsteps to the point where we first got off. Only then can we make the slight correction needed to get back on the right path.

One way I saw this repeated many years later was when I was walking with a close friend down the path of life. We had sweet fellowship together and walked as one. But later, he changed his mind about some commonly held beliefs and began to veer ever so slightly off. I told him I thought he was making a mistake, but he had made up his mind. And besides, weren't we still close? Though he had taken a slightly different course, we could still see and talk to each other as we walked down the path of life. It was all right, wasn't it?

But within a short space of time, maybe a year, we were as far apart as those two ridges with the chasm in between. Fellowship ceased; we had gone separate ways, and they only took us farther and farther apart. To this day, he's still wandering around in the brushy canyons, while I've had to go on sadly without him. How can I say that our original commonly held beliefs were right and he was wrong by changing? Because over the years I've held the same beliefs without wavering, while his beliefs have gone through change after change. As far as I know, he's never been able to come up with the final alternative that settles it for him.

Marriages can be like that. What can start as a little breathing space, a "little time to be myself," a little hobby that just I like to do, can lead to different interests, different friends, different experiences, different worlds. One day you wake up and you're on one ridge and your spouse is on another, and there's a big chasm in between. You wonder, "How did this happen?" Just like it did to me: back on the trail of life where things weren't too clear and the differences between the two of you were so slight you didn't even notice. Now it's gotten to this and the only way to fix it is to abandon your separate ways and go back to where the common ground was and start over again.

ANOTHER SUMMER IN YREKA

The Year of the Big Screw-up

The summer of 1970 saw the forces of a perfect moral storm gather and break upon us in fury. By the time the storm was over, the lives of many, including me, would never be the same—careers were blotted, scandal exploded, the helicopter was taken away, and thirty-seven years later, our example would still be held up to the then-members of the helitack crew as a warning of something to be avoided at all costs. It altered my course dramatically; setting me on a path that almost ended in my destruction, but in the end, pushed me into the arms of my salvation. The story is at times uncomfortable and I apologize for that. I will spare details where I can.

The summer of 1970 picked up where the summer of 1969 left off. The one thing that was new was the second pilot, a young Vietnam veteran named Rick Inderbitzen. Rick was crazy, as you would expect from a helicopter pilot in Vietnam, where the average life expectancy was measured in days. But what was amazing was, he was crazy in a lighthearted way. Flying around on a fire for instance, when it was just us and him, he might suddenly roll the helicopter on its side and start screaming, "Charlie in the tree line! Charlie in the tree line!" Then, gripping the cyclic stick like the trigger of a machine gun, he would blast away, "Rat-a-tat-a-tat-a-tatta!" all the while with an impish grin on his face.

He always seemed to have a grin on his broad, blue-eyed, handsome face under a shock of blond hair. With his "pretty-boy" looks, outgoing good humor, war stories, and position as helicopter pilot, Rick was perfectly suited to pick up women, which he did with the same youthful exuberance that he did everything else.

The mechanic was a tall, muscular, mustachioed fellow named Tony, who brought his petite wife and two kids up from Arizona with him. They lived in a tiny travel trailer in an R.V. park outside town.

On our very first out-of-town fire, I rode with Tony in the fuel truck. Before leaving Yreka, we pulled into a convenience store to gas up. After paying for the gas, Tony came back with something I'd never seen before, a copy of *Hustler* magazine and some detective magazines.

The timing of the thing, as we were leaving town for our first fire, seemed to indicate this was what "the boys" did when they were off by themselves. I had no idea at the time that it was an omen of things to come. From then on, every time we left town, there was no shortage of such magazines in Tony's truck or at the motels where we stayed.

A FLY IN THE OINTMENT

The summer was moving along full swing, but something was going wrong, and Jim Kuphaldt seemed to be at the heart of it.

This was the second fire season I'd worked with Jim. We'd spent a lot of evenings in bars. Jim wasn't a wild partier or reveler, but drinking seemed to be a necessary part of his functioning. It loosened him up to talk.

I was surprised to find that he had somewhat of a repressed personality. While sober he could be quite gregarious: telling jokes, stories, kidding around, etc. But he couldn't open up to the deeper realms of personal feelings, hopes, and fears of the inner man.

However, after a few drinks, Jim could access those deeper levels of his soul. I've had many deep conversations alone with him after a few beers got him into the right mood.

And, of course, we always eyed the women. Eyeing and flirting with women seemed to go hand-in-hand with the drinking lifestyle and the bar scene, even for married men. But it rarely goes any farther than that.

Jim seemed to be a good father to his three small children, with a fairly good relationship with his wife, Linda. If there was a lack of pizzazz in their marriage, that wasn't unusual in a ten-year marriage. How their story would have played out had we remained working on the River is impossible to say. But the dynamics certainly changed when we went to Yreka.

At Seiad, there was little opportunity to spend time in the bars, and even less time to mess around. But in Yreka, we had abundant leisure time in the evenings—plenty of opportunities for "checking out the action." And we had the bad examples of the playboy bachelor pilots like John Worley and Rick Inderbitzen to follow. The restraining forces of wife, kids, and friends were far away down the River.

The first year in Yreka, Jim had run around a little, picking up girls here and there. We just accepted it as the way he was and didn't think much about it. I have no idea whether any of those bar flirtations ended up becoming intimate—I didn't think so at the time—but at least none of them ever became ongoing relationships. It was just a normal part of life.

But this year, we weren't in Yreka long before Jim had a regular girlfriend. Then pretty soon he had another. These were affairs, not flirtations. They would come to the Grapesteak looking for him, or would call him on our phone at the CDF barracks. I don't know that Jim ever confided in anybody, so it's impossible to say what was going on in his head, but it looked like either intentionally or unintentionally his marriage was heading toward the rocks.

LAKE CHELAN FIRE

The Pacific Northwest was having an especially dry summer. In addition, it had experienced scattered but severe infestations of the gypsy moth that killed whole stands of trees. After the trees baked dry in the sun, they became a dangerous fire hazard.

About halfway through the summer, we were sent to a large fire near Lake Chelan, a big lake in the central part of Washington.

The fire was burning in what seemed to be a wilderness area on the north side of the lake, in endless stands of timber, much of which had been killed by the gypsy moth.

It proved to be the longest, most arduous, and in some ways, the most perplexing fire of our two years in Yreka. Though the fire was on the north side of the lake, for reasons we could never fathom, the fire camp was established on the south side in grassy fields near orchards of the famous Washington apples.

Twice a day, we had to conduct massive airlifts of hundreds of men and their tools from the fire camp across several miles of lake to helispots around the fire. In between these airlifts, we were kept busy ferrying endless supplies of food and drinking water to other crews in remote areas of the fire.

The Forest Service must have hired nearly every Huey in the western United States for the fire, without helitack crews. One was even brought from Alaska. Because there were no other helitack crews, we found ourselves running the whole base heliport, loading and unloading all the Hueys.

We were flying literally from the first light of dawn until the last dwindling rays after sunset, every day, day after day. Fortunately, we didn't have to stay at the fire camp, but were allowed to fly into town in the evenings. The town was five to ten miles away at the foot of the lake. We booked a motel where we could clean up and sleep in a good bed. We would get in about 9:00 p.m., get a bite at a nearby hamburger stand, shower, and be in bed by 10:00. Then about 4:00 the next morning, we would roll out of the rack, get dressed, and fly out at the very first light back to the fire camp where the crews were already lined up waiting for us.

After the heaviest part of the morning airlift, we would take turns going through the chow line and getting breakfast, wolfing it down as fast as we could or taking it back to the heliport. This process was repeated at lunch and supper.

The fire was perplexing because from where we were across the lake, we hardly saw any smoke, let alone flames. And yet, the fire continued day after day. We couldn't figure out why the fire camp was not established across the lake nearer the fire and save the expense of this massive airlift. But answers were hard to come by.

Fatigue became an important factor, as we were gradually worn down by the long hours and hard work. In addition, the constant noise level and the continual blast of the rotor wash required us to shout every word at the top of our lungs.

The motel was a godsend. We had a room in a converted basement with cement block walls. It was dark and as quiet as a tomb—a perfect tonic for our days of constant noise and motion.

Jim, who spent his entire time flying shotgun, got extremely fatigued. The pilots could only fly so many hours per day: eight the first day and six thereafter. But Jim was always in the helicopter, no matter which pilot was flying. Sometimes he would let one of us spell him for a time, but then after getting some food and using the porta-potty, he would be back at it again.

THE UNSAVORY UNDERBELLY OF FIRE FIGHTING

Fire fighting is a lot like war, both in the job and in the fire fighters' lives. Being away from home and family, in difficult and dangerous situations, soldiers and fire fighters will cut up and let loose, if given half a chance.

Out of the Fire

Of course, keeping the fire fighters in fire camp lessens the opportunities for hanky-panky. The work is hard and they need their rest. Other than occasionally smuggling in some beer, they generally behave themselves, at least until the fire is over.

But those of us with the helicopter had more freedom, often staying in motels away from the fire camp. Although the helitack crew usually worked hard and was exhausted at the end of the day, the pilots, mechanics, and fuel handlers had a much easier time. Each pilot could only get six hours of flying time each day after the first day, and he had to take every seventh day off.

And on this fire, the nightlife seemed to seek us! From the very beginning of our stay in the motel, there were "groupies," mostly small town high school girls, bored, wide-eyed, stirred by the excitement of a major fire, and drawn to the glamour of the helicopters and those who flew them. So almost immediately, there sprang up a nightlife party scene in the motel with booze and these girls supplying the action.

For a few nights, Saffell, Jimmy Gould, and I joined in, sitting around in a motel room–drinking and talking for an hour or two. But as the fire wore on and fatigue accumulated, we dropped out, greedily soaking up every minute of sleep we could get after our eighteen-hour days. But the pilots, mechanics, and fuel handlers, with plenty of time to nap during the day, carried on full blast for half the night.

Jim was caught in the middle. He wanted to party with the helicopter guys, but he had the same work hours as the rest of us on the helitack crew. For awhile, he tried burning the candle at both ends. By the end of the first week, he looked catatonic.

For a time, only the presence of these female groupies marked this fire as being different from a number of others, that is, until the Alaskan helicopter came to town.

We didn't have a lot of respect for the Alaskan pilots' flying capabilities. They parked their Huey at the heliport and drove to town the first night they were there. The next morning, we loaded their helicopter with cargo for one of the helispots before the pilot showed up. We loaded it the same as we loaded the other helicopters. When the pilot finally did show up at midmorning, Jim rode shotgun with him to show him where the helispots were on the fire.

Later, Jim came up and asked, "What in the world did you load that Alaskan helicopter with? Was he loaded any heavier than the rest of the loads we've been running? He almost crashed at the helispot!"

"What? How'd that happen?"

Jim continued, "I thought he was coming in way too steep on his approach. I couldn't even see the helispot any more through the windshield as we were coming in. I had to look down through the bubble in the bottom of the helicopter under the foot pedals, so we were coming in almost straight down. I told him on the intercom I thought he was going to overshoot it, but he didn't have enough power to pull out!

"The spot was right on a narrow ridge top. We hit hard past the pad, bounced back into the air and came down again even farther down the hill, stopping at a cockeyed angle that came very close to tipping the whole thing over. The pilot started cursing and swearing, shouting, 'Who in the #$&% loaded this *!@^+ thing anyway? And what'd they load it with, rocks?'"

Saffell and I assured Jim that we'd loaded it the same as any of the other helicopters. "We had some weight in it, what with containers of drinking water and canned goods. But Jim, no matter what cargo you load it with, it's almost impossible to get more weight in that cramped space than when you're carrying thirteen people back there."

Jim was obviously shaken by the close call. "Listen, no matter what anybody tells you, load that Alaskan helicopter light! I don't know if he's got a smaller engine than the others, or if he's just not used to mountain flying, but he can't handle what the others can. Don't even fill him up with people. Just give him half a load."

But whatever expertise these pilots lacked in flying, they more than made up for in partying. What had been pretty average carrying on quickly escalated into wild affairs that bordered on orgies. Now not only was I too tired to join in, but I was repulsed by some of the stories I heard.

I had spent time talking with some of the girls during the first days of the fire and had found them pretty normal, even likeable. They had all the hopes and dreams and naiveté of most teenagers. Trying hard to enter the adult world, they were still half children: unsophisticated in a lot of their ways of looking at things, child-like in relating to most men as they were used to relating to their teachers and parents.

Now, from the stories I was hearing, they were being exploited by these men who seemed so charming and glamorous, but who would soon be gone, leaving with no thought for the consequences in these girls' lives for their brief fling with life in the fast lane.

The worst seemed to be Alaskan's main pilot, the one who had almost crashed: a smooth talking man named Dick. In his early 40s, he was old enough to be their father. He quite possibly had a wife and children at home in Alaska. But there he was, with his friendly, disarming manner, preying on these starry-eyed teenagers, plying them with booze and then robbing them of their purity and self-respect.

There was not much morally I would have condemned in those days, but something about the stories Tony told me each day about the goings-on the night before, troubled me. More than the drinking and the sex, here were innocent people being ripped off. Maybe some would end up pregnant. Maybe some would discover they had contracted an incurable venereal disease. At the very least, they would wake up to the realization that they had been exploited, used, and discarded. These men would not want those things done to their daughters or sisters, but here they were doing them to somebody else's daughters and sisters, and reveling in their conquests.

Somewhere during the summer, Jim had met a young lady from Seattle, perhaps on an earlier fire, since we were in Oregon and Washington a lot that summer. He had quickly struck up a relationship with her in addition to his girlfriend in Yreka. Now back in the area, he called her from Lake Chelan. She drove out from Seattle and got a room in a nearby motel.

This gave Jim more focus in his evening's activities than the wild partying of the others. But he, more than anyone else, was burning the candle at both ends. He looked so bad that after a week, Tom Pfeiffer—who pretty much kept aloof from the carryings on—insisted he take a full day off and rest.

Jim did take a day off. But he spent it with his girlfriend who drove him to Seattle. From what little he said later, it seemed to have been a profound experience, a time of emotional bonding, a time of falling in love. She was a quiet, thoughtful person, not a partying type. They seemed to be two people discovering each other.

But how was that going to figure in with his current family? I couldn't figure out his thinking on that. He seemed to be a man driven by desires deep within himself that even he didn't fully understand. He looked to be riding the wave of unfolding events, being carried along by powerful forces, with no comprehension of the consequences his present actions would bring.

Even a close call we had with the helicopter one evening couldn't cool the reckless, partying spirit of the time. It was evening, with just enough light left in the day to get from fire camp to the motel. Rick was flying and Jim was riding shotgun. The rest of us were driving back in the helitack truck.

Rick was hot-dogging it, flying just above the surface of the lake, screaming along "under the radar." They came upon a water skier in the lake going in the same direction. Their plan was to sneak up from behind and "buzz" him—suddenly roar by right over his head. They got so caught up in their plan that they failed to notice some power lines stretched across the lake until they were right on them. Rick pulled up in an emergency maneuver, putting the helicopter into a panic climb that just did get over them instead of crashing into them.

But even that scare didn't dampen the partying mood for more than a night.

TIE A YELLOW CHAINSAW 'ROUND THE OLD OAK TREE

Once back in Yreka things didn't slow down.

It wasn't long before the Oak Knoll District was getting thunderhead buildups. Oak Knoll was just a hop over the mountains from Yreka. We were on alert and ready to roll when the call of a lightning fire came in. We were over the scene in a matter of minutes.

There were no roads close to the fire, but we found a spot not far uphill on top of a rocky bluff where we could get one skid on the ground. That was enough for Jimmy Gould and me to scramble out with some fire tools and make our way down to the fire.

When we got there, who did we find to our surprise but Glen Robinson! Now Glen was remarkably savvy about fire. It was not at all uncommon during times of thunderstorm buildups for him to disappear. He would quietly get into his pickup and drive off into the woods, and nobody would know where he was for hours. But often as not, if a thunderstorm did develop and a fire started, Glen would suddenly reappear in the immediate vicinity of the fire, just like he did this time. Thus right before our eyes another tale was added to the already substantial lore about Glen Robinson.

Soon more fire fighters had hiked in and also were dropped off by the helicopter.

As the fire fighting progressed and we began to get a line around the perimeter, Glen decided we were going to need a chainsaw. He had just purchased a brand new, bright yellow, McCullough chainsaw for fire use, and it was grabbed from the warehouse and taken to the heliport at the ranger station. Instead of partially landing up the hill where we had been dropped and handing it out to someone, it was decided to bring it right to the fire and lower it down to us on a rope. Bill Saffell was in charge of this project.

The first I knew about it was when Glen came over and pulled Jimmy Gould and me off the fire line and sent us out into a clearing to receive the chainsaw. Soon the helicopter came into sight. Jimmy Gould was standing back at a distance giving hand signals to the pilot, while I was stationed underneath to grab the saw.

We were using the same, ubiquitous, light nylon rope that we used for everything, the same rope we used to sling that chainsaw on the Indian Ridge Fire. It was light, easy to use, and had surprising strength for its weight. It was not supposed to be elastic, yet it could stretch surprisingly far with weight on it.

So there I was in the clearing looking up at the helicopter hovering overhead. The first thing I saw out of the door was a bright yellow chainsaw with Saffell's face above it. Saffell started to lower it with the nylon rope. But chainsaws are heavy, and Saffell was letting it down way too fast!

As it approached the ground he realized it was going too fast and tried to slow it down by increasing the tension on the rope. But as he increased the tension, the rope simply stretched, with the chainsaw maintaining the same speed as before. The rope kept stretching and stretching, even though by now Saffell had it almost completely stopped in his hand. As a matter of fact, by now he was clutching it desperately, hoping to stop it before it hit the ground.

At this point memory fails me, maybe because I was scrambling to get out of the way of the careening chainsaw swinging wildly through the trees like a pendulum. So I don't remember if the rope was still stretching *as* the chainsaw hit the rocks, or if the rope, having stretched to the limit, finally snapped *and then* the chain saw hit the rocks.

But I do remember very clearly that the saw *hit* the rocks, sending pieces flying. And I do remember very clearly Glen Robinson picking up the broken carcass of his brand new chainsaw with a faraway look on his face, as, the fire now forgotten, he kept repeating in hushed disbelief, "My chainsaw! My chainsaw! They broke my chainsaw! They broke my brand new chainsaw!"

So, in the end, just as this fire further fueled the legend of Glen Robinson and his instinct for lightning fires, so I'm sorry to say it also further fueled the legend of the helitack crew as bumblers and screw-ups.

LACK OF ABILITY OR LACK OF GUTS?

While we were still at Oak Knoll on standby, in the hottest part of an afternoon, the fire alarm sounded for a fire across the river. Once again we were over the fire in minutes. It was by a gravel road that goes over the mountains into Yreka through the "back door." The fire started beside the road about halfway up the mountain. This usually means either a cigarette from a car or arson.

It had started on a dry, steep slope, and by the time we got there in the helicopter, the fire had already taken off up the hill. Jim dropped Jimmy, Saffell, and me off at a wide spot on the road below the fire and took off in the usual cloud of dust.

This was a throwback to the fires of last year, when we kept getting dumped off at hot, fast moving fires, only this time we were completely on our own until the tanker and ground crews could get there from Oak Knoll. Without taking time to scout out the fire, we adopted a conservative plan of starting our fire line at the road, hoping to go up the side of the fire and pinch it off at its head.

The hillside was steep and the gravel-like soil was loose. For each two steps up the hill, we'd slide back one. Nevertheless we were working away in a cloud of dust when a pickup truck drove up beneath us and a man climbed out, got a shovel from the back and walked up to us. "Whatcha doing, boys?"

We were out of breath from the exertion and excitement, though our fire trail up from the road hadn't yet reached the fire, hidden behind thick brush somewhere above us. "Well, we've got this fire... up the hill... and we're building a fire line up to it...."

He nodded appreciatively, "I used to be in the Forest Service myself. Maybe I'll go up and take a look."

He went up the hill while we continued scratching and sliding around in the loose soil. "Hmm," I thought dourly, "might be a suspicious character. How do we know he didn't start the fire? Maybe I should go down and get his license plate number."

About ten minutes later he came back. Nobody else had shown up, and we still hadn't reached the fire with our line from the road. He reported in like a junior officer back from an assignment: "I scouted the fire all the way to its head. It's burning in grass and brush and scattered trees. I hot-spotted around it to slow it down...."

He paused and looked at us closely, for the first time perhaps fully comprehending what we were doing. "You know you fellas might be money ahead to forget about your line here, go up the hill to where the fire is really moving and try to knock it down and slow it up." Then he returned to his pickup and drove off just as the first troops were arriving.

Standing there on the slippery, sliding hillside, I suddenly felt very foolish. Here we were, three helitack hotshots, supposedly fire fighting experts, accomplishing nothing, while one ex-Forest Service civilian comes along and does everything that we should have been doing. First, he'd scouted out the whole fire: what it was doing, where it was going, and where the greatest danger was. Yet none of us had so much as gone up to look at it. Next, he'd hot-spotted the fire to contain the worst spots before they could build any more speed or intensity, ignoring the rest until help came.

His had been the classic, textbook response, while our response was ruled by fear and intimidation. It was a continuation of our response on that inferno on the Goosenest last year when even after the air tanker had knocked the raging heart of the fire into submission, we were still scratching around in the sod in the clearing, afraid to enter the thicket where the fire had so recently been rampaging. I was still thoroughly intimidated by hot, aggressive fires and so responded with defensive, conservative, mostly ineffectual tactics whose aim was insuring our own safety rather than attacking the fire.

Once the ground troops started arriving, we all headed up the hill and joined the battle in earnest. The fire was moving up a spur ridge that put it in a good place for the air tankers. I saw some of the most spectacular retardant drops ever, with the big planes practically at treetop level and the retardant thundering down through the canopy. With their help, we soon had the fire knocked down and begging for mercy, with more than a little credit to this anonymous, quick thinking, ex-Forest Servicer.

However, our own dismal performance did nothing to help our reputations. In effect, getting us there first by helicopter didn't buy the Forest Service any advantage. We didn't accomplish anything significant until the ground troops arrived, so what was the point in having us? I realized that nothing that had happened since last year had changed anything—I was still paralyzed by fear in the tough situations. Once again, I was face-to-face with my own inadequacies and there seemed no solution.

THE THICKENING WEB

Linda finally found out about Jim. It was the classic case of the wife being the last to know. She reacted with the usual emotions of shock, disbelief, hurt, and anger. The crowning blow was that nobody had told her; all her friends knew, but not one had told her.

After the initial shock, she responded with a noble attempt to win Jim back, to try to save her marriage and her home. She started coming up and spending time with us, leaving the kids down on the river. This complicated Jim's social life.

We'd all pretty much stayed out of Jim's personal affairs, though Tom Pfeiffer kept trying to get him to go home at night when we were in Yreka. But Jim was a troubled man, and seemed to have no desire to patch up his marriage. Meanwhile, I was getting more impressed with Linda as I watched her shake off her dowdy housewife look and put some fire back into her appearance as she girded up for battle for her man. There was something of the heroic but also of the pitiful about it: heroic in that she was putting forth her maximum effort; pitiful in that by now it was probably too late.

I found myself being attracted to Linda and thinking about her. She seemed so innocent and vulnerable. And her personality had a perkiness and spontaneity in spite of the current difficulties that I found attractive. It was pleasant to joke with her, and this interaction seemed harmless enough. I didn't realize the seeds that were being planted and what fruit they would bring.

I befriended Linda. I liked her spunky spirit and disarming manner, and she found in me someone with whom she could talk. I can't say I was angry with Jim, or took her side over his. But none of us could understand him and the forces driving him. Looking back, I don't think he understood himself. Underneath his sociable exterior was an enigmatic and troubled person. But it was so hard to access that person, both for those who desired to help him, and even for Jim himself.

Perhaps in the final analysis, the glamorous life with the helicopter had awakened in him a hunger for that fast life, where booze and broads were readily available, and there was no tomorrow. To him it might have looked better than a fading wife with three small children in a backwater town on the Klamath. He should have known that he couldn't have both, but I'm not sure he did. I'm not sure of anything in his mind. He didn't seem to be thinking. He seemed to have relinquished control of his own destiny.

Out of the Fire

In the midst of the moral implosion of the summer, I started smoking marijuana again. The religious and spiritual side of marijuana we had experienced when first using it was all gone now—it was just another way to get blasted.

At the barracks, while we were admired by some, we weren't popular with others. During the day, we spent a lot of time zonked out on our beds recovering or just lying around reading, to the resentment of some of the state fire fighters, who had to stay busy in the hot sun on work details. Just as we had a reputation with some of our own people for being screw-ups, so with many of the state people, we had a reputation for laziness and moral depravity.

One day it so happened we were supposed to be in Seiad the next morning for the monthly safety meeting. The helicopter was going to stay in Yreka and come get us in case of fire. Linda heard about it and came up to get Jim and take him back home with her to spend the night. She prepared a good meal, left the kids with a sitter, and showed up right before quitting time while we were playing volleyball in front of the barracks. She kept trying to get Jim to come with her but he wouldn't go. He wanted to stay in Yreka that evening and come home later that night. "Fine," she said, "then I'll stay in Yreka tonight too and you can take me out to eat." When he wouldn't agree to that either, she tried to keep the conversation light by "teasing" him that he must have a heavy date and asking him coyly who his date was with, all of which he stonily ignored.

She was naturally put out with his refusal to come with her. But in front of everybody she didn't want to lose her composure. So she looked at the rest of us and said in her lighthearted way, "Well then, does anybody *else* want to go home with me?"

Keeping in the spirit of the thing, and just on a lark I piped up, "Sure, I'll go with you."

And she, also on a lark said, "Well, get in then, let's go."

Looking at Jim, I inquired, "Is that OK Jim?"

He shrugged and looked away, "Whatever floats your boat."

It had just turned six and we were off work, so I climbed into her car and we took off. I figured she'd just cruise around the driveway of the CDF complex and bring me back, that I was just humoring her attempt to needle Jim a little, and get him off the dime. Instead she headed out to the road and started toward town.

"Uh, where are we going?" I finally asked.

"Hey Hobe, just like I said, I'm taking you home with me; screw Jim," she said, still in her lighthearted way. "I'm not waiting around for him to see that little honey of his and tell her goodbye or tuck her in bed or whatever it is he wants to do."

It gradually dawned on me that she was serious; she was taking me home with her. "Wow, this is crazy," I thought; "I can't believe this is happening; I don't even have my toothbrush."

On the way down the river, she stopped at the Oak Knoll compound to see her friend Elsie Allen, wife of Ed Allen, the station foreman. Elsie had been babysitting her kids. I waited in the car, feeling a little uncomfortable yet also a little wild and carefree, while she went in to talk with Elsie and get her children.

"Ed treats her just like Jim treats me," she confided, as we drove away. "He ignores her, doesn't spend any time with the kids, is always out with his buddies... but at least he doesn't go out on her." Her eyes flashed for a moment before she resumed her lighthearted manner.

We chatted all the way downriver to their house. I had spent years learning about the men of the Forest Service—who was hard to work for, what they had done before the Forest Service, etc. Now a whole new dimension was filled in: who was a good husband and who was not; information about their children; which men's wives were discontented and why; even details of their love lives—she seemed to know everything!

Linda had three very cute kids: Kellie, the oldest at ten, Jimmy Jr., about seven, and little Eric who was three.

We sat at the table at her house while she served us the beef stroganoff dinner she had planned on serving Jim. After doing the dishes and putting the kids to bed, we sat back down at the kitchen table and this time had a very deep and serious discussion about the situation. She filled me in on details of their marriage, and I filled her in on details of the summer from my perspective. We were each trying to get a fuller picture of Jim from the other's point of view to help figure him out.

"Jim's totally different here at home than he is at work with you guys," she said. "There he's always telling war stories about fire fighting and smoke jumping... here at home, he hardly talks at all."

I asked her about the story he had told me when he tried smoking marijuana, got freaked out, and ended up talking to her half the night. He said it had really given their marriage a boost. "You know that was really something. Jim broke down and cried and told me things he had never told me before. Hobe, what you see is all a show; it's all a sham. Really, deep down, he's so empty inside; he's so insecure.

"He came from a really poor home life, Hobe. His dad was an alcoholic who didn't work at anything long. He was never there for

Jim. His mom was a shrew who berated Jim all the time about everything he did. He could never please her."

When 10:00 p.m. rolled around and Jim still hadn't shown up, I went to bed in a sleeping bag on the couch. About midnight, I was awakened by voices. Jim had come home at last. Linda had heard him pull in the driveway and gone to the back door to meet him. As he walked through the kitchen and into the front room, he must have seen my form on the couch.

"Who's that?" he asked, apparently having forgotten that I had come home with her, or maybe expecting she had taken me to the barracks in Seiad.

"Oh, that's Hobe," she replied matter-of-factly.

"What's he doing here?" Jim's words cut my heart like a knife. My conscience assailed me, because the meaning of his words went deeper than a question of why I was in his house—he was asking why she had brought me into the affairs of their heart.

FINAL DAYS

Autumn came early that year. Though the summer had been hot and the fire season—especially in the Pacific Northwest—had been intense, August was barely over when the season started turning. Clouds moved in, the temperature dropped. Change was in the air. If only we had known how many areas of our lives would be affected by that change!

I had gotten tired of having no transportation and having to depend on everyone else. In Yreka, I heard that one of Bill Cadola's—the FCO at Happy Camp—sons had a motorcycle for sale. I took Tony the mechanic up to check it out. It was a Honda 175, only about a year old. Though not large, it could still get up to highway speeds. I bought it for $450, and I would never be without some kind of transportation again.

The fire weather went south, so to speak. It got cold and drizzly. A storm even dumped snow on the summit to Scott Valley—very unusual for September. Finally we had some serious "down time."

Tony the mechanic invited Saffell and me over to his travel trailer out in the woods south of town to drive out the chill with some "hot toddies" made with heated rum, sticks of cinnamon, and hot apple cider. I was surprised when Saffell, normally a straight arrow, also accepted. Sitting crammed into the travel trailer with Tony and his wife, I was amazed that she and their two children had spent the whole summer in this thing. It was only sixteen feet long, and half of that was a bed. There was barely room for four adults.

It was cold and damp outside, but inside we were getting warmed by the hot drinks and loosened by the alcohol.

Then Tony's wife started flirting with me in a very obvious way.

She was just the opposite of Tony. He was about six-four with a rough, gravelly voice, while she was petite and demure. But though small in stature, she was not lacking fire in her personality. She started looking into my eyes and fixing all her attention on me as though captivated by everything I had to say. When she spoke to me she would reach out and lay her hand on my arm. I didn't know what in the world was going on, but it was hard not to feel flattered by this sudden gush of attention.

Tony had to notice because she was doing it right in front of him. He seemed be taken aback by it and didn't know how to respond. "Wha... wha... what," he was growling like a provoked bear at some of her more obvious moves.

Then just as abruptly she turned her attention to Saffell and started the same flirtations with him. Unable to resist the sudden rush of feminine attention in the cramped trailer, he came alive to her flattery just like I had.

Tony was miserable and angry, disgusted yet not wanting to create a scene in front of us, his friends. We on the other hand wanted to be true to Tony, but her pointed flirtations were hard to ignore. Meanwhile, she seemed to be enjoying herself immensely.

In looking back on this bizarre evening, I've concluded that she was taking her revenge against Tony for his high jinks that summer: his running around, partying, and chasing women, while she sat in a tiny travel trailer with two kids in the woods far away from home and friends. Somehow word of his doings had filtered back (like it always does) and now it was payback time. Just as he had cheated on her openly in front of us on the crew, she was now paying him back openly in front of us on the crew, even using us to do it!

And who could blame her really? It was he who had sown the seeds of "wild oats" all summer. And now his feisty wife was throwing it back in his face by pouring out her flirtations on us right in front of him—whew!

I report this episode only because it seemed to be a fitting finale to the entire summer. Fire season was finished. The party was over. I loaded all my stuff in the back of Saffell's pickup and on a glorious Indian summer day, he followed me on my new "Hog" over to Arcata.

BRIEF RETURN TO NORMALCY

September 1970

Again I was coming back to Arcata with no place to live. Somehow, I found a place in a house on Union Street, on a hill south of campus. The house had a basement that had been converted into a big bedroom that I shared with one other guy.

This was to be my sixth and last year of college, although I had no idea of what I would do next. But with the balmy Indian summer setting in, the joy of roaring over the steep hills on my new motorcycle, a nice place to live, another exciting summer of fire fighting over and my bank account comfortably full—well you could say that life was rosy, and I didn't have many cares. I was as clueless as I could be over the significance of all that had happened during the summer, and what was still left to play out.

Friday, October 9, dawned just like the other days, sunny and warm. After breakfast, I lingered in the living room upstairs doing some reading for a class.

The phone rang. It was Linda on the other end of the line! She was broken up and very emotional. I must admit that at that point she and Jim and their problems were a long way from my mind. Now it all came rushing back as I listened to the words of her story tumble out.

She had not been able to make any progress toward winning Jim back. He remained distant and involved in his other life. After a particularly disturbing conversation with him on the phone, she had taken the kids, jumped in the car and headed upriver. Exactly what happened next she couldn't remember. But apparently she had run off the road and up a cut bank at an angle, flipping the car over. She had been bruised, but Kellie and Eric were all right. Jimmy, however, had a broken arm and was in the hospital.

In the hospital! "Wait a minute, where are you now?" My mind was spinning, trying to catch up with this sudden turn of events.

"I'm here at the hospital in Yreka. Jimmy's here in traction; the other two are with friends."

"Where's Jim? Isn't he there with you?"

"No, he's down in Redding. When he heard about the accident he came up to see us. When he found out we were all right, he went back to Redding. Oh Hobe can you come...? I need you."

It was like an emotional whirlpool sucking me into its vortex. All the seeds that had been so casually planted and forgotten: the heart-to-heart talks, the ride down the river, the bantering back and forth and the pleasurable thoughts about her in my mind— now they all came sweeping back in through that plaintive cry for help, "Hobe, can you come? I need you."

Without a moment's hesitation I responded, "Hang on. I'll be there as soon as I can."

I packed up quickly, getting some basics together. My mind was a spinning torrent of emotions—fear and excitement, apprehension and elation. I had no idea what I was riding into, what would happen once I got there, and what life would be like on the other side. Having no idea when I'd be back, or even if I'd be back, I scribbled off a quick, emotional note to my mother, thanking her for being such a good mother. Then I hopped on my motorcycle and headed up 299, back over the mountains.

TAKING THE PLUNGE

I pulled into the Yreka hospital about three in the afternoon and a nurse steered me in the right direction toward Jimmy's room.

Linda saw me through the door and came out into the dimly lit hall. Without a word we embraced. We held each other tightly, while the pent-up emotions flowed. What began as a simple embrace of greeting and comfort became an embrace of deeply felt, heart commitment. As we clung to each other, we were committing ourselves to the other for the duration. She was placing herself in my hands in trust, and I was committing myself to her and her needs above anything else in my life. Though neither one of us could have articulated it that way, we both could sense it. She was no longer alone; I was no longer my own.

Then we went in to see Jimmy. He didn't have major injuries, just a broken arm. But he was a young boy in a strange place after a traumatic experience, and it was good having Mom nearby.

After spending some time with Jimmy, Linda and I retired to a quiet corner where we could talk.

Though I didn't say so to Linda, my own analysis and gut feeling of the situation was this: she'd tried everything she knew to get Jim back. After nothing had worked, her subconscious had taken over and made one last-ditch, desperate effort to get his attention by wrecking the car. It was the loudest cry for help she could make.

Now even that had failed. Jim had not rushed to her side; he had not miraculously awakened to how much he really loved her. Now, even this last, desperate cry had fallen on deaf ears, and Linda was devastated. She was finally face-to-face with the fact that her ten-year marriage was finished.

Linda had been the product of a broken home. She had never known her father, and her mother had abandoned her as a baby, running off with some man, never to be seen or heard from again. She had grown up with a clan of Mormons who had passed her around to different families within the clan for a few years at a time. Some of them she had grown attached to, others not. But through it all she had lacked a sense of security and permanence. Then at age fifteen, she had gotten pregnant by her high school sweetheart Jim. She dropped out of school and married him, finding the permanent family she longed for in Jim and their children. Now even that had collapsed. Where had she failed him that he was so set on leaving, that he wouldn't even try to work things out? That secret has always remained hidden in his heart. As it was, once he turned away, he never hesitated, never vacillated, never looked back.

Linda didn't even have any transportation, now that her car was wrecked. She was stuck in Yreka, staying at a motel.

But though she was devastated and numb, she was not unaware of what was happening between us. The seeds that had been planted in our lives had grown unnoticed. Now, amidst the ashes of her relationship with Jim, they were blossoming into love. Our initial embrace had both sealed and started something. She wanted to put her devastated life in my hands and say, "Tell me what to do." And I wanted to put my arms around her and say, "It's all right, I'm here. I won't let anything happen to you."

She was desperate to get away for awhile and calm down from the swirling events of the past few days. Besides, it wouldn't do for me to go with her to her motel, and she didn't want to be alone. I hit upon the idea of taking her to Eslie's ranch. It was way out in the country, and there was only Eslie there in that big old house. So she told Jimmy she'd be gone for a day or so, climbed on back of my Honda, and we headed out of town in the gathering dusk up Ft. Jones Mountain.

It was after dark when we got to Eslie's. I explained the situation to him, and accommodating Eslie gave us full use of the upstairs of his solitary farmhouse.

The Cory Ranch had been built by Eslie's father and his brother at the turn of the century, and it had been quite the house in its day. It was a full two-story house with nine foot ceilings plus an attic. It had been wallpapered throughout, even the ceilings, though now the wallpaper was faded and water-stained from long forgotten storms. Upstairs, dead flies covered the windowsills, but at last we were alone and away from it all.

We chose the south bedroom, which had an ambiance of straw. It seemed like there was straw everywhere—under the carpet, inside the mattress, maybe even in the pillows.

We lay down together in the double bed and for the moment, everything else in our lives took a back seat to what was happening between us. We talked, we held each other, we laughed, we cried, we relaxed.

I've never been in a house with more solitude than Eslie's. Set well back from a little-used gravel road, looking out over the French Creek Valley to the towering mountains beyond, with the nearby pine forest whispering in the wind—here was the perfect spot for Linda to unwind and for me to make one of the most delightful discoveries of my life.

Let me draw a delicate curtain over the details of that night, other than to say we were intimate but not sexual. I'd never been in love with a woman until that night, and there was nothing lustful about it. It was as pure and tender an emotion as I'd ever felt. And I was deeply touched by her simple dependence on me. Her child-like faith made me want to rise to the occasion, to be all I could for her.

The next day was like a day of gauzy fantasy from a romantic novel. It was a perfect Indian summer day and I was in love. I was floating on cloud nine, with a singing in my soul and lightness to everything around me. I was intoxicated with love.

We took Eslie for a walk in the warm afternoon sun through his property above the road. The squirrels were scurrying around the oak trees getting ready for winter, but we were totally caught up in the day at hand. Eslie didn't know what to make of these two love-birds, but he was the kind of guy who could pretty much go along with anything. Linda thought he was a trip, with his slow manner of speech and methodical ways, and she loved to tease him and provoke him to smile. When the hill got steep and Eslie began to get winded, we lay down on the dead grass under a tree and rested, enjoying the peacefulness of the setting. She kept saying, "Hobe this is perfect; this is just perfect!"

That night was a repeat of the first night.

The next day, I could have stayed on and on, but there was a stirring in Linda's soul for her son. The rest was over; now her mother's instinct was calling her back to duty. So in midmorning we headed back through the valley and over the summit to Yreka.

Jimmy was OK and doing better. He was glad to see us. While we were there, a friend from the Oak Knoll District came by to see how things were going with Linda and Jimmy. When instead, he saw how things were going with Linda and me, he invited us to his house in Montague that night for a party with him and his girlfriend. He even offered to pick us up.

For the two nights we had been together at Eslie's, we had ignored the sexual pressure building from our intimate closeness. Linda seemed surer of my love and commitment now, and she was opening up more all the time.

It wasn't much of a party, just the four of us. We sat around drinking and listening to music. After awhile, without saying much, he and his girlfriend retired to his bedroom and didn't return. When it became apparent they weren't coming out again, we turned our attention to each other. The alcohol and pent up passion quickly carried us over the final threshold of our relationship.

Afterwards, Linda went into the bathroom, but I, partially stupefied from drink, remained still, frozen in time and space, trying to comprehend the significance of what had just happened.

Sex was something I had longed for and dreamed of my whole life. Finally, at age twenty-three, it had happened, but in such a shoddy way: drunk and with somebody else's wife. Where was the love in that? I was overwhelmed, trying to sort it out—where were the correlations between what I had imagined all my life and what had just happened?

BETRAYAL

Linda and I were entering into a degree of paranoia, running around trying to keep our relationship a secret. Already what had started out at Eslie's as pure love was being compromised. First it was compromised in Montague with lust, now it was further clouded with the fear of discovery, knowing it would be wrong in the eyes of others.

I paid for a motel room that I never entered so I'd have a place to park my motorcycle for the night. I'd drop her off at some distance from her motel so she could walk up to her room just to get a change of clothes.

But Yreka was small town America. Even with such precautions, we couldn't stay hidden forever. Our Montague friend already knew about us, and it was only a matter of time before Jim found out. In the meantime, now that we were committed to each other, Linda needed to deal with dissolving her marriage: the legal paperwork, interlocutory decree, child custody, financial settlement, alimony and child support payments. In the meantime, in the eyes of God and society, we were committing adultery. Such was the thicket that young love had to struggle through. Not to mention the fact that I was supposed to be attending college 250 miles away.

But we were in love. There was no doubt about that. For the first time in my life, I was head over heels. I was prepared to do anything for her, while she transferred to me the devotion she had once given to Jim. I found her love and trust heady wine indeed, and I was determined not to let her down. At the moment, we found the mountain of difficulties forcing us closer together and strengthening our commitment to each other.

The next day, we were at the hospital with Jimmy. She had begun telling him about us, preparing his heart. I was getting ready to ride back to Arcata to be in class again Tuesday morning.

Suddenly, without warning, Jim walked through the door and found us together.

It was funny, but that summer, as Jim's life had begun to spin out of control, he and I had actually gotten closer. We didn't talk about what was going on in his life, but we shared about other things, like the time he got a big buck in his sights but couldn't pull the trigger, because it was such a noble animal. Around other people, it was impossible, because he would revert to the story-telling, good-time Jim. But there were those times, rare quiet times, when we were alone together and could talk about things of a deeper nature—things that revealed the hidden man within. He had a sensitive part to him—a tender place inside that amazed me. There had been times I thought, "Wow; this could be my best friend for life."

Now here we were, unexpectedly face-to-face. He was startled to find me there, just as I was startled to find him walking through the door. He quickly recovered, however, and after casting only a brief glance at Linda and me together, ignored us and went to Jimmy's bed and began talking to him.

Linda and I slipped out of the room into the hall. It was a tense moment, and neither of us said much. Jim came out, walked up, and ignoring me, said to Linda, "I want to talk to you."

Thus began a time of bitter arguments between them that was to last throughout the fall. Before I came into the picture, there were not many arguments. He mostly stonewalled her and her questions about his activities. But now the floodgates opened, breaking loose the bottled-up emotions in them both.

One of the greatest wrongs I committed was that with one blow I destroyed my deepening relationship with Jim forever. Jim had many friends, but few he could open up to—the thing he desperately needed. I have no doubt that I helped Linda through a very difficult time, but at such a price! If I could have avoided becoming emotionally involved with her, if I still could have helped her while maintaining my integrity in the Forest Service and my relationship with Jim… what a difference it would have made! Jim also needed me. Maybe not as much as she did, but he still needed me. He needed someone he could open up his real heart to, someone he didn't have to maintain his good-time front with.

As it was, by allowing myself to become involved with Linda, I inserted myself into the equation. Now my own desires, needs, emotions, and destiny were mixed in with theirs, and became one more part of the mess that had to be sorted out. Instead of playing the part of the true friend and working for peace and reconciliation, I had played the part of the false friend and pounced upon the spoils of the breakup.

I must judge myself, that, in trying to help Linda, and by pursuing my own agenda of finding love and happiness, I failed Jim in his time of need and betrayed our friendship.

SLEEPING IN THE BED WE HAD MADE

So followed an autumn of strife. With me in her corner, Linda seemed more emboldened to fight back against the one who had done her wrong. And with me in her corner, Jim had a focus for his grievances against her.

Between skirmishes, Linda strengthened herself by calling me or by running over to see me. Once I picked out a piece of jewelry, a gold chain with a cross on it, and sent it to her as a gift. Jim discovered her wearing it, found out that I gave it to her, and ripped it off her neck and flung it into the wood burning furnace. Another time she went over to their bank in Ft. Jones and pulled all the money out of their joint checking account, built up from Jim's summer's work, leaving him penniless.

Inside, I was feeling a lot of guilt over Jim. That, and using marijuana again, resulted in fresh paranoia attacks on my part. Once when she came over to see me, I was so overwhelmed by the fear that he might follow her, find out where I lived, and break through the door at night in a jealous rage, that I put a heavy monkey wrench under my bed for protection.

Another time, I was at her place for the weekend. It was stormy and the rain was pelting down outside. Late in the evening as the storm was raging, just after we put the kids to bed, the power went out and the dogs started barking furiously outside. I started to have a panic attack, thinking maybe Jim had cut the power to the house in preparation for breaking in and killing me. Then we noticed that the lights were out at the neighbor's across the field too, and realized it was because of the storm. Later I thought how stupid I had been to think the dogs barking furiously outside were a sign that he was out there coming for me. After all, they were *his* dogs!

Once in December, Linda left the kids with friends and came over to see me. Afterward, she wanted me to come back with her to their house to get some things. We drove up the river together. Though the sun was shining, it was cold, and the first snow of the winter had blanketed everything with a thin coat of white.

As we came around the last bend in the road and saw their house, our hearts stopped. There, rising straight up in the clear air was a plume of smoke from the chimney. "Jim's home!" she gasped. My heart sank. I had not seen Jim since that afternoon in the hospital. He had his own place now, but still came around occasionally.

But there we were, and all we could do was go through with it. We parked off the highway and walked in the front door. Linda wanted to go first because she thought he might pulverize me.

As we walked in, he looked up with an expression of anger and deep pain on his face. He was a man in anguish.

He made a nasty remark to me—the only time gentle Jim ever cut me down—then he and Linda launched into a heated, bitter argument that went on and on throughout various rooms of the house. It was one of the most uncomfortable experiences of my life, sitting on the Naugahyde couch in the cold living room while the anger and arguing swirled around me, and the nervous sweat dripped from my armpits. There was nothing I could say, nothing I could do. I couldn't be part of the solution, because I had become part of the problem. Such was the misery that flowed into all of our lives for what we had done.

BITS AND PIECES

I have many memories associated with my visits that winter to Linda's house along the Klamath, such as lying beside her late at night in the cold bedroom, listening to the lumber trucks plying their solitary way on the highway above the house. They ran twenty-four hours a day, taking the cut lumber from the mills in Happy Camp to wherever they were going. Or sometimes it would be the scraping of the snowplows keeping lonely vigil during the many snowfalls that winter.

Being with a woman had a profound effect on me. There was the bonding, the incredible feeling of oneness with another human being, sleeping in each other's arms, feeling her breath on my face. One of the most wonderful things was breathing together—lying there so unconsciously tuned in to each other that our breathing would synchronize—the two would breathe as one! Being a loner and never physically close to anyone, I found this relationship meeting deep needs I didn't even know I had.

BONDING AND WRENCHING

Now that Linda's marriage was over she was considering her options. Things she wouldn't have dreamed of doing before, like going back to school and getting a high school diploma, now became possibilities. After Christmas, she enrolled in night school in Yreka.

She picked me up from Arcata late in January and took me to her place for a visit. She had class one night and asked me to baby-sit while she was gone. I did the dinner dishes with the kids, played with them, and read them a story before putting them to bed. Then I stayed up studying, waiting for her return. Since class was over at nine, I expected her back by 10:00 p.m. so we could have our time together. But ten o'clock came and went with no sign of her. Then eleven, still no Linda. Midnight rolled by with no familiar crunch of gravel in the driveway.

Now I was getting worried; where could she be? I thought of the forty-five miles of lonely river road between there and Yreka. If she happened to fall asleep at the wheel, or got distracted and drifted off the road.... She might not be found till morning.

Shortly after midnight, I called the sheriff's department in Yreka. I told them my story and my fears. Did they have any bodies or accident victims they were unable to identify? The dispatcher said no, things had been pretty quiet that night. They were not working any major accidents. But she would alert any officers patrolling this stretch of river road to be on the lookout for a red Maverick.

Sometime after that, I finally went to bed, falling into a fitful sleep filled with worry.

Later in the night, I awoke with a start. I knew that a long time had passed and her side of the bed was still empty. I looked over toward her clock; the lighted dial said 4:00 a.m. I jumped awake. Four a.m.! How could it be that she was still not back! My fear and worry that had gradually been building all night, now took a quantum leap. What could have happened? Was there any doubt left that she was the victim of foul play? There was no other reasonable explanation. But what did this mean? What would happen to the kids? Should I call the police again? Maybe the Highway Patrol this time? Who could I call to watch the kids while I went out searching for her? And how could I search for her? She'd driven off in the car! I lay back on the bed in uncertainty and dozed off again fitfully.

Finally, at 5:00 a.m., Linda walked into the bedroom. "Linda, where have you been? What's happened to you? Are you all right?" My worry and fears gushed out in a stream of questions.

"Oh sure, I'm fine; sorry I'm late."

"You're sorry you're late? But what happened?"

"Oh well, after class one of my classmates invited me down to this bar for a drink. Then this other guy told us about this great party going on, so we went there. Hobe, we had the greatest time! It was so much fun."

I felt so relieved that she was all right that I was almost speechless. But now her answers were troubling me almost as much. "But why didn't you call? Why didn't you let me know? I don't understand; out partying all night with other guys? What about us?"

We had met like two ships in the night. Though we had been going in different directions, her ship was sinking so she jumped into mine. For a short season, we went together in my ship, but that only masked the fact that we were still going in different directions.

I, never married or even serious with a girl, was looking for a permanent dose of that closeness and intimacy that I had so happily found in her.

Linda, coming out of a tragically ended marriage she had entered into at only fifteen years old, was trying to find herself. And even more significantly, she was trying to recover the missing years of her youth. She had lost those carefree teenage years of boys and dances and fun—to babies, diapers, laundry, and cooking. But now she had been given another chance, and was determined to find and relive those years, no matter what it took.

Though we patched things over and continued on, still that night was the beginning of a two-year wrenching slide that I could not understand nor stop. Later, when I asked her about why and how it started to go, she said there was a time in January when she was desperate and alone, and I was at school in Arcata. She had needed me, and I hadn't been there, so she'd turned away from me in her heart. When she said that, it sounded so unfair. No person can *be there* every second, only God can do that. But be that as it may, from that time onward her complete and childlike dependence on me ended, and more and more she began following her own agenda: having fun, partying, looking for those lost years, and avoiding commitment.

I looked on marriage as the perfect thing to cement together all the glorious pieces of this wonderful relationship. For her, marriage was what had robbed her of the best ten years of her life and then spit her out, wounded and impoverished. She was certainly not going to make that mistake again! It would take years to sort it all out, but we were each going in profoundly different directions, and no amount of bonding could alter that fact.

RELOCATION

Linda wanted out of her house on the Klamath; it had too many painful memories. She wanted to return to her roots—back to Etna in Scott Valley where she had grown up. There she could pick up the pieces and get re-established in life. As for me, I wanted to be with her. She was still the biggest thing happening in my life. And things hadn't been going very well with us lately. She was not interested in coming to the coast to live with me, and being separated from each other wasn't working. Her life was going through constant turmoil, certainly not stable enough to support a long distance relationship.

When it became clear that she would not come to the coast but would return to Etna, I decided to go to Etna to live also. I didn't understand that our boats were trying to go in different directions. Since she had gotten out of my boat, I would get in her boat and go with her for awhile. So it was on February 1, 1971 that I

dropped out of Humboldt State to move to Etna and live with my great uncle Eslie in his house up French Creek.

I got some help from my hippie roommate. We loaded my stuff in his VW bus and he and his girlfriend followed me on my motorcycle. It was an unseasonably warm, sunny afternoon with the temperature in the 60s as we headed up 299. But the sun set as we were leaving Gazelle and the cold settled in quickly. Luckily, he had wanted a turn riding my bike, so we switched and I drove his VW, sitting inside where it was warm. It was well below freezing when we got to Eslie's, and he was one cold dude!

Meanwhile, Linda had found half a duplex to live in just outside town. I helped her move in one cold, blustery day with snow squalls coming down out of the mountains. She hadn't wanted me to move in with her. So I spent my days at Eslie's, my evenings with her, and my nights back at Eslie's.

Linda began to improve. Away from the barrenness and memories of the Klamath, back among her own people, she was healing and getting hold of life again. But our own relationship didn't seem to be going anywhere, and I couldn't figure out why.

SUMMER AFTERMATH'S DELAYED HIT

As the winter wore on, I thought I'd better get in touch with Glen Robinson about the next fire season. So I wrote to him, letting him know my address and my availability for work. I was stunned when he wrote back a week or so later. Glen said Oak Knoll didn't have the helicopter anymore. The Forest had decided to eliminate the small helicopter on the Callahan District and keep just the one Huey on the Forest. Because they would only have the one, they were moving it to the Scott River District where it would be more centrally located. If I still wanted to be with the helicopter, I could check with them. Otherwise, Stan Austin, the foreman at Oak Knoll, was interested in having me on his tanker crew.

Naturally, I didn't waste any time contacting the FCO at Ft. Jones. Ft. Jones was right across the Valley from Etna anyway, less than twenty miles from Eslie's, much closer than Oak Knoll. If I could get on there, it would be perfect. I could even commute and not have to live in the barracks.

I went over and filled out an application, and was soon ushered in to talk to the FCO in his office. He was an older man, definitely from the "old school." He looked at me strangely, like I both interested and repulsed him at the same time, like the morbid fascination people find in gazing upon a serial killer. I was so naive about life; I really knew nothing about gossip. I just lived my own life, such as it was, and figured other people did the same.

"Why, no," he said to me, after I told him my desire to continue working with the helicopter, "I can't offer you a job. The helitack positions are already filled." Then he went into a long-winded explanation of why the helicopter was over there now, why it wasn't at Oak Knoll or Yreka, and why there weren't any openings. He just kept going on and on, which seemed unnecessary and evasive. But I couldn't figure out what he was trying to evade.

I still hadn't figured it out. I didn't realize how badly we had blown it and become a disgrace throughout the forest—the object of gossip and shaking of heads. The consolidation and relocation made sense as far as where to put the helicopter, but the new crew made sense only in light of the moral failures of the old one. I had yet to learn that a good reputation is a great asset, but it only takes a little folly to destroy it. And in the eyes of many people, we had committed more than a little folly last summer. I'm sure in many quarters, it was a full-blown scandal. When you combined our lackluster fire fighting abilities, our reputation as general screw-ups, the out-of-control partying, Jim's failed marriage, and my involvement with his ex-wife... well there was something for everyone to shake their heads over.

And I was probably seen as the guiltiest. Jim was only doing what most red-blooded American men could be expected to do; he just got a little carried away. But I—I was a home wrecker.

Actually, I never heard anything other than the official reasons why the helicopter was moved and given a new crew, so maybe the embarrassment over the lack of our supervision went deeper than I know. We were given more freedom than we were able to handle, and the results looked bad for everybody.

So there I was, face to face with this old-line Ft. Jones FCO looking at me strangely and offering evasive answers as to why there was no longer a job for me in helitack. It was one more of a long string of unpleasant results for what I had done. After four seasons, my helitack days were over.

FIRE SEASON AT OAK KNOLL

April 1971

It was a long, hard winter, but eventually spring did come. In early April, I got a call from Jim Benson at Oak Knoll. He wanted me to come over and start work April 19, heading up a trail crew. It was the first time I had been put in charge of anything so I was pretty excited about it. The job lasted until June when the fire season began. I had a three to five-man crew, and we worked trails on the old Seiad part of the District. This was real woods work like as a boy I had dreamed of doing. Capping it off, they packed in three of us on horses to the Lower Devils Lookout where we stayed for a week at a time, working the trails in the high country.

One afternoon while we were working far from the lookout, a cold rain began that gradually changed to a wet snow. Before we knew it, a blizzard swept down on us from the Middle and Upper Devils' Peaks! We could barely see through the blinding snow to make it back to the tower where the wind howled around us all night. In spite of the weather, we did eventually complete the trails around the lookout. By then it was time to report to the Oak Knoll Ranger Station for the start of fire season.

You know how everybody likes to have their own little claim to fame, like "George Washington slept here?" Oak Knoll's claim to fame, which I heard soon after arriving, was, "We have the tallest Red Fir tree in the world." Apparently, it had just been discovered that spring.

The change in the weather we had experienced on the lookout continued throughout the month of June. It was the coolest, cloudiest June I'd ever seen. The powerful winter was not yet ready to relax its icy fingers and yield to summer.

This cool dampness made June seem to go on forever. We should have rejoiced that the weather was helping us in our task of protecting the forest. But instead, we were beside ourselves, waiting week after week for the weather to break and for the first fire of the season. However, at least I had a job. Neither Saffell nor Jimmy Gould came back that year. Jim had been promoted to Fire Control Technician, working as assistant to Glen Robinson.

Not only did I still have a job, but for some reason, we had two class II tankers at the station instead of just one. I was chosen to be TTO of the second one, while a husky, good looking guy named Monte was TTO on the first one.

SUMMER MOSAIC

Summer finally came in July and August, and the weather got hot and dry. But the fire season never amounted to much.

It was a bad summer for substance abuse. Almost every night I went down to the bar for a hamburger-fries-and-beer supper. Then I would stay and drink through the evening till bedtime.

Things were not going well with Linda and me, and I was blue. I was stuck back on the River, and she was going out partying, meeting guys, and having fun. I couldn't figure why our relationship wasn't enough for her. Why wasn't it enough just to have each other? I was a long way from understanding what she needed. I had plunged headlong into a relationship that had almost no chance of success, and now I was reaping the bitter fruit. If only my life had been guided by some principles of wisdom, rather than just my own ideas of right and wrong, I would have been spared much agony and frustration that instead were mine in abundance. As it was, I spent countless hours sitting in the bar sulking in my beer, singing along with the mournful songs on the jukebox:

Country Roads, take me home, to the place I be-lo-o-o-ng
West Virginia, mountain mama, take me home,
my country roads.

Sometimes, after getting half drunk and thinking about her for awhile, I'd go out to the pay phone outside the bar and call her, being sentimental and stupid, or worse yet, finding she was gone for the evening!

SPREADING RIPPLES AND A DEAD-END ROAD

One late summer evening, I decided to go for a cruise on my bike up in the mountains. A lot of logging had been going on behind the ranger station, and there were logging roads everywhere. It was a great place to cruise around and explore the district.

But the sun was going down earlier now and it wasn't long before it started getting dark. I had come quite a ways, and was now on a new logging road going through some fresh cut-blocks. I had never been on this road, but the road was headed in the direction I wanted to go—gradually working its way across the face of the ridge—and I figured at some point, it would have to come out to the main access road I was aiming for that would take me back to civilization. Meanwhile, darkness was coming on fast, now that the sun had set. I sped up a little, forgetting the beautiful scenery. I just wanted to get out before it got dark and I had to navigate through this maze of roads and cut-blocks by my one headlight. "A guy could get lost up here at night," I thought.

I came to another fresh cut-block. "Boy, they're sure doing a lot of logging on this road," I thought, as I bounced over the ruts caused by the logging equipment. I rounded a turn and came to the end of the cut-block, and, horrors of horrors, to the end of the road! Only the forest was left, marching on in undisturbed grandeur.

"Wow, this is crazy," I thought, remembering all the miles I had traveled along this road while thinking it would take me to the main road out, only to have it end deep in the very forest I was trying to get out of.

If only I could have seen it, my life at this point was also on a dead-end road. I was back into drugs, though I had been free of them for several years. I was drinking more heavily than ever before. Somewhere along the way, I had even started smoking a pipe after being miraculously delivered from cigarettes a couple of years ago. I was in a dead-end relationship with Linda that had started out so well, but now was steadily worsening while its ripples continued to spread out to touch others in negative ways.

During the first week after I arrived at Oak Knoll, there had been a dance at the Community Hall. I went to meet some of the new people with whom I'd be working. During the dance I found myself sitting next to a young, auburn-haired woman. She smiled and introduced herself as Mary, the wife of Forest Service regular Carl in the timber department. They lived on the compound in a trailer with some of the other married couples. We had quite an animated conversation. "This woman is so friendly," I thought. "It almost seems like she's coming on to me." I returned her friendliness, but no more than that. I didn't want to chance another entanglement with a married woman.

During the summer, I found out that Mary and Carl were having marital problems, but I didn't know any more than that

Linda later told me that one day Mary had called up Elsie Allen and told her she had decided to have an affair and that she was having it with Monte. She had been very open about it, much as if she had called to say she had decided to buy a new pair of shoes. Although I certainly was not one of very high moral standards, I was sickened by this latest turn of events; sickened and amazed at how the bloody footprints seemed to lead back to my house!

And so the ripples kept spreading. Could it be that our unintended example—that there could be "life after marriage"—was now being repeated by others who didn't have any business going there. Apparently Mary had heard about Linda and me and decided that, "If they can do it and get away with it, so can I!" No wonder a lot of the men secretly wanted me pulverized!

I had always been one of those who wanted to change the world. From the civil rights movement to the antiwar movement, I was there. Last spring, May 1970, I had boycotted classes for a week and gone to demonstrations every night after the National Guard killed the five students at Kent State, where my dad taught. Discovering drugs had only heightened my conviction that "change must come to our society."

And so I had introduced Linda to marijuana "to take her to a higher plane of existence," but instead, it had been a gateway drug to launch her into a world of drinking, partying, and chasing guys.

And now, by helping Linda find "life after marriage," it looked like others were being encouraged in that direction, others who had no idea of the devastation it had brought to all of us.

I was very grateful that it wasn't I who had gotten mixed up with Mary back at the first of the summer when she was "looking around." My integrity was already in tatters over Linda; it would have been destroyed beyond recovery by Mary. Little did I know what lay only one year ahead for me!

"You're going the wrong way! There's a dead end ahead!" Life was shouting at me. But I wasn't listening; I wasn't ready to hear. Tragically, I would have to go still deeper into the fire before being ready to admit I was lost and needed help getting out.

In the immediate situation, I did manage to retrace my course in the dark through the many cut-blocks and fortunately find another road that went all the way through, arriving safely at the station around bedtime.

Would I ever find my way to a safe harbor in life?

AN EARLY SLASH SEASON

Since the fire season had been such a bust, slash burning was scheduled to start early. The usual policy was to wait till after the first rain. But even though there had been no rain, the weather had been so cooperative all year that Glen, Jim Allen, and the Fire Control staff in the Supervisor's Office decided to go ahead and start burning the slash blocks.

The first one was a large block on Buckhorn Ridge.

The fire was fun. The early fall air was bracing after the heat of summer. All the guys were there: the station fire crews; the outlying guard stations of Beaver Creek and Colestine; and Glen and his leadership team. Jim Kuphaldt was in his glory telling war stories. People were drinking coffee, laughing, and having a good time.

The burn went well. Around midnight, most of us went home, while one crew stayed for the night.

A few days later, we torched another one down on the old Seiad District in the mountains above Walker Creek.

Of course, once a block was burned, you had to watch it until winter set in. It was like a forest fire: logs and stump holes would burn for a month or more.

Most of the temporaries had left by now. I planned to go back to college also and finish up, but since I had completed fall quarter last year before withdrawing, I was in no hurry to leave. I was excited about participating in my first slash burning season.

The burning of the third block was planned, but the weather went screwy again. It started warming up a little each day. A monster high-pressure ridge was building over the West Coast, pushing the jet stream far to the north. Hot air from the desert southwest flooded in.

"All burns are off!" the word came down from the S.O. Suddenly we were back into fire season. Still there didn't seem to be much reason for alarm. If a major fire had occurred that year, we'd be watching it and patrolling it just like these slash fires.

The big danger was wind. Our first burn had straddled the top of a ridge, where winds can blow hard. And these monster high-pressure systems, when they finally do break down, can kick up some powerful gradient winds.

As the high pressure system and fire danger continued to build, it was decided to start mop-up operations inside the burned blocks, first sending in crews to extinguish all hot spots within 100 feet of the line, then 100 yards and so forth, gradually separating the remaining hot spots farther and farther from the surrounding forest. But what was *good* still might not be good *enough*.

The high pressure continued through a second week, and then at last it began to break down.

"High winds expected tonight over peaks and ridges." The weather report was passed around by word of mouth. By this time, crews were manning the slash blocks around the clock. That night they fortified the crews. The rest of us were to be ready to go.

I was jolted awake about midnight by Stan yelling up the barrack's stairs, "A high wind's come up and the fire's gone over the top! Let's go! Roll the tankers!"

The treetops were whipping crazily in the wind as we headed up the twisting logging roads to the slash block. When we got to the ridge top, the wind was howling out of the east with gale-like force. Glowing embers were streaming like tracer bullets from hotspots in the burned block across the line into the neighboring forest—mostly scattered clumps of trees with heavy grass in between. The embers were already starting little grass fires here and there.

"Hose lay! Hose lay!" someone was shouting. It was obvious that hand tools weren't going to make it in this wind and in the thickly-sodded grass, so we pulled out the inch and a half hose, accordioned in the back of the tanker.

We fought the fire gamely all night, but in the end were overwhelmed by the wind and the time it took to refill the tankers. We had to pull out and relocate our line below.

THE LARGEST RED FIR TREE IN THE WORLD

Morning light found us far below in the middle of the forest with our tankers, trying to establish a new line. For once, the terrain was not steep, and a cat was bulldozing a fire line through the trees.

We were taking a break while the cat worked. The night's adrenaline had drained away and we were sitting listlessly. Tim from Colestine came up to me and said in a low voice, "Hey Dave, you wanna come see something?"

"Yeah, sure," I replied. He seemed pretty mysterious about it. "What is it?"

"It's the largest Red Fir tree in the world," Tim muttered. "I'm supposed to protect it, but it's burning and I can't stop it."

"Wow! It seems that's all I've been hearing about this summer—this giant Red Fir tree." I knew it was here on our district but had never known where. And now Tim was telling me it was here *in* the fire. This was too much. "You mean it's right around *here*?" I asked incredulously.

"Yeah, right over there through the trees. Come check it out."

"Now this I've got to see!" I was galvanized to action. I took my leave of Stan and headed into the woods after Tim. Embers from the fire, pushed by the strong winds, had fallen like snow the night before, leaving little spot fires burning here and there.

A couple of hundred yards away, he stopped and motioned to me through the undergrowth. There it was, towering over the rest of the forest, the tallest Red Fir tree in the world! But it was old, and partially hollowed out. By some chance of fate, a spot fire had started near its base the night before and had burned up into its exposed, hollow trunk. Now the trunk was acting like a chimney, holding in the heat and allowing the fire to climb far up inside the tree. Fifty feet or more up the trunk, there was a hole where smoke and flickering flames could be seen venting themselves from inside.

I quickly grasped Tim's dilemma. Without water, there was nothing he could do to extinguish the fire. "I can't even put the fire out here in the lower part." He pointed to the base of the tree where the trunk was hollowed out from the ground up about twenty feet. Here, the whole inside of the tree was a mass of glowing coals. "I've been throwing dirt on these burning coals like crazy, but the dirt just falls back to the ground and the coals keep burning."

It was midmorning when the cat-road was completed. It came within fifty feet of the tree. With the hard line, my crewman sprayed the large hollowed out area at the base of the tree and got that fire out, but even with the water under full pressure, we couldn't push it high enough inside the tree to extinguish the upper, internal fire. The fire was too well entrenched inside the tree; all we could do was let it burn and go on to other mop-up areas.

The next day things had quieted down a lot. Even the Red Fir tree was barely smoking now. As I was mopping up in the area, I saw a guy walking up with a .22 caliber rifle. Someone said he was a Forest Service marksman. The Forest Service was pretty sure the Red Fir tree would die now, being cooked to death by the fire inside it. So this marksman was sent to shoot the seed cones off the branches to salvage all the seeds possible from this behemoth. It was thought there might be something special in the genes that made this tree grow so big, and maybe with the seeds a race of giant Red Fir trees could be started.

The marksman was there most of the morning shooting at the hundreds of cones on the branches. Seeds were all over the ground from the shattered cones. I picked up a handful to keep as a memento of the fire that destroyed the tallest Red Fir tree in the world.

As for me, my life was getting cooked inside too. It was still not certain whether I would end up a burned out hulk, or whether something like the marksman could separate me from the growing body of death and free me to find the life I was meant to have.

NEW START IN ARCATA

October 1971

There was a remarkable similarity between my experiences of the past year with Linda and the LSD trips I had taken back in 1967. There had been that same heady rush of excitement, then the plethora of new experiences: the bonding, the intimacy, the intoxication of first love. But just as with the LSD high, these exciting new experiences had a downside: the double life, the fear and anxiety, even panic attacks, the loss of integrity, and the destruction of my friendship with Jim.

Then, after the initial rush, there was the beginning of the gradual pulling away, the "high" beginning to lift: Linda pulling away to pursue her own life. With LSD, there had been the excruciatingly long coming down: the slow descent to reality that lasted longer than the actual high. So in "coming down" from Linda, I spent a summer's worth of nights in the bar drinking beer and listening to mournful country music, feeling sorry for myself and wondering what went wrong.

Many people minimize the negative aspects of drugs and take them again and again in the search of that elusive "first high" experience until they get so hooked they take them because they can't live without them. Also in love, many people put the negatives behind them and go right out again in search of that elusive "first love" experience—that "romantic rush"—and end up going through one painful relationship after another, never finding anything of lasting value.

Though I was a long way from catching on to all this, I had figured out that my future didn't lie in Etna with Linda. I was ready to take up my life again where I left off. So, sometime in early October, after the winding down of the "Red Fir Fire," I returned to Arcata.

Once again, I was coming back to town with no place to live. I looked up my old friend Ron Dupuy, who was now living with his future wife, Jan. They let me stay with them while I was looking for a place of my own.

I was facing some slack time because I couldn't start college again until January. In the meantime, I was looking for a solution to the perennial problem of where to live. Since apartments were always scarce because of the college, I got the idea of buying a house. If I could buy a house big enough to have additional rooms to rent in the ever-demanding student rental market, the rent could help me make house payments while giving me a permanent place to live. All it would take was some capital to get started—my summer's work money!

I checked out a nice three bedroom house in a residential area of Arcata for $23,000. Too much! Then I saw an ad for a three bedroom house out on Old Arcata Road—$7,500, with $2,000 down. "Now that's more like it."

The house wasn't much, wedged between Old Arcata Road and Freshwater Slough, with the slough's levee right in the backyard. It was originally a one-bedroom house, but two additional bedrooms had been added. The lot was in the shape of a triangle. On the tight end of the triangle, the corner of the house was so close to the slough that you walked off the steps from the back porch right onto the top of the levee. The front yard ended only about twenty-five feet from the raised berm of the road! The nicest feature of the house was the hardwood floors in the living room and the master bedroom.

It was for sale by a widow named Ruby, who lived there with her teenage son but wanted to move to town. I agreed to her terms—

$2,000 down and $70/month for seven years at seven and one-half percent interest. I gave her $100 to bind the deal until it closed escrow.

The down payment took nearly all my savings from the summer's work. But I was a homeowner at age twenty-four, and that seemed pretty exciting.

THE HOUSE

I was lying in bed in my new house, a proud homeowner. The fall rains had finally come and were dropping almost silently on the roof. I lay there at rest, savoring the moment. I had two roomers for the other two bedrooms who, at $45 per month each, were meeting my house payment of $70, plus my share of the three-way split of the utility bills. Now I had my own permanent place to live, building equity, yet not costing anything out-of-pocket. I was essentially living for free!

Meanwhile, since I was not presently a student, I was eligible for unemployment compensation. Because of all the money I had made in the few months I was working, I was eligible for the maximum benefit paid. I was living for free and making money doing nothing! It was great being an American!

My reverie was interrupted by a sound I couldn't immediately place. It sounded like a dripping noise, but not a dull thud, like you'd expect from water dripping on the roof. It had a hard, metallic sound to it, and strangely, seemed to be coming from the attic above the closet in the bedroom.

It was getting dark, but curiosity was getting the better of me. I got a flashlight, and moved a chair underneath the attic access in the closet. Standing on the chair, I pushed aside the plywood cover and scrambled up into the attic.

With the help of the flashlight, I soon found the source of the dripping sound. Suspended above the open access door was a coffee can. Since there was nothing directly above it to hang it from, it was suspended by the curious device of a couple of strings tied off to the roof trusses on either side and then threaded through holes punched in the can, so the can was hanging on the taut strings. Why it was there quickly became apparent—there was a steady drip from a leak in the roof above the can, each drip hitting the bottom with the metallic thud I had heard.

"Hmm, interesting." I swung the flashlight around through the rest of the attic. Everywhere bright, shiny coffee cans looked back at me. The attic was full of coffee cans, each under a drip from the roof!

After taking a moment for the impact of this to sink in, a thought occurred to me: "Why, with so many coffee cans under drips, was only one making a noise?" Closer examination revealed the answer: the rest of the coffee cans had scraps of fabric in their bottoms, which cushioned the falling drips so they made no noise. But whoever had devised this scheme had forgotten to put a piece of cloth in the one above the crawl hole, hence the dripping sound that led me to discover the whole plot. And it was indeed a clever plan! The scraps of cloth acted both as sound deadeners and as wicks to evaporate the water out of the cans between storms.

There's no telling how long it might have taken the cans to fill up or for me to catch on to their existence, except for the one without the cloth suspended above the opening. That was the Achilles heel of the whole affair. "Ruby, Ruby, Ruby, where did you come up with this scheme—*Sunset Magazine*?"

The roof turned out to be made with overlapping strips of rolled roofing running the length of the roof, not exactly code. To make emergency repairs, I had to buy several 5 gallon buckets of a tar-like roof patching substance and brush it over the entire roof with a big laundry brush. That sealed up the tiny cracks in the rolled roofing and stopped the leaks.

One day, not long after that, I came home in the afternoon and one of my roomers said, "There's no water."

Now Ruby had said something about her water well being down at a neighbor's farm. She said that although the pump used his electricity, he never charged her for it. But "it would be a good idea for [me] to check with him." I had meant to, but hadn't gotten around to it. Now it looked like the issue was forced.

I found the farmer—an older man with a wizened face—down at the barn and introduced myself as the new owner of Ruby's house. I mentioned that she had said the well was on his property, but now for some reason there wasn't any water.

He looked at me hard and said, "So you think I'm going to keep supplying you with free water forever?"

I apologized profusely for not coming to see him and working out some kind of agreement. "I'll gladly pay you for your power."

That seemed to mollify him, and we agreed on $4 per month.

Later in the fall, after a particularly heavy rain, I got up in the morning to take a bath. As I lay in the tub with the hot water cascading out of the faucet, I noticed its color was dark, like weak tea. It also had an offensive odor: a barnyard kind of smell. "Man I don't know if this is getting me cleaner or making me worse," I said aloud. I got out without finishing the bath.

On my way to Arcata, I stopped by his barn and surveyed the well. It was the old fashioned type, built of bricks, five feet in diameter, sticking two feet out of the ground. There had been low spots around the base of the well that he had filled in with what looked like manure from his barn floor. "Yecch," I gagged, "I wonder if the manure around the base of the well is seeping through the bricks and getting in the water?" It certainly smelled like it, especially after being heated in the hot water heater.

I didn't have the guts to confront the raspy old farmer about this latest development. I knew it didn't matter to him; it wasn't his drinking water. He had city water. He used this water for his animals. So we had to adjust to the situation. We didn't dare drink the water or bathe in it. For dishes, we filled the sinks with hot water and sterilized it with bleach. Ruby had been drinking bottled water—now I knew why! Baths were the biggest problem. We had to take them wherever we could at friends or even at the dorms at the college.

I had asked the farmer about getting hooked up to his water district. He told me it would cost $7,000 to pay my property's share of getting the service out there. That was wild when the whole house only cost me $7,500.00!

I don't remember what it was that prompted me to get a termite inspection. I probably read something in the paper that made me think of it. Anyway, I called a company from the phone book and asked for a checkup. I wasn't there when the fellow came, but when I returned, Carol, my first and most faithful roommate, met me at the door and handed me a sheaf of papers. "Hey Dave, this termite guy was here and boy are you in trouble!"

"Why, what's the problem?"

"Oh it's all in here," she said, waving the sheaf of papers.

"Yeah," my other roommate chimed in. "He said it's the worst house he's ever inspected."

Dumbfounded, I sat down and leafed through the papers. There were pages of things found wrong: dry rot, soil-wood contact, grade problems, termite evidence—pages of itemized deficiencies.

The whole house was built on pillars instead of a foundation. Many of the pillars were resting on rocks buried in the ground, with the soil touching their bases. The house was built on a slope, that ran from the raised road down toward the slough. Because there was no foundation, all the storm runoff ran under the house, making the dirt wet most of the time. At the low end of the house, the water rose above the ground in the winter. In fact, the whole backyard was under a few inches of water all winter, that also backed up under part of the house.

After the water table had risen during the winter and the backyard was under a few inches of water, somebody noticed that every time the toilet flushed, there was a disturbance in the water in the backyard. "Well I wonder if the septic tank is plugged up, or full, or has a leak in it," I thought. So I called the county to see if they would come out and inspect the septic system.

Again, I wasn't there when the inspector came out, but he left a message that he wanted to see me in his office downtown.

"Does this mean I have a problem with my septic system?" I inquired innocently after being seated in his office.

"Man, you don't even *have* a septic system," he exploded. "You don't have a septic *system*; you don't have a septic *tank*; you don't have leach lines . . . you don't have anything!"

"But what about that wooden cover in the middle of the back yard? Ruby said that was the septic tank."

"Septic tanks don't have *wooden* covers," he corrected me, pausing for emphasis; "Septic tanks are made out of *cement*, with *cement* covers."

"Then what is that thing in the backyard with the cover over it?" My world was spinning.

"That, my friend, is a cesspool, basically just a hole in the ground. Your toilet," his voice was stern, "empties out into nothing more than a hole in the backyard, contaminating the backyard and everywhere else the water seeps along the outside of the levee."

It's amazing how revelations will come to you at the oddest moments. As soon as he said that, my memory flashed on the scene of Ruby showing me the house. I was really impressed with the backyard with its lush green grass shaded by trees growing on the levee. I had loved its quiet privacy with the house on one side and the levee on the other. "Wow, this would be a great spot to set up a barbecue," I had gushed. To my surprise, Ruby's response had been restrained to say the least. Now, suddenly, I knew why.

With a jolt, I returned to the present. "But what can I do?" A wave of helplessness swept over me. This whole home ownership thing was becoming more than I could handle.

"You've got to fix it, bring it up to code."

"But I just bought the house; I had no idea it had this problem; I'm just a poor college student....

I told him about buying the house from Ruby and the many problems I had discovered, and about how Ruby had insisted on putting a clause in the contract that the house was being sold "as is," with no guarantees about anything. All this, plus the fact that I had first contacted him, seemed to placate him somewhat.

"Frankly, I don't know how you're going to fix it, but like I said, you've got to do something. What you need to do is hire an engineering firm to survey the problem and come up with a plan. Then you can submit it to us for approval."

Since by this time summer was near, I asked to be granted a stay while I was gone for the summer, promising that I would have a plan ready for him to approve when I came back in the fall.

FLOOD!

Then there were the floods. The winter of '71-'72 was a wet one. Three times that winter heavy storms brought floodwaters, filling the slough behind the house to dangerous levels. All three times the floodwaters overran the road to the north towards Arcata. But the third storm even put water over the road on the south towards Eureka. I had been waiting out the storm at the home of my friends John and Jeannette in Arcata. I drove to my house in the evening as the storm was letting up to see if the house was still there. I was especially afraid of high water under the house shorting out the electrical wires and starting a fire.

I finally got there after riding my motorcycle through the flooded roadway and around fallen tree limbs from Eureka. I took my flashlight and went to the back to view the surging, murky waters of the slough. The light revealed the water had come up on the outside of the levee so high it had actually flowed over the levee back into the slough! Yet the high water stopped a foot and a half below the floor of the house. The house had ridden out the flood!

I was thankful and relieved to have escaped the flood; not everyone was so lucky. The realization of what life would have been like if I had been one of the unlucky ones hit me like a chill wind a few days later, as the news of the flooding receded from the local paper as quickly as the flood waters had in the slough, and life went on.

It can be a great big, impersonal world out there, and this time I felt it. If I had been flooded, I wouldn't have had the least idea of what to do about it. It was a local flood, not of any big proportions. There was no media out there checking up on people; nobody knocked on my door to see if I had made it. There were no governmental agencies offering help. There were no neighbors, friends, or family to rally around, no fellow church members to give advice and emotional support. In fact, there was one house up the road that got flooded all three times. It was pathetic riding by there on my way to school and seeing their muddy possessions out in the cold air to dry. With no money and very few friends, the house flooding might have wiped me out without so much as making a ripple in the world around me. I would have lost my renters. I wouldn't have had the money, knowledge, or skill to fix the house, and without the rent coming in, I couldn't have made the house payments. It would have been nobody's problem but my own.

If I had been flooded out, it might have been like the man said: the county wouldn't even let me rebuild unless I could bring everything up to code. I would have lost my $2,000 investment and my place to live. I had never realized my own vulnerability so clearly.

This sense of aloneness was something I often felt during the winter when I was not part of a fire crew. Fighting fires in the summer, at least I was part of a team. Here on the coast, fighting water in the winter, I was on my own.

Sometimes I would lie in bed at night, or even lie in the bathtub after turning the water off while taking a bath (before the water went bad). In the stillness of the house, I could feel my own heart beat. The thought would come to me, "What if your heart stops beating?" I couldn't do anything to keep it beating; it was completely beyond my control. So what if it just stopped? My whole world would collapse in an irreversible moment of time without there being a single thing I could do about it.

And what then? What *would* happen after life ended? I knew that day would come. Nothing I could do would prevent it. Would I cease to exist forever? Or would there be some kind of existence beyond the grave? If so, would it be good or bad? If it was good, why did I have such a fear of dying? It seems like nature itself teaches that what lies beyond the grave is not so good. If it is good, why do all living things fight so hard to stay alive? Why do we have that survival instinct that bites and claws frantically to hang on to life at all costs, if there is automatically a better existence after death?

I was thankful to have escaped the flood, but the whole house episode left me feeling overwhelmed and vulnerable. What had seemed like the key to unlocking the Great American Dream had become instead an Albatross around my neck.

It seemed like every time I made what I thought was a big advance in life—like discovering drugs, or my relationship with Linda, and now buying this house–it always ended badly. What kept going wrong? Each time it had seemed like the right thing to do at the time. How could I anticipate these negative outcomes, and how could I make better decisions in the first place? There seemed no easy answers.

MAKING IT TO THE END

While all this was going on, I was back in school working on the final two quarters of my music degree. To give myself a break from all the music, I continued doing some creative writing on the side, toying around with the idea for a book. I would write a fictional autobiography of a man who never made it big but went ahead and wrote his memoir anyway, trying to show between the lines the reasons for his failure.

Along about the middle of the winter, I was feeling the financial pinch of spending most of my last summer's earnings on the down payment for the house. Unemployment had carried me until school began in January. Now the winter quarter was ending, and I was hurting. I contacted the Forest Service to see if by any chance I could work with them over spring break. Jim Benson, my supervisor on the trail crew the previous spring, said he could use me for a week planting trees.

Planting trees was a lot like life. The working conditions were terrible: the weather was cold, the work was boring, and the ground was muddy and full of rocks. Yet if you did it right, you were planting trees that would outlive you!

I spent the week working with a small group of regulars. One of them was the new foreman at Seiad, a fellow from the Modoc National Forest by the name of Dave Drury. Stan, my last year's foreman at Oak Knoll, was gone and nobody else at Oak Knoll wanted me back this year. But Dave said he had asked for me so I would be working at Seiad again. I asked him about the TTO position, but he said he had already offered it to a guy by the name of Tom Rosenthal. I knew Tom and had always thought of him as being a goof-off, but at least I had a job.

With the help of that little bit of money, I just squeezed by to the end of the spring term. That at least gave me one major accomplishment that year. In spite of the troubles with the house, flooding, polluted water, and poverty, I graduated with a degree in music. Finally, after six years of college stretching over seven years, I finished my music major and graduated.

But though I was graduating in music, my real goal at this point became writing. I would support myself by working for the Forest Service during the summers. But in the winters, I would work on writing instead of school. Now I would be eligible for unemployment benefits all winter while I wrote. My first project would be completing this fictional autobiography. After that, who knew what would happen? I had solidified my life goals into three parts: fame, fortune, and love.

The idea of getting a regular job never crossed my mind. A permanent job still looked like the kiss of death. I wanted the free lifestyle and the creativity of the counterculture, not the stable and productive life of the regular worker in society.

Mine was the Peter Pan mentality. I thought that if I never did what most people do upon graduation—get a job, get married and raise a family—then I would never grow old. As long as I could maintain the free and unencumbered lifestyle of the single college student, I would remain young forever.

So I graduated, arranged to keep my house rented over the summer, and headed off for Etna and Seiad Valley again. College was at last behind me, and in spite of past failures, I was sure I was back on the right track.

1972 FIRE SEASON—RETURN TO SEIAD

June 1972

Being at Seiad working again after all that had happened in the meantime was a *déjà-vu* experience. It was especially poignant, since it was the first place I had worked for the Forest Service and memories of that first summer came flooding back.

Yet it was so different now. The ranger station was virtually abandoned. It was just a shell of what it had been before everything had been consolidated and moved to Oak Knoll. Instead of a family atmosphere it was bachelor quarters. All of us guys on the crew lived in the old barracks and cooked for ourselves. This included Tom Rosenthal, the fellow Dave chose to be his new TTO. The washer and dryer were gone. The only thing new was Dave's office that had been built in part of the old horse barn.

Dave Drury was as colorful a character as any I met in the Forest Service. He had transferred from his home district on the Modoc National Forest for some off-forest experience. Dave was heavy-set, extremely nearsighted with thick glasses, and a hearty, friendly manner. He also had an irreverent sense of humor. He might be sitting in his office working on some paperwork when suddenly he would launch into a parody of a religious song at the top of his voice. Something like:

On a hill far away, stood an old Chevrolet

He had a whole host of such songs that he would sing with great gusto and the utmost seriousness until he reached the punch line. Then he would stop and laugh heartily, greatly pleased with himself,

Ama-zing grapes, how sweet and round,
That made a lush like me-e-e

Dave had a comical way of screwing up his face and peering at you through his thick glasses when surprised by something unusual. Though jolly most of the time, like a big old bear, he was not one you wanted to get riled up.

Dave was the consummate bureaucrat. He had almost no well-developed physical skills or abilities. His specialties were: delegating responsibility to others, doing paperwork, and steering his career on a sure course through the rocky shoals of bureaucracy and political infighting.

Dave had a well developed "us" and "them" mentality. In his mind, everybody was in one group or the other. "Us" included Dave, his family, and his inner circle such as Tom and me. "Them" were the ones over him—those who had the power to affect him for good or ill, and to a lesser extent, the rest of humanity.

The very first day I arrived, Dave invited Tom and me over to his trailer in the mobile home park across the highway. We met his family, had a beer together, and got acquainted. As we were leaving, Dave took us aside and warned us darkly, "Hey listen you guys: when you need to do laundry, come over here and use our washer and dryer; don't use the Laundromat at the trailer court."

"Gee that's real nice of you Dave, but what's wrong with the Laundromat?"

He screwed up his face and peered out at us through his thick glasses, "The women here at the trailer court wash out their [poopy] diapers in them."

I didn't know who these women were, but immediately a dark cloud of suspicion fell over my mind regarding them.

Dave's "default setting" was delegating. It was his response to everything. So whenever he encountered difficulty, he would turn the task over to another instead of sticking with it until he mastered it himself. Therefore, he hardly knew how to operate the tanker, which was his main responsibility. He just delegated it to Tom—who didn't know that much about it either. I remember one blazing hot afternoon when Dave was trying to show the new guys how to fill the tanker by sucking water from a pond. He hooked up the heavy draft line, threw it in the water, revved up the pump motor. Nothing. With sweat pouring down his face and every eye on him, he checked his connections, revved up the pump motor nearly to red-line, threw open various valves on the control panel. Still nothing.

Suddenly, "Tom!" he bellowed.

"Yes Dave."

"Take over; I've got some paperwork to do." Without another word he turned on his heel and stalked off.

But when it came to politics: the pecking order, the balance of power, who had it and who didn't, Dave was the Master. I'd been on the district for six years while he was a newcomer, yet he could tell me things about the inner workings of the district that I wouldn't have figured out in a thousand years—much as Linda knew the intricacies of every marriage on the district even down to details about their sex lives. Dave told me about the feud that Glen was having with the new district ranger, and about how those in the S.O. wanted to get rid of Glen because he was too powerful—and therefore independent of them. But they were afraid to try because he had built up a power base in the community outside the Forest Service. Dave always knew which way the wind was blowing.

I couldn't help liking Dave, but philosophically, we were total opposites. The qualities I respected most were competence and character. I figured if those were present, the politics would take care of itself. On the other hand, if competence and character were absent, even the greatest political instincts in the world would eventually fail, and you'd end up a loser in life.

Tom Rosenthal was a little guy with disdain for authority and the system. He was fun to be around and we quickly became friends, though he didn't have much competence <u>or</u> character. But he was personable and Dave liked him.

I was put in charge of another vehicle assigned to us, a heavy duty four-wheel drive pickup with a big winch on the front. We used it all summer to winch down old buildings at abandoned mining claims—now *that* was fun!

BAD COMPANY

Tom seemed to live for two things: for the moment, and for Tom. Teamed up with him, I found myself effortlessly fulfilling the second half of the ancient proverb that says if a person walks with wise men, he will become wise; while a companion of fools will be destroyed.

Back in the hills was a site where we were doing some construction work. There was a little pond, and we were clearing the dam area of logs and debris. One afternoon, Dave was going to take Tom and me to work on the project. But at the last minute, he was informed that officials were coming to our station and he would have to show them around.

So Dave said to Tom, "Why don't you guys get lost for awhile. You know, go up to the pond and do something there while I'm showing these guys around the station. Just stay in touch by radio."

To us, that sounded like an invitation to goldbrick. I'm sure Dave had in mind that we would *do* something up there, but that's not how we heard it. Our first order of business was for Tom to swing by the store and pick up some beer in his own car. Then we transferred it to our Forest Service vehicle, went up to the pond, hung out and drank it. By the time we came back down the hill late in the afternoon, I was sloshed.

Before this summer I would never have done this—*never* have gotten drunk during working hours, and especially when we were supposed to be guarding the Forest. Jim Kuphaldt would often have a hangover during working hours from the night before, but he would never drink while on duty; we were scrupulous about that. Not only was I doing what I never would have done before, but the scary part was I was justifying it to myself while I was doing it, with hardly a whimper from my conscience. We convinced ourselves that we were just carrying out Dave's orders, and that he would have approved had he known what we were doing. We were sure that if he could have, Dave would have been up there drinking and having a good time with us.

Tom had this way about him, like this kind of stuff was just business as usual, no big deal. While at one time, I had thought of

Tom as a goof-off, now I was one with him. And because I was one with him, I was seeing everything from his perspective. Now he seemed just fine—a good friend in fact.

OVER THE RIVER AND THROUGH THE WOODS

It was another slow summer for fires. I was sent on a ten-man crew to the Bear Fire down on the Los Padres National Forest for a week. But even there, though the fire was huge, all we did was cold trail the edge where the fire was already out. We spent a week plodding through charcoal and ashes without seeing a flicker of flame or a whiff of smoke.

Then out of nowhere, the jet stream started pumping subtropical moisture up over the state. Big, billowing thunderheads appeared early in the morning and continued building throughout the day. With these clouds, there was no question about *whether* the thunderstorms would come. The only question was where and when would they strike.

The spell lasted the better part of a week with new thunderstorms every day. Before it was over, we had fire fighters from as far away as the Angeles National Forest, 600 miles to the south. We had over a hundred lightning fires on our district alone. Luckily, there was enough rain with most of them for the first crew to stop them.

It was exciting but also frustrating. I didn't go out on the first fires because the few of us on the station were assisting crews from out of the area. So while there was activity, it was not fire fighting.

"What a drag," I thought. "I go down south, and they do all the fire fighting, and we don't even see any smoke. Then we have fires on our own district, and they come in and fight them here too! It's not fair."

Then it happened. It was late in the afternoon of the third day and most of the crews had been sent out. Dave Drury appeared and told me he was sending me to a fire that had just been reported upriver. It was on the far side of the river and he said I needed our boat to get to it.

We always had a boat, but I had never seen it used. It was just a big rowboat without a motor we kept on hand for rescues or other emergencies. I could tell already this experience was going to be different.

We loaded the boat upside down in the back of a pickup and stacked fire tools, lightning packs, and a couple of paddles underneath it and started out. Dave sent a young man with me without any fire experience; he was all we had left.

We had no trouble finding the fire. As we rounded a bend, we could see the blue-white plume of smoke rising through the canopy of trees across the river and a few hundred yards up the other side. As we pulled off the road on a turnout, I noticed that other cars had pulled over too. Their occupants had gotten out and were watching the rising smoke with great concern.

As we struggled to untie Dave's fancy hitches, a man came up and asked, "Do you need any help fighting the fire?"

"Oh no," I assured him, "we'll do all right."

"I don't mind, I really don't," he insisted. "Hey, here I am; take me with you."

A little sadly I turned down the Good Samaritan's offer. "I think it would probably be against Forest Service policy," I explained. "Thanks but... we'll be all right."

Without further ado, we carried our boat to the water's edge, loaded our gear, and pushed away from the bank. The Klamath River was not formidable at this point, probably no more than waist deep at the deepest point, and thirty feet across. Still, it would have been difficult without the boat because of the current and the slippery rocks. But with the boat, it was simple. The current carried us downstream to a gravel bar, perfect for beaching the boat. We unloaded our gear and started up toward the fire.

We had no trouble finding it. As the smoke indicated, it was burning briskly on the ground in dry leaves and pine needles over a gently sloping area.

The bulk of the thunderstorm that spawned this lightning strike had been farther upriver. This strike had come down on the fringe of the storm, far enough from the storm's center that there had been no rain to dampen the forest litter. Consequently, the fire was burning merrily away. At least there was no wind to fan it and no heavy fuels to cause it to crown. Still the situation was serious enough. It already covered about one quarter acre and was steadily building in size and momentum.

We both started scratching fire line on the lower corner of the fire where we first encountered it, my crewman going one way along the bottom, and I going the opposite direction up the west side. He was inexperienced and worked rather slowly, but thoroughly. Meanwhile, I moved as quickly up the side as I could. Remembering past experiences, I didn't build a finished line, but scratched a quick one to slow the fire's spread while I tried to get to the top of the fire as quickly as possible to nip off the head. The easiest place to scratch this quick line was along a little ridge that went straight uphill.

It was a good thing that I adopted this strategy, for when I reached the head of the fire, I saw that it was starting up a little draw between the ridge I was on and an identical ridge on the other side. This draw was not large, probably sixty feet from ridge top to ridge top.

The fire was burning hottest in this draw that narrowed as it went up the hill. Heat and smoke were coming up it like a chimney, making working in it uncomfortable. So I scratched my line well up the draw from the fire. Then I started down the other little ridge on the far side of the fire, hoping to tie in with my crewman working up from below.

It was hot and still and I was sweating profusely. The sun had set and darkness had almost taken over the forest. As I worked down the second ridge, the slightest whisper of a breeze brushed my face. To my horror, I saw the fire below me start to move. The amount of heat it was generating was now sufficient to start a draft of air moving through the draw. As this draft increased, the flames were accelerating up the draw. Right before my eyes, the fire was changing from a static fire to a moving one. In fire fighter parlance, it was starting to "make a run" up the hill.

I realized at once that my paltry scratched line through the top of the draw wouldn't be enough to stop it—the flames would lick over that like it wasn't even there.

I looked around quickly, taking stock. My crewman was like I used to be, slogging along below, building a fire line where it was needed least, oblivious to what was happening here at the top. But this time there wasn't anybody else to come to my rescue. There wasn't some ex-Forest Service worker driving by in his pickup to jump out with a shovel and race around the fire, "hot-spotting" it at the most dangerous places. The Goosenest FCO wasn't there to tell me to "get in there and start building your line." There was no air tanker thundering in to save the day. This time there was no one to tell me what to do. There was only the dusk, the wind, the fire, and me.

I looked above the fire in the direction the flames were heading. Not far above, the draw opened up into a large brush field. Once the fire got going in the dry brush, it would make another run for the timber above. After that, there was only one mountain road somewhere above before it would hit the top of Johnny O'Neil Ridge, two to three miles from the river. If it got away here, we might not be able to stop it until it reached the ridge. "This is it," I thought; "it's got to be now."

I took my McLeod scraping tool and headed down into the draw. Sucking in a giant mouthful of air, I advanced to just beyond the licking flames. Turning around quickly with my back to the fire, I reached up the draw as far as I could, and started pulling the leaves and duff down toward the fire. After only a few quick strokes the heat and smoke were too much for me, and I darted up out of the draw, gasping for breath, sucking in the fresh, clean air of the forest. After a moment's respite, I jumped down again, grabbed one last lungful of air, made my stand, and pulled a few more bladefulls of duff from as far as I could reach down toward the fire; then quickly jumped out again.

At first, the fire burned even more brightly as it got the additional fuel that I was scraping down from above. But my strategy was to greatly expand the width of the line above the fire so it could not possibly jump it.

I was sweating even more profusely now in the humid evening air under the forest canopy. I had to stop and hurriedly put on my sweatband above my glasses to keep the sweat from running in my eyes or turning the dust on my glasses to mud. I could feel the sweat running down my body inside my clothes.

On and on the silent battle went. Again and again, the fire drove me out of the draw. Again and again, I dove back in to get a few more quick scrapes before being driven out again by the smoke and heat. For the first time in my life, it was just me against the fire.

Panting, with sweat pouring off me, I finally succeeded in scraping the entire draw above the fire as far as I could reach with the McLeod. There was now at least a ten-foot swath of pure dirt across the draw above the fire. The fire was still burning hotly, but now it had nowhere to go. It was hungrily consuming the extra fuel I had given it, but there was no more within its reach.

Exultantly, I realized I had stopped it; now to disarm it.

Once again I dove down into the draw, grabbing a last breath of air, only this time I stayed facing the fire. Pushing on the McLeod with all my might, I shoved the burning material down the draw as far as I could reach, scattering it among the embers of what had already burned below. Then it was over. The once hotly moving fire was now just smoldering ruins, no longer even giving off enough light to see by, in what was now total darkness under the forest canopy.

I got out my headlamp and hooked it up; then went down the far side of the fire to find my crewman working away, slowly building the line up towards me.

"How's the fire up above"? He inquired innocently.

"It's fine," I smiled and shook my head, "just fine."

At first light, I was up walking through the fire checking it out. Near the bottom, I found where the lightning had struck. It had started down one of the taller fir trees, and then jumped to an oak to travel the rest of the way to the ground. "So much for the conventional wisdom of not sitting under tall trees," I thought. "If you'd sat under the tall fir tree, you'd be alive today; but if you'd sat under that insignificant oak tree, you'd be fried!"

After C-rations for breakfast, my partner cleaned up the camp and got ready to leave, while I filled out my Fireman's Report Form. I mapped the fire carefully, pacing off the distances around the circumference because I wanted to know just how big this fire was. It turned out to be one-third acre.

"Hmm, that makes it a class B fire, not bad," I thought. A class A fire is less than one-tenth acre, while a class B fire is at least one-tenth acre but less than one acre.

Back at Seiad, I was pretty proud of our accomplishment in stopping the fire. I was especially excited because it had been a personal victory for me over myself. I had finally come through in a clutch situation where many other times I had choked. But how do you communicate that to someone else?

I filed my report with Dave and tried to tell him about the drama we faced and our ultimate triumph. He gave his perfunctory approval, but I could tell it didn't register.

After that I never heard another word about it. Nobody from the ranger station, from Glen on down, ever asked me a thing about the fire, the fire that almost got away. I was bummed; I wanted to share my victory with someone, and I wanted Glen to be proud of me. It just seemed like it was not to be.

At the end of the week of continual lightning fires, as the weather pattern was changing, I heard it announced over the radio that Glen had reported that the district had had 176 lightning fires that week, and had stopped them all without letting a single one get bigger than a class A fire!

"But mine was a class B and the two of us stopped it all by ourselves!" I was angry and hurt. "He's taken away from my glory to add to his own," I thought gloomily, "and it's not even true."

I had experienced personal breakthrough in my battle against fire's intimidation and my own fear. The sad thing was it didn't seem to matter as my life continued its downward spiral. I was still hung up on the seemingly impossible task of getting the approval of men, and more and more I was seeing the Forest Service as just another governmental bureaucracy—my idealism was evaporating like the morning mist under the hot sun.

DABBLING WITH THE SPIRITS

After the episode of the lightning fires, Tom was fired, a story too lengthy to go into at this point.

All this time, my relationship with Linda continued its slow, steady decline. I still spent quite a bit of time with her and the children, and we had some good times together. But bit by bit the dying embers of the fire were being extinguished. It had already become mostly platonic as she continued her pursuit of the fast life. It was about this time she got her first serious boyfriend, who happened to live down south in some place called Yuba City. All this was hard, as I kept hoping she would eventually get this running around out of her system and settle down with me.

Now Linda had been dabbling in the occult. She and her neighbor, a divorced woman who lived in the other half of the duplex, got an Ouija Board and were experimenting with it. Linda thought it was a real kick. She talked me into trying it with her once, but it didn't work for us because I wouldn't take it seriously enough. You had to believe in it enough to yield your hands to it. Then the spirit could move through all four hands, moving the board to the right answers to your questions. If faith is required for spiritual work, I must say I didn't have it for this thing.

About this time, Linda informed me that her house was haunted. She thought there were two spirits living in the walk-in closet in the kid's bedroom where a hodge-podge of things from their previous home on the Klamath were stored.

"Why there?" I asked.

"Because they like the clutter and disorderliness."

Now this was more interesting than an Ouija Board. I wanted to meet some "spirits." I had an interest in them dating back to when I was a young boy and had a very vivid dream about meeting some spirit beings of light in the attic in our house in Brimfield. For awhile in my teens as an atheist, I had rejected all such possibilities. But after encountering the unseen spiritual realm again through drugs, I was still keenly interested in finding out more about it. So I determined to make myself available to these spirits to see if they would contact me. I went to Linda's house one Saturday morning and closed all the curtains in her bedroom to make it as dark as possible. Then I lay on her bed, hoping the spirits would show up, but nothing happened.

She continued having occasional encounters with her spirit residents. Gradually however, her experiences with them turned sour. She got to feeling that they were abusing their welcome in her home by scaring the children. The straw that broke the camel's back was one night when she was gone and her daughter, Kellie, was babysitting the boys. Since Linda was out late, Kellie had gotten a blanket and was lying on the couch in the front room after the boys had gone to bed. Kellie felt the spirits come to the hallway door and stand there for a long time looking at her, frightening her.

Now with Linda, you can do a lot of things, but don't mess with her kids! When Kellie told her about the incident, she snapped. "That's it. No more spirits in this house!"

As she was telling me the story later, I blurted out, "But how did you get rid of them? I wouldn't have had a clue."

"The first thing I did was to go into that closet and take everything out. I threw a bunch of stuff away, and tidied up the rest. That took away the mess that made them comfortable. Then I stood there and shouted in a loud voice that they were to get out and stay out!"

I was amazed at her authoritative grasp of spirit-ology. And it worked. They never showed up again.

Linda had driven the spirits out of her house, but I had opened myself up to them. There is a difference between interest in spirits —which I always had—and taking actual steps to meet them, such as offering a sacrifice, holding a séance, or merely setting up a time and preparing a place as I had. Though nothing had happened at the time, and I thought my quest to meet them had failed, I didn't understand that when you open yourself up to them, they *will* respond. I was going to meet them all right—who they *really* were—but at a time and in a manner of *their* choosing.

SURPRISED BY TEMPTATION

After his dismissal, Tom took his girlfriend Crystal and moved upriver past Horse Creek. I stayed in touch with him. He was in a country western rock band. One weekend in September, he invited me over to watch him play at a bar in Ft. Jones. I smoked a joint on the way over, enjoying my brand new Toyota truck which I'd just purchased in Redding. My motorcycle riding days were over!

The bar was an old-style bar with a big room and high ceilings. The wives and girlfriends of the band members had a table along the wall.

The crowd was not large and seemed comprised of the local rednecks. Here in Scott Valley were the *cowboy* rednecks, as opposed to the *logger* rednecks in the bars on the Klamath.

At the end of their set, Tom and the others joined us, and we sat around talking and drinking. Meanwhile, with the band on break, people began feeding the jukebox.

This was 1972 and a backlash was underway against the excesses of the hippies and "peaceniks." Someone played "Okie from Muskogee," a raucous affirmation of our nation's "traditional values"—like getting drunk instead of stoned—and a sarcastic put-down of the hippies and anti-war types. This really enlivened the crowd. You could feel the spirits rise as the patrons shouted or howled their approval.

Furtively looking at them and then at us, I wondered if any of their "hootin' and hollerin" had us in mind. We weren't exactly hippie looking, but we weren't cowboy looking either! In truth, we lived closer to the hippie lifestyle than we did to theirs.

I was glad when the song was over. Then someone put on a real hoedown song and a few of the young bucks started dancing. It was still pretty lifeless, but they were trying hard to have fun. Sometime during the midst of the carrying on, I saw a guy hide his face in his hand, turn his head and emit a loud "EEEYYY-HAH." It was weird because you would think that cry was an expression of exuberance, yet his face was so lifeless, it made the sound seem empty and forced. It was also strange that he had to hide his face and turn away before he could make his cry. What was he ashamed of? I'd had enough. The crowd made me uneasy—the marijuana-induced paranoia didn't help! I finished my beer and said goodbye to the group.

Once outside in the fresh air, I felt better.

I was surprised to see several young people hanging around outside, listening to the music and the carrying on in the bar. I studied their faces with a few quick, penetrating glances. Suddenly, I caught on to what it was all about! Out here in the cool night air, they couldn't see what was happening inside. They had to draw a picture with their ears. I considered it from their perspective, hearing the upbeat music and the occasional cries of exuberance.

"Hmm," I thought, "just listening out here makes it sound like they're having a great time. You can't see the deadness on their faces out here, their joylessness as they work so hard at *having* a good time. Out here the banshee cries sound real. You can't tell they're hollow and forced."

The kids were actually looking with longing toward where the sounds were coming from, undoubtedly wishing fervently for the day they would be old enough to gain admittance to those "sacred portals" where everyone was having such a good time, where real living could be had.

"Wow, what a rip-off! They have no idea that what they're longing for is an illusion; it doesn't exist!"

Then I got another revelation, "So that's how the lie is passed from generation to generation. These kids outside right now are being prepared to be the adults on the inside tomorrow. But once on the inside and aware of the sham, they'll be afraid to admit it: afraid to face that emptiness, too ashamed to admit they've been duped. Instead, *they'll* start propagating the sham themselves like the others are doing now, trying hard to convince each other and the *next* generation of kids waiting outside that they really *are* having a good time, that this really *is* living!"

I was stirred from my reverie by Tom and Crystal coming out of the bar. They had followed me out to smoke a joint before the next set started. We smoked one together in my pickup, and talked about the scene inside and the bad vibes we felt from the rednecks. Then Tom left to start the next set.

I talked with Crystal some more and asked her about life with Tom and how the children were doing. I had known her when she was living in a hippie commune in Seiad before she and Tom started going together. I think it was the first time we'd ever just talked since then. I got the feeling she wasn't used to someone wanting to listen to her, and be concerned about her welfare. After finishing our joint and the conversation, I went home to Eslie's.

Tom had hit me up for $20 earlier in the evening. A few weeks later, after work, I happened to be going home through Yreka instead of up the Scott River, so I found myself driving past their place. I thought I'd better stop and see about getting my $20 back. I knew that, with Tom, unless I took the initiative it would be gone forever.

It was early evening, but already dark. I had never been to their new place. It was on a side road up a creek, on some level ground with a gravel driveway stretching back through the trees. It might have been built as a community of vacation cabins. Now, years later, these tiny, rundown cabins could only be called "squalid."

I finally found their cabin. Crystal answered the door and told me that Tom had gone to Yreka. She invited me in.

There was one small room that doubled as a kitchen and living room. Behind that was a hall going back to the bedroom and bathroom.

She had a boy and a girl, both under five. I felt sorry for them. They had expressive, almost haunted eyes. I wondered if Tom beat them.

Crystal expected him home soon, so I hated to leave. Coming up here was out of my way, and I did want my $20 back. I waited in the front room while she put the kids to bed.

When she came back in, I stood up to go, ready to give it up. She stopped in front of me. We stood there looking at each other for a moment. I don't quite know what happened next, but suddenly we were in each other's arms, embracing and kissing each other. I have never seen anyone act so passionately! She started breathing hard and moaning, bringing my own passion quickly to a boil. This was a new experience for me, being caught totally flatfooted and instantly overpowered by lust. There's no doubt what would have happened next, and very soon, but I was called back to earth by a pounding on the front door.

"Crystal, Crystal, open up; it's me, Tom!

Instantly we were thrown into confusion. Crystal was running around, wanting me to hide somewhere, yelling to Tom to wait a minute, trying but failing to sound normal. We still had our clothes on, but I couldn't face Tom until my passion had cooled. I retreated to the bathroom and locked the door where I straightened my clothes and hair and tried to return to normal.

By the time I got back to the living room, Crystal had let Tom in. Things were strained to say the least. Tom kept looking from her to me and back again. Neither one of us could look him in the eye.

Well, needless to say, I didn't get my $20, and soon left. At least he hadn't pulled a gun and plugged us both.

I ran into Tom unexpectedly a year or more later. He still "didn't have" the $20, but surprisingly enough he was able to chuckle about the incident. Apparently he and Crystal had never talked about it, because he still thought we had had sex that night and that he had come in at the end of it. I assured him that he had come just in time to *prevent* it. He told me how when they were living at Happy Camp, he had come home and found her walking down the road to the bar, or other times he'd had to go down to the bar and get her out after men had already picked her up. He also told me that back when she was living at the commune, when she seemed so available, she had in fact been sleeping with the George guy who ran it! By this time, Tom had left her. I think you could possibly classify her as a nymphomaniac; a condition that people joke about, but is really no laughing matter.

I was glad that Tom came home when he did. Crystal was a woman who was desperately searching for something, but she wouldn't have found it in me. Nor would I have found the love and stable relationship I was searching for in her. If we had completed the Act, there is no telling what further problems it would have created. As it was, I was able to walk away without looking back.

I never saw Crystal again, so I don't know what happened to her. The thing I remember most about that evening was the sad and expressive faces of her children before she put them to bed. If those eyes could talk, what sad tales they would tell!

Spirits pick the weak and vulnerable areas in us to attack. I had just been jumped by the spirit of lust and escaped almost unscathed. But the second spirit, adultery, was about to body-slam me good.

JUDY

Linda had a good friend whom I knew slightly. I'll call her Judy. Judy was an intelligent, intense woman about our age, with a daughter and son in school. She was skinny, not particularly attractive, with an affinity for black, and tended to live on the tragic side of life.

Her husband was a large, quiet fellow, a square shooter. Much mellower than Judy, he tended to balance out her intensity.

I used to joke with Linda a lot about sex. She was always amazed at how much my world seemed to revolve around it compared to hers, which revolved around partying and dancing.

We were into the fall slash-burning season by now, and I was home each weekend. One Friday evening, I stopped by Linda's on my way to Eslie's, and we were spending some time relaxing on the couch after her kids had gone to bed. We were in a light-hearted mood, and Linda, laughing and teasing, said something like she bet my greatest fantasy was making love to two women at the same time.

"Yeah," I said, "that'd be the best thing that could happen to me since the Indians invented the tobacco pipe."

Linda continued the fantasy, "I should get my friend Judy and take you out on a campout down by the river some night and fulfill your wildest dreams."

A week went by, and I was back in her living room again, unwinding after the week.

"Hey Hobbsie," she said with a mischievous smile, "Remember what we were talking about? You know, fulfilling your fantasies? Well it just so happens your dreams might be coming true. "

"How's that?"

"I mentioned it to Judy, and she's really into it!"

"What?"

"She wants to have an affair with you."

Judy wanted to have an affair with *me*? I didn't know why. I didn't care why. Do you ask a stranger "why?" when he hands you a check for a million dollars? She wanted to have an affair with me, of all people. It seemed so exciting, so gratifying to my ego, so "out-of-the-box."

I immediately accepted the idea, and the conspiracy gradually took shape. My work would be ending soon, so I would be available during the day. Linda had her new boyfriend in Yuba City. She wanted to see him for a few days, but needed someone to watch her children. So I would stay at her house, babysitting the children. Then, during the day, while the children were in school and Judy's husband was at work, Judy would come over and rendezvous with me at Linda's house.

So at 1:00 p.m. on the appointed day, we met in Linda's home. I double-locked the door and pulled all the shades. We were nervous, cold and clammy. But we had sex. There was no love, no romance, no enticing seduction, no yielding to overpowering temptation. We hardly knew each other! It was something we had made up our minds to do beforehand for our own reasons, and now we just did it.

When Adam and Eve ate the apple, they each had their own reasons. But once they ate, their reasons no longer mattered; they were swept into a new spiritual realm that was out of their hands and from which they could never return. It was the same with us. For whatever reasons we did it, once it was done, a whole new set of circumstances came into being, circumstances beyond our power to control.

The first thing that happened was we decided we loved each other. The sex, even in the loveless way we had gone about it, now bound us together and established a whole new reality in our lives, a reality that was now carrying us along—like jumping into a swiftly moving stream and immediately being swept downstream by it.

The one act of sex changed everything: feelings for each other were kindled. We were becoming a couple; we were something that was happening. But there were problems. She had a husband and children. We each had individual, complex lives that up to moments ago were going blithely along in completely different directions. Now, suddenly, she and I became *we*.

She had to get home because her children would be back from school soon. She invited me to follow her back to her house, where we sat and talked for a long time in her living room.

Then her son and daughter walked in from school. We were just sitting there talking in separate chairs. Yet when Judy introduced us, something in Judy's face, her body language, her eyes—her daughter picked up on. She looked suddenly hurt and confused. She sensed I was another man. The fabric of her world was tearing asunder.

We had no plan. We were improvising as we went along. Now I was the one who had to go. Linda's kids would be getting home, and I had to fix them dinner. Soon Judy's husband would be coming home too. We agreed not to tell him about us yet. We needed more time to work things out, to plan, to figure out what to do. The safest thing at this point was to say nothing, let it ride, stonewall it. We parted and I went back to Linda's.

I had arranged to have Eslie come in and eat with us, since I wasn't out at the ranch to help him cook. I drove out to get him and then rushed back to get supper started. Even in the midst of earth-shaking events, life must go on.

That evening, as we were gathered around the table eating, I was suddenly seized by panic. There was no reason for it. Nobody said anything. Nobody did anything. Everything was just as normal as could be. But suddenly I was awash in panic. I wanted to run outside, load everybody in my pickup, and take off as fast as I could go, deep into the mountains, high up on some deserted logging road. I had to get away; I HAD TO GET OUT!

The feeling of panic persisted. I couldn't shake it. I couldn't understand it. But in a flash of unexpected insight, I knew what it meant. Judy had told her husband about us! In spite of our agreement, she had told him, and he was furious! Though we were miles apart, I was feeling his rage, something I had never experienced. It was like the very heavens were angry, like God Himself was raging on His throne!

Then, just as suddenly as it began, it was over, followed by a great calm. It wasn't just quiet, it was *calm.* The rage was gone; it had been pacified.

I was greatly unnerved by this whole turn of events. Somehow I got Eslie home and put the kids to bed, though my mind was spinning. I lay down that night deeply shaken.

Up to this point, my life had been deteriorating in a steady downward spiral. Each year saw me do things I had never done and would hardly have imagined doing only a few years before. This summer, I had gotten drunk during regular working hours and hadn't seen anything wrong with it. I was filled with bad attitudes at work. Now I was involved in an affair with a married woman with absolutely no justification. And worst of all I had no idea of the great wrong I was doing. In me, the new morality had fully triumphed: "If it feels good, do it!" That was it. Life was no more complicated than that. Or was it?

Her husband was in a rage. Intuitively, I knew that. I felt like I had finally and unknowingly crossed some line in life that was threatening to topple my whole house of cards. This was the "straw that broke the camel's back." And when you finally push the envelope too far, things happen. I could have hidden from her husband. But this was bigger than her husband. This time there were cosmic forces involved that I didn't understand but could only feel. And I've never felt such fear and terror in all my life—panic so great, I lost my ability to think.

But then what happened? Why did the fear suddenly lift to be replaced by a great calm? What pacified that great anger?

I woke up early in the morning. The house was quiet. I still felt that sense of calm, but also that sense of being shaken and unnerved, like I'd blown it big-time but didn't quite know how.

On the nightstand was a Bible. Never in my whole life had I actually read the Bible. I was familiar with certain parts—like the Sermon on the Mount—from Sunday school and Vacation Bible School, but that was it. Now, for some reason, in this strange, calm-yet-troubled mood, I picked up the Bible and began to read.

I found myself reading in the Gospel of John, where Jesus was teaching the people and doing verbal battle with the scribes and Pharisees. I was fascinated by the interaction between Jesus and his detractors. His words seemed so profound on the one hand, yet so hard to understand on the other. I found I could identify more with the Pharisees and the people than I could with Jesus. It seemed to me like it seemed to them—that he was talking in circles, that he wouldn't come out and plainly say what he wanted to tell them. Especially when it came to telling them who He was! At one point, in exasperation, the people said something like, "How long are you going to keep us in suspense? If you are the Christ, why don't you tell us?" In response to this straightforward question, He again gave them a "beating-around-the-bush" answer, something like, "I am who I've been telling you I am, the same thing I've told you from the beginning...." As I read, I felt their frustration as I read statement after statement by Jesus, but always with the meaning veiled. "What was He trying to say?" I wondered. "Why didn't He come out and tell them, so I could find out too?"

My reflections were broken by a quiet knock at the door. It was a very quiet knock, yet it was a knock. I swallowed hard, thoughts of my present situation flooding back over me,

I got up and went to the door. It was, indeed, Judy's husband.

"I didn't knock loud because I didn't want to wake the kids," he said in a low but intense voice. "Listen, I know about you and Judy; she told me everything last night. And I just want you to know this: if I ever so much as hear about you seeing her again, I'll kill you. It's that simple. I'll kill you. Got it?"

Once again my meek spirit in the face of great anger probably saved me. I nodded, "Yes, I understand."

"Good." He turned and stalked off, got into his pickup, and powered out of the driveway.

"Whew," I turned around at the door, relieved. But my relief turned to shock as I beheld the terrified eyes of Jimmy looking at me. I realized that he had heard every word. "Don't worry Jimmy," I assured him, "it'll be all right."

As I stood there pondering the brief appearance and terse threat of Judy's husband, the thought hit me that it couldn't be as simple as that. Never see her again? Never talk this thing out? It couldn't be so. There was too much fat in the fire now to just end it like that. "I've got to go after him," I thought. "We've got to talk this thing through." I hurried into the bedroom and finished getting dressed.

"Where are you going, Hobe?" There was real alarm in Jimmy's 8-year-old voice.

"I've got to go after him and talk with him," I replied.

"Hobe, no, don't go..." I looked closely at Jimmy, for the first time focusing on him alone. "He really thinks I'm going to get killed out there," I thought. "He really thinks he'll never see me again if I go."

I felt a sudden wave of compassion for the sincerity and concern of Jimmy's heart. I tried to take away his fear. I put my hands on his shoulders and looked him in the eye. "Don't worry, it's going to be all right. Tell Kellie to take care of you and Eric till I get back."

I truly believed that. I didn't have any fear as I left Linda's. They say that fools rush in where angels fear to tread! I thought I would catch up with him somewhere on the road to Greenview, but he was driving fast, and before I knew it I was pulling into their driveway.

As I got out of my pickup and walked toward their house I saw him in back splitting wood. He was obviously taking his anger out on the wood, bringing the splitting maul down on the rounds with mighty blows.

He looked up, startled to see me. Before he had a chance to register another emotion, I started talking, talking fast... something to the effect that we've got to talk this thing out, solve this problem, address this situation. Then Judy came out and saw us standing there. Worry mixed with anger on her face as she joined the heated discussion. Her complaints about their marriage now tumbled out. Finding himself outnumbered and suddenly on defense, her husband suggested we all go inside to talk.

Then began a difficult and painful time. We took turns talking in different groups. The three of us talked. Then she and he went off and talked. Then she and I talked. Even he and I took a turn. It was very intense, very uncomfortable, very confusing.

He came to the point where he was willing to move out of this new house he'd been building for them, and turn everything over to me. He even went so far as to say that he and I would have to get together so he could go over the details of what still had to be done on the house to complete it. He was completely serious. When he heard from her lips that she really did "love" me and wanted me instead of him, he was willing to step out of her life completely and give her everything they'd built together.

I couldn't live with such a deal. I could take Judy but not the house he had built—*that* would have made me feel guilty! "No," I told him, "I don't want your house. I just want Judy. You keep the house. I'll take Judy. We'll make our own life together." And just 24 hours ago, I barely knew her!

Somehow, I got back to Linda's, assuring the kids that I was OK. And Linda returned, freeing me from the babysitting chores to ride this wild tiger I had mounted.

After Linda's return, I had to go to Yreka. Coming back over the mountain at night, I kept going over the events of the past few days in my mind. The burden of this whole thing was getting heavier and heavier. This was not what I wanted: the anger, the strife, the guilt, the hornet's nest of trouble that had been stirred up.

Near the summit of the mountain, I felt overwhelmed. I turned off the highway onto a gravel road and pulled over to the side. I turned off the motor, got out and climbed the hill a little ways in the brush and darkness. Completely alone at last, I began to weep. All the intense emotions of the past few days came pouring out in great sobs and cries. I never intended for all this to happen; I never knew all this would happen; I just hadn't thought it through....

All my tears finally spent, I got back into my pickup and drove over the summit and down into the valley's darkness.

I retired to Eslie's ranch and hung out by the phone while Judy tried to sort out her relationship with her husband and her own conflicting desires. Every few hours, she would call me for advice. I tried to walk in this new role in which I found myself and did the best I could to counsel her. Judy, highly intelligent and articulate, would pick my brain for my best counsel, absorb all my advice, and then do everything her own way.

She had to come out to see me again, to strengthen our bond and reaffirm our relationship.

We had sex again, thus re-establishing the only basis of our relationship, then lay together in the narrow little bed and talked. She was nervous and intense, smoking cigarettes constantly.

Between 11:00 p.m. and midnight she got up and began getting dressed.

"What are you doing?" I asked.

"I'm going home."

"But what... I mean why, I mean I guess I don't understand."

"I'm going home, that's all; I'm going home."

I accompanied her downstairs through the darkened house and out the door. Something was different about her. I could sense it but couldn't grasp its meaning. She promised to finish up her affairs in the valley, then come over and meet me in Eureka. She drove off, and I never saw or heard from her again.

I had just met the second spirit. It had come out of the blue, used my vulnerability in the area of women, and easily duped me into making horrible decisions that nearly cost my life. Now, just as suddenly as the attack had come, it was over. It would take months to realize Judy wasn't coming to Eureka, and years to understand the connection between the bizarre happenings with Crystal and

Judy and when I had earlier opened myself up to the spirits in Linda's house.

Judy and her husband got back together, made another go of their marriage, forgave each other, put the past behind them, and went on with their lives.

As for me, I was left "holding the bag"—emotionally. All my hopes were blown away like so much chaff. A driving goal of my life—to find a loving, long-term relationship—had been stymied again. Now the emotional bonds that had been forged had to be severed, piece by broken piece, opening up painful wounds in my heart. In many ways, just like with the drug bust, I certainly got what I deserved, but that didn't make it hurt any less.

Was It Really the Spirits?

Some people have a hard time accepting that it was the spirits that set me up with Crystal and Judy. They say, "Isn't this 'the devil made me do it' defense?" Well, actually "the devil made me do it" is not a bona fide defense at all, because we are all responsible for what we do. The devil can influence us to do evil, just like running with a set of bad companions can, but we are still responsible for what we do. That's why in the Lord's Prayer it says, "Lead us not into temptation." Being led into temptation can result in us doing wrong things that we would not have done had we not been led there. Hence the cry, "Lead me not into temptation." If you get three teenage boys together they will do things that none of them would do alone! But are they still responsible? Surely. So I don't mean to lessen my guilt in the slightest by saying I was set up by the spirits.

I have pondered for years the meaning of the two incidents with Crystal and Judy. They were each such powerful events in my life that I felt I had to include them in this story, but was mystified as to their meaning. I had never connected them to the incident with seeking the spirits. In fact, I had deleted the story of spirit-seeking from the manuscript in the editing process because it didn't seem to be relevant to anything. Then one Saturday morning in prayer before working on the final manuscript for publication, out of the blue the Holy Spirit showed me the linkage. I had to dig up the old account of seeking the spirits from the discard pile and look at it again in a new light. That was one of the very few things once deleted from the story that ever made it back in.

Let me offer the following reasons that have confirmed to me what I was told in prayer.

With neither Crystal nor Judy did I seek them out. I had been attracted to Crystal at one time briefly before she connected with Tom. I had never been attracted to Judy. But in both cases, it was as if they were thrown at me suddenly. There was no buildup—like with Linda where I planted seeds of fantasy and attraction in my soul that grew over time. These two came out of nowhere.

While the events existed, they were extremely intense, more intense than there was any justification for.

They ended as suddenly as they came; after one encounter with Crystal, and less than a week with Judy.

When they ended, they ended abruptly and completely. I never saw either one of them again.

These two events were utterly unique. Nothing even remotely similar has happened before or since in my life.

There were two affairs, just like the two spirits. The timing was perfect, probably within a month of my trying to contact the spirits.

They attacked in my greatest area of vulnerability, as can be seen by my initial reaction to Linda's proposal.

Since then, I have learned a lot about how the spirit realm operates, and it's totally consistent with the events as they happened to me here. No attempt to contact the spiritual realm is without effect. But the response will frequently come in ways we don't expect, and so we often miss it when it comes—like I missed it in this case for years.

DEAD IN TRESPASSES?

October 1972

One of the first things I did upon getting back to my house in Eureka was to look up my friends Ron and John. The three of us got together and went out for some beers and shared notes on the summer. I was real excited and couldn't wait to tell them of this new woman with whom I was involved. After all, I expected her to show up any day and start our new life together, get married, have a family, live happily ever after—the whole shot.

Ron and John wanted to know more about this woman, who was she? How did I meet her?

So I told them how we'd had this affair and fallen in love, and how her husband had been against it.

"Wait a minute, you mean she's married?"

"Well sure, but she doesn't love her husband. She loves me and she's going to divorce him and marry me and...."

After getting all the facts, Ron and John were aghast. "Dave I can't believe you've done this. Why that's adultery!"

"Well maybe technically, but isn't that an old-fashioned concept? I mean what's wrong with that?"

They couldn't believe their ears. They couldn't believe that I was so casually breaking up a functioning marriage.

I couldn't believe they were having such trouble accepting it. I tried every way I could think of, every different angle: "Why is it my fault if she chooses me over her husband"; and every kind of platitude: "You've got to fish where the fish are biting," trying to convince them it was OK. But they wouldn't be persuaded, remaining dumfounded at my blatant transgression. "What are you guys, a couple of religious fanatics?"

Their refusal to accept what I had done began getting to me. I was hurt. My ego was bruised. Here I had come in with what I thought was a dynamite summertime story for "show-and-tell," and now they were making me out to be the bad guy. But at the same time, light was slowly beginning to dawn in my darkness.

I was morally comatose, and my two friends were shaking me, trying to wake me up. "Dave, Dave, it's wrong, Dave; it's adultery, Dave; it's not right, Dave; her husband was right, Dave...." Shaking me and shaking me, slapping me on the cheeks, yelling in my ear, giving me closed heart massage—anything to rouse me out of my moral stupor.

Gradually, reluctantly, I began to come around to their way of thinking. They were so insistent, and trashed all of my arguments. Even John's wife, Jeannette, had no sympathy. And so my friends, few though they were, did what friends are supposed to do—they began drawing me back from the brink of the moral abyss.

I had not given a single thought to what society would be like if everyone did what I was doing. What would the world be like if all marriages were temporary arrangements until someone "better" came along, if children were shunted around at the adults' convenience, if each person defined morality according to his own conscience and shifting desires?

I still kept expecting to see Judy's car. Every time I drove into town or returned home, my eyes kept searching the road for it. It took months to dawn on me that she wasn't coming; and even longer to realize that whatever had happened between us was over—all the hopes I had invested in her as being the answer to the unfulfilled longing within me were dashed. To which I can only say now, "Thank goodness."

THE HOUSE: THE GOOD NEWS AND THE BAD NEWS

One of the first things I resolved to do when I got back was to deal with the water situation at the house. It was intolerable having such foul water. I decided to quit relying on what other people had told me and go directly to the source. So I went to the water district's office in Eureka and asked the lady exactly what it would cost to get hooked up to their water. She basically confirmed what the raspy farmer had said—that I would have to pay a hookup cost of $7,000 to pay my share of the cost of building the system. Then she said "Here, let me give you the exact amount."

She looked it up but suddenly exclaimed, "Wow! Look at this!

The special assessment was for a period of seven years. But the seventh year just expired! Now you can connect to the system for the normal hookup charges... let's see... across the road.... In your case, that would be $85.00.

Eighty-five dollars! To have good city water! No more sneaking into the dorms to bathe! No more drinking bottled water and using bleach to wash dishes! "Where do I sign up?"

Just as promised, within a week workers came out and started jack hammering the road. Soon crystal clear, chlorinated water was pulsing through the lines! Isn't life good?

I wasn't able to solve the septic problem, however. In the weird-shaped lot, there was just no place to put in a leach field. The only real solution was to wait for city sewer service. Luckily, I never heard from the man from the county again (and this time I kept my big mouth shut!).

LIFE'S WORK

School and work were over, and it was time to get involved in my career. I had completely bought into the hippie notion that the straight life was the living death. To go out and get an eight to five job, raise a family, pay taxes, etc. was to lose my existence and join the amorphous mass of anonymous humanity. We, after all, were the generation raised on protest songs like Pete Seeger's "Little Boxes":

Little boxes on the hillside, little boxes made of ticky tacky,
Little boxes, little boxes, little boxes all the same.
There's a green one and a pink one and a blue one and a yellow one,
And they're all made out of ticky tacky and they all look just the same.

As an alternative to a traditional career, I wanted to work in a creative field. I had taken classes in creative writing, and I had briefly made a stab at channeling my creative impulses into music composition. Now I was back to writing again, though I missed music's ability to allow me to soar.

My first project was the completion of my novel, the fictional memoir of the writer who never became successful but wrote his memoirs anyway. I had started writing the book last year as a diversion from my music theory and composition classes.

The idea was simple enough. It was a protest and satire on the classic story I was always hearing about the unknown genius striving for years in his field before finally breaking through to great success. His recognition might come sometime in life, or even after death, but it always seemed to come.

So how about a counterculture theme? My hero would be the same struggling artist, but would *never* be discovered; he would remain forever in obscurity. And this book would be *his* memoir. This was my theme and challenge—what kind of memoir would such a man write, one who had struggled all his life but never prevailed? And why wasn't he discovered? Because he wasn't a real genius at all? Or did something hinder the acknowledgement of his greatness?

I had toyed around with it for awhile. Now it was time to give it my full attention and finish it, thereby embarking on my career as a writer. Besides, it would be a great spoof on the cliché that a writer's first work was always an autobiography. This book would spike that canon!

Fortune and fame were waiting. As for love, well perhaps there was another bus coming down the line.

WAITING FOR THE DAWN

Writing the book became my top priority for the winter. I resolved to work on it every day. The rest of my time was spent on the foundation problems of the house.

From the start, a combination of factors hindered the book project. For one thing, I didn't know how it was going to end. It just grew chapter by chapter, in whatever direction the last chapter—my last "good idea"—had taken it.

Also, its main character remained elusive. Was he truly an unrecognized, creative genius or a self-deluded fraud, forever pretending to be someone he was not? And what was my actual point in the book—that society was arbitrary and unfair by giving recognition to some while withholding it from others? Or was the problem not society at all, but people who can be completely self-deluded? My problem was that I didn't know the answer myself. I toyed first with one theme, then another, as the ideas for different chapters came forth. But instead of forcing my plan on the writing, the writing was leading *me,* first one way and then another.

All winter long, I struggled with these things. It kept getting more complex and insoluble the longer I worked on it. There was no one I could share my struggles with, or offer me insight.

And I couldn't bear to throw away anything I'd written. At one point I'd write a cute chapter that made the whole thing seem like a charming little farce. Later, another chapter indicated that this was a tragedy of heroic proportions. But I couldn't make up my mind which it was going to be and I couldn't bring myself to discard either chapter. Instead of eliminating anything, I tried to find ways to reconcile everything! And the more I wrote, the more impossible this became.

As the winter wore on, I gradually developed a headache unlike any I ever had before. It was very slight at first, but wouldn't go away. Normally, I could handle tension headaches by taking three aspirins and sleeping it off. But this headache was different. It didn't respond to pain relievers, nor did it respond to sleep.

As I continued to work, it gradually got worse, until it became a knot in the middle of my head that I could find no way to loosen. It was there from my first waking moment until my last feeling at night. The pain was not sharp or excruciating like a migraine, but dull and uncomfortable like pressure. The freaky thing about it was that it would never leave or let up.

This was uncharted territory, and I began to get worried. I felt it was related to the impasse of the book. But I also realized I had gotten to a place I couldn't leave. Setting the book aside didn't help, exercise didn't help, and sleep didn't help. Without knowing when, I had passed a point of no return.

The book got harder and harder to work on, as it seemed to be the source of my growing misery. And yet everything else—my summer job, house with the rented rooms, and five months unemployment compensation—was set up to give me the freedom to write. If I failed at that, the rest would be meaningless.

In the midst of this struggle over the book and my headache, I got a letter from Glen Robinson at Oak Knoll.

"I have put your name out to the various foremen on the district," Glen wrote, "and no one has chosen you. Therefore, I am unable to offer you a position this summer."

I was thunderstruck. Though I had realized that my career at Oak Knoll was going nowhere, the possibility that I might be let go never entered my mind. I had gotten used to thinking of myself as a good worker. The only problem was that an employer might be ignorant of what I could do for him. But once he knew, he would certainly want to hire me. I had the same attitudes towards women. Many were ignorant of how good I would be for them, but once they knew, none would refuse me. That's why Linda's continued drift away from me was incomprehensible, and the idea that Judy would prefer going back to her own husband rather than forging a new life with me was unfathomable.

"But I have experience!" I thought, "I know fire fighting; how can they get along without me?" But if you were an employer, who would you rather have? Me as I was when I first went to work in 1966: earnest, sincere, zealous, eager to learn, but *inexperienced*? Or me as I was then: a drinker, a druggie, anti-establishment, questionable morals, bad attitudes, but *experienced*?

It was a blow to my pride. Since my high school days working on my uncle's farm in Indiana during the summer, I was used to being a good worker, to being praised for my work, and desired as a valuable asset. Now, for the first time, those who knew me best didn't want me; the place I had worked for six summers had had enough.

Coming in the midst of the struggle over writing my book, it was a heavy blow. With no summer job, my whole game plan was overturned. What would I do with myself? How could I support myself? I had no other talents or marketable skills.

However, there was one very slim ray of hope. I had already realized I wasn't getting anywhere at Oak Knoll. In the last three years, I had gone from crewman on the big helicopter, to tanker operator, to driver of a four-wheel drive pickup at an outlying station. What was next, weed eradication? Not content to languish in perceived mediocrity, I had begun looking around for something more challenging.

The area that seemed most promising was the hotshots. Hotshots were highly trained line building crews of twenty to twenty-five men, organized for one purpose—to fight major fires. They traveled throughout the western states working on the biggest, toughest fires. They were a cut above the run-of-the-mill fire fighter just like the Special Forces members were a cut above the average soldier.

Our region had a hotshot crew at Redding, but after all the wild stories I heard about its foreman from Jim Kuphaldt, I was leery of it. But there was another one just north of us in Oregon, the Rogue River Hotshots. I had seen them a couple of times on fires with their distinctive blue hard hats, so I decided to send them an application just for the heck of it. It would beat filling potholes at Oak Knoll.

This all happened back in January and I hadn't heard anything about it since. Suddenly, this casual act represented my only hope for the summer.

I had gotten into a place in life where the only way out was rescue from an external source. It was like the time when I was a preteen, before I learned how to swim. I was out playing in the water at a lake with my brother Howard and a friend. But I got a little too far out to where the water level was up to my nostrils. I tried to walk in toward shore when I realized, horrified, that the force of water against my body was too great and I couldn't move. Neither could I speak nor cry out for help as my mouth was already submerged. All I could do was stand there on tiptoes blowing bubbles with each breath, waiting to panic and drown.

Rescue had come at that time in the form of an inner tube floating by. I lunged upward and grabbed it desperately, shouting for my taller friend to give me a push toward shore.

So likewise in the present situation. I was already too far out in the water to push back to shore. I couldn't resolve the conflicts in my book by thinking my way out of them. My headache was growing more intense. It was with me all the time and responded to nothing. I couldn't even drown it in drink. In the meantime, my unemployment was running out, and I had just lost my job.

However, unknown to me, the rescue had started. One day I got a phone call from the Prospect Ranger Station on the Rogue River National Forest. The call was about the hotshot crew. Had I accepted another position? Was I still interested? It sounded like I was being seriously considered.

A few weeks later, I got a formal job offer in the mail. I could hardly believe it—accepted on this elite hotshot crew! A whole new vista of Forest Service fire fighting had opened up for me. Greatly relieved by this unexpected turn of events, I made arrangements to fly back to Ohio and visit the folks once my unemployment benefits ran out and I didn't have to be "available for work." Maybe the change of scenery would help my headache.

It was good to get home again and see the folks. Spring had come to Northeastern Ohio. But though it thawed the winter snows and frozen ground, it did nothing to relax the clenched fist in my head.

Once, when I was alone with my mom, my anguish poured out. Sometimes even as an adult, it's necessary to "go back to Mom." She recommended I seek help from a medical doctor she knew. He had a peculiar ability of being able to see into the "other side" where problems often originate. At that point, I was ready for anything. I already felt sure the problem wasn't physical.

After he conducted a physical examination, he asked me what was going on in my life, and I poured out the story of my book.

He listened as I talked. When it came his turn he startled me by asking, "Who are you writing this book for? Who are you trying to please with this book?"

I thought for a moment but had no answer. "I guess I don't know," was all I could say. "Why do you ask?"

He replied, "As you were talking, I saw a mental picture of you with the book in your hands holding it up to someone for their approval. But I couldn't see who that person was. Identifying that person could be the key to breaking the impasse. Who could it be? Your father perhaps?"

I had no answer for him. It was a question I had never considered, that I might be writing the book to gain someone's approval.

I went seeking answers to my predicament, and instead got a question that was just as insoluble as my problem.

Though he didn't do me any immediate good, still, the question he provoked in my mind, proved to be, over time, not only the key to the resolution of my current predicament, but the key to the resolution of the entire predicament of my life.

Without any present help, however, I returned to Eureka still burdened with my book and my head. The time had come, however, to lay the book aside and get my affairs in order for the summer. After securing some renters for my house, I moved to Eslie's in preparation for this new experience on the Rogue River hotshot crew, the "Rough Riders."

As I drove out of town on Highway 299 for Etna, I had the manuscript for the book in a binder on the front seat of the pickup, still hoping for some flash of inspiration to resolve the conflicts. After crossing the second summit on the way to Willow Creek, I pulled off the road and opened the manuscript one last time. But it was like opening Pandora's Box! The words on the page fairly shouted out at me as if they were alive, accusing me, mocking me, throwing it all up in my face. Writing was my chosen path in life. Everything I did revolved around this writing career I had embarked on as my ticket to fame and fortune. And now I had been completely check-mated by some power I couldn't even identify.

Abashed, I hurriedly closed the binder for the last time that summer, and resumed the journey to Etna, thoroughly beaten down by life.

THE ROGUE RIVER ROUGH RIDERS

June 1973

I arrived June 15 at the Rough Rider barracks in Union Creek, Oregon, twelve miles up the highway from Prospect. Union Creek, the *town*, was a gas station/convenience store on one side of the highway and a restaurant on the other. Union Creek, the *creek*, was a robust body of water rushing under the highway on its way from the base of Crater Lake to the Rogue River. Union Creek, the *water*, was some of the best drinking water in the world.

A quarter of a mile up the road from Union Creek, on an unmarked gravel road, mostly hidden in the tall trees, was the hotshot crew's barracks—my home for the next ninety days. It consisted of two dormitory buildings plus an eating hall surrounded by lawn in a large clearing in the forest.

The first guy I met was a big guy with a cheerful disposition who introduced himself as Pete. He welcomed me and told me where I could find a bunk. Since I was late, most of the beds were taken, but I did find one in the first building by the front door.

The crew was a bunch of good-spirited guys in their late teens or early twenties, most in some stage of going to college and choosing a career.

I had arrived pale and wan from a rough winter tangling with my book. The knot in the middle of my head followed me there, as did the cloud of depression and despair that had gradually settled over me. They told me later that as I got out of my pickup, some of the guys saw me from the barracks and were amazed at my appearance. John Lacey, a squad leader, had said, "Wow, who's the *old* guy?" I had just turned 26.

However, in the warm, dry air and perennial sunshine of the Oregon summer, in the friendly and boisterous atmosphere of the hotshot crew, and under the physical demands of the rigorous training program, my cares and burdens began to melt—imperceptibly but continually, as a glacier in the heat of summer.

I was in no way prepared for the physical training I encountered, having sat around all winter, my only exercise being the work on the house. I knew I was supposed to arrive in shape, and I had gone early to Eslie's to work out, but I lacked the discipline to do it myself. Now I was paying the price.

Even the very first morning the calisthenics were rugged. They were topped off by a mile run in our work clothes and heavy boots down a dirt road and then through the woods. Only dogged determination and a desire not to be humiliated kept me going as I quickly ran out of gas. It took supreme effort to get back to the starting point at the barracks, after which I was "through for the day." After a short breather, we set off for the Visitor's Center for classes on line building and fire fighting. It was a quarter mile away and, of course, we ran.

At break time, we sprawled on the lawn. I was amazed at the closeness of the core group of the crew. One would be lying on the ground on his back, and another would by lying with his head on the stomach of the first. They had an easy familiarity with each other that was spontaneous and natural. I think from the very beginning it was the glue that held us so closely together.

Then we were back on our feet and running to the barracks for more training with tools. So it went throughout the week. As the days wore on, muscles unaccustomed to such strain became progressively sorer and the agony increased. Physically it was probably the roughest week of my life.

That weekend, safely back at Eslie's, all I could do was to sit and stare at the wall. I was too exhausted and sore to notice that my headache was gone.

ORGANIZED FOR ACTION

The purpose of a hotshot crew is to build fire line quickly and efficiently around major fires in rough terrain where only hand crews can operate. To this end, the crew was broken into different teams, each with its own tools.

Everybody on the crew was on one of these tool teams except the foreman and assistant foreman. The assistant foreman's job was to flag where the line was to be cut. The foreman supervised the whole operation, and communicated with the fire bosses on the radio.

The second week, we were all assigned to squads and given tools and positions on the line. I was made a hoe—the hardest, most backbreaking work. Then we began the training in line building under the hot Oregon sun in full fire fighting gear.

The crew foreman was a tall, lanky fellow named Dale Alter, the only Forest Service regular on the crew. Dale was one of the most dedicated men I'd ever met. If you ever wanted a no-nonsense, straight talking, hard working, individual, look no further than Dale Alter.

Next to Dale was the assistant foreman Don Bailey. Don was a short, stocky, laid-back guy. Don was the perfect link between Dale and the rest of the crew, half serious and half rowdy.

Then came John Lacey, the most colorful and dominating figure on the crew. Barrel-chested and powerful in body and personality, Lacey was the man in charge of physical fitness, and the unofficial leader in team spirit and culture, as well as the last hoe on line-building "digs."

Lacey had an animal side of him that lived for the world of the crew. He was totally a man's man, and responded to life at the physical level. He was the champion of the Copenhagen chewin', beer drinkin' and cussin' crowd. He was truly happy only when he was "pitted up." You were "pitted up" when, after heavy exertion, the sweat from your armpits formed a wet circle on your shirt.

Then there were the Lever brothers, Jeff and "Luke"—loud and colorful, they were sawyers and part of the core group that kept the crew together.

From the beginning, the crew worked well together. Though many were first-timers like me, and some even new to fire fighting, everyone seemed to catch on fast and have a zealous spirit. It wasn't long before we were zipping through the practice digs like we'd been doing them all our lives. The foremen and squad leaders pow-wowed, then declared us ready for the real thing. We were added to the Forest's list of fire fighting resources available for dispatch. Let the fires begin!

WAITING FOR THE FIRES

We were trained; we were in good physical shape; we were psyched up. Now we had to wait for the fires, which can be tedious. Instead of sitting around the barracks waiting for fires however, they sent us to work on projects on the Forest.

After a week of projects, we finally got our first fire call, on a nearby ranger district. But it wasn't much. By the time we got there the line was already built. We spent the afternoon watching it, and were sent home.

Our next call was to Colorado. It was a nice trip, and we saw some beautiful scenery, but again, the fire was contained by the time we got there. We spent a couple of shifts guarding the line and mopping up; then we were sent home.

Then we had a fire on the Applegate District of our own forest, just over the Siskiyou Mountains from my old Seiad District. The trip was beautiful along the winding Applegate River.

We arrived all pumped up, thinking at last we would get some hot line and a chance to prove our stuff. But again, we were disappointed. This fire proved to be the deadest of the lot. By the time we got there in late afternoon, there was hardly a smoke left, though there was a four inch thick layer of ashes, and black, charred trees to attest to the fire's earlier power.

Next we were sent to a fire in New Mexico. Fires in the Southwest are totally different from the timber fires we were used to. Traveling through the countryside, you wonder what could burn. There aren't any trees and only patches of grass and scattered brush with plenty of cacti of all shapes and sizes. Nevertheless, the country does burn, and burn hot!

We got to do some line construction in New Mexico, but it was entirely different for which we had been trained. We even got some hot line experience when the fire made a run down a ravine toward us while we were building line across its mouth. But this brief moment of excitement still didn't satisfy our craving for a real "dig," as we called fire line building.

HELLS CANYON

The fire call came again. This time it was north, to Hells Canyon, the mile-deep river gorge of the Snake River between Oregon and Idaho. This was a "real fire" we were told and it certainly was in one of the worst imaginable locations. Precipitous to the point of being inaccessible in places, the steepness of the canyon walls facilitated the rapid spread of the fire even as it hindered the efforts of the fire fighters.

Finally, after an all-day drive, we arrived at fire camp on the canyon's rim.

The next day we assembled at the heliport, preparing to be flown into the canyon to our fire assignment.

Helicopters were the only way to get around on the broken cliffs and ridges of the fire area. The terrain was too steep for roads, and the fire was spread out over a broad expanse from the river all the way to the top of the plateau. But it was spread unevenly. There seemed to be a series of fires loosely connected, scattered over the jumbled canyon slopes.

Our first destination was a knob near the top of a spur ridge going down into the canyon. But after only a short time, it was decided to send us halfway down the canyon to another ridge with the fire mostly below us. We started digging line parallel to the ridge top but a hundred yards below it. Farther up the ridge, other crews were putting in line that would eventually tie into our line. Though there were patches of trees, the predominant cover was grass, which made a lot of work for the hoes, not as much for the pulaskis or shovels, and none for the saws.

We were swinging away, moving steadily up the ridge, just passing a large tract of trees, when somebody pointed back down the hill behind us. A large cloud of black smoke was boiling up from somewhere below—the fire was blowing up! Soon the roiling smoke was blotting out the sun, and an eerie, red twilight settled over the land. I have learned that red-tinted, unearthly twilight on a fire is a sure sign of danger, though at the time there was no other indication of trouble. The wind that had been sporadic all morning, had died down to a complete calm. There had not been any sound from the direction of the smoke to indicate what was happening below. Instead, an eerie, orange silence covered the land, the calm before the storm!

Suddenly, an onrushing wave of fire came sweeping up the ridge toward us; the wind sprang to life with a roar and burning embers rained down around us in the dry grass. "Run for it!" Dale and Don shouted, and we took off sprinting up the hill. All along the line, everyone ran for the top of the ridge.

We pulled up just short of the ridge top, panting from exertion, and regrouped. I was pretty panicked, and was thinking more about safety than anything else. But some of the crew leaders were looking back to see what the fire was doing.

Initially, it had swept up the hill, overrunning some of our line. But now the fickle wind had quit again and the fire's progress had stalled. It was still burning briskly in the grass, but now it was creeping instead of running towards us.

"Hey, I think we can stop this thing," someone said. The idea caught on; the crew began to get fired up; somebody issued the orders; we started running down the hill toward the fire, screaming that we could stop it. All except me. I was running with the rest, but not exactly sharing their enthusiasm.

Life can be full of surprises, and boy was I surprised when

what I thought was a futile effort inspired by excessive machismo turned out to be successful at stopping the fire! We got our relocated line tied in and backfired before the wind came up again. While everyone else farther up the hill was still retreating, we turned back and stopped our part of it cold. I never would have believed it if I hadn't seen it happen.

But I wasn't the only one watching. Farther up the ridge, the sector boss was looking on in amazement. He rushed up to us all excited and impressed with how we had stopped the fire. In fact, he was so impressed that he swore he was going to put every one of us in for an award for heroism or valor or something.

However, because the other crews had fled and hadn't held their line farther up the ridge, there the fire slopped over and started burning in the next drainage. So our victory celebration was short-lived. We had to join the other crews and go over the ridge to put a line around the slop-over.

It was rough and jumbled country. There were many rock outcroppings. We had another moment of excitement when the fire spotted in the grass below us. Dale saw the flames and took a contingent of men to put a line around it. While they were trying to corral it, the wind came up again and the fire started coming at them. They were above the fire retreating backwards. But as they retreated, they ran into a wall of rocks from an outcropping and realized their escape was cut off. It was nip and tuck for a moment. Some tried beating the fire down to stop it, while others tried to figure out a way to escape. They finally realized that the rocks were going to stop the fire anyway, and all they had to do was get out. Some managed to clamber up and over the rock face, while others escaped by making a quick dash through the flames.

The fire was finally subdued, and we were glad to get out of that steep and rugged terrain with its angry yellow jackets that buzzed us everywhere we went. We left for home still pumped up beyond measure by our triumph over the blowup on the first day.

Good as his word, the sector boss did nominate the whole crew for an award for valor that we each received later in certificate form. In his cover letter of nomination, he said that when the fire blew up, he looked down and saw his entire sector fleeing from it. But then he looked again and saw one crew of blue hard hats running in the opposite direction, *toward* the fire! We were the only crew on his sector to turn and attack the fire head-on, hitting it with such gusto that we stopped it cold in its tracks.

LEE BOGG

I awoke on my bed in the barracks sensing that something was wrong. I tried to move, but couldn't. It was like I was paralyzed. With a start I came fully awake. I couldn't move my body!

Our latest project was installing barrier posts in campgrounds to prevent cars from driving out-of-bounds. We had to dig the holes by hand and bury the posts exactly three feet deep so they all stuck out of the ground at the same height. This involved a lot of work from a bent-over position.

Though I hadn't experienced any problems while working, now my back was frozen stiff. I could move my arms but not my torso. I couldn't get out of bed! In fact, I couldn't bend at all! It was a sudden, unexpected, monkey wrench thrown into the smoothly meshing gears of my life. I struggled and struggled, moving everything that would move, but found no way to get out of bed.

Finally, with help, I was pulled out of bed and taken to a doctor near Medford who specialized in muscular and skeletal injuries. By this time I could sit stiffly, but could walk only with great difficulty.

Not only was I in physical distress from the sudden turnaround, I was in absolute emotional shock! Everything had been going so well this summer—the fires, the camaraderie, the money, the total change in my mental outlook. And now this! This had never happened to me before. What was going on?

The doctor was not encouraging. His prognosis boiled down to a belief that my fire fighting days were over; I could never recover from this kind of back injury. His advice: "Look for a job in a different field."

"Like what?"

"Well, like maybe being a mail carrier."

A *mail carrier*? Done forever with fire fighting? A virtual cripple the rest of my life? Disability license plates with my name on them? It was a tremendous shock. My whole life changed in a moment, as I went to bed feeling fine, and woke up a semi-invalid for life.

His ho-hum attitude seemed to say, "Well here's another one for the scrap heap of life."

He sent me away with a prescription for muscle relaxants, and one of those "whalebone corsets" that kept my lower back from bending at all. There was no other attempt at treatment. "Take a week off from work, and then come see me again."

Needless to say, there was a great feeling of gloom as I painfully squeezed into my pickup and headed for Etna and my prescribed week's rest.

Sometime during the two-hour drive to Etna, I remembered Linda telling me once about this family she used to live with. I thought she said this fellow worked on backs, and that he was quite talented. A ray of hope appeared. Maybe he was still around somewhere; maybe he could help me.

The next day I called Linda and gave her the bad news. Then I asked her about this fellow. She said his name was Lee Bogg (long "o"). She thought he might still be around, but would have to check with her "grandmother" to find out where. Later in the day she called back and said Lee was living in the little town of Tennant over in the Goosenest District. She gave me his phone number; I called him and made an appointment for the next day.

The next morning I once more painfully wedged myself behind the wheel of my pickup and headed to Tennant, over eighty miles from Eslie's. A Forest Service work station and tanker were located there, but getting there was harder than I thought; it was thirteen miles off Highway 97, all on gravel road!

The town was small, but there was a store. The directions to his house were obscure. There were no house numbers and the "city streets" were gravel lanes. I went into the store and asked where Lee Bogg lived, "You know, the guy who works on backs."

To my surprise, in spite of the small size of the town, nobody knew him. Somebody had heard of a stranger who had moved there recently, but didn't know that he worked on backs.

Perplexed, I went outside and studied my meager directions again, trying to make them jive with the lanes and houses now before me. I made my best guess and started knocking on doors. On my second try, I found him.

He lived with his wife in a little frame house. They were an older couple, but youthful in appearance. Later, I found to my surprise that they were both in their 70s! He was a talkative fellow, and soon told me much of his story.

He made no bones about it—God had given him a gift with backs. He took no credit for it, but attributed it to an impartation of understanding from God. After receiving this gift and realizing what he had, he began studying anatomy and muscle structure to develop and deepen what God had given him. All this time he was examining me on his table. He had me lie face down and measured both legs. "Here's your problem!" he exulted, "one of your legs is half an inch shorter than the other!"

"But how could that happen all of a sudden?"

"You know how a shoulder or hip goes out, when the ball slips out of the socket? Well this is similar except it's the muscles, not the joint. You stretched or pulled too hard, and the muscles that connect the lower back to the hip on your right side were stretched out of place. Once stretched out, they won't return on their own, and everything you do only aggravates the situation.

"Your doctor told you to rest for a week, but nothing's going to change during that week; your muscles will still be out. Only the secondary swelling and pain caused when you further aggravated those muscles will gradually subside. But once you go back to work again and start using your back..., it'll happen all over again because the problem hasn't been fixed."

"Well can you...?"

"Can I fix the problem? Sure, we'll have you good as new before you leave here today."

As he continued to work he resumed his discourse.

"You see, what God showed me about the back was that most of the problems are muscle related. What happens is that every time you cause a strain on the back and feel a little twinge of pain...that's a tiny muscle somewhere that just spasmed and froze into a knot. This muscle spasm—this knot—never releases itself on its own, but remains permanently in that state. As you go through life and these little knots build up, your back gets stiffer and stiffer. Most people attribute this to the normal process of aging and don't do anything about it. But it can all be undone by releasing the muscle spasms!"

By now his massage had my back muscles all loosened up.

"Now let's fix the main problem."

He grasped my right leg at the foot and began working it around in small circles, at the same time applying a gentle pushing pressure as though pushing my leg into my body.

"There it went. Feel it? Back into place! Now to loosen up your back."

His tool for releasing the muscle spasms was his elbow! I knew when he found a spasm, because it felt like a hard little knot under his massaging fingers. After finding one, he placed his elbow directly on it, and gave just the right amount of pressure, like squishing a bug. That pressure, applied directly to the spasm, brought a gasp of short-lived pain as the spasm released itself and the muscle returned to its normal state.

"There're four different levels of muscle spasms. I'll start at the surface ones and gradually work to deeper levels."

After making his discovery on the cause of most back problems and how to cure them, he went into business, hanging out his shingle in Ukiah.

But his technique was so successful that the demand for his services skyrocketed. People were coming to see him at all hours of the day and night, *demanding* to see him, refusing to leave the waiting room, desperate people. Overwhelmed, he began running from his gift, ending up here, in one of the remotest towns in the state, at the end of thirteen miles of gravel road. And even here, he told nobody what he did!

If true—and it seemed reasonable—it was certainly a sad state of affairs: a man who had received a gift from God of tremendous benefit to his fellowman, now hiding it almost completely from those it was supposed to help. What would happen if I ever received such a gift? Would I be able to handle it any better, or would I either fall into pride thinking I was great, or flee from its demands like Lee had?

But he was glad to work on me. I winced and gasped each time he released another knot with his elbow, causing him to chuckle, "Oh, that was a good one, wasn't it?" After releasing the surface ones, he moved progressively deeper into my back. I was sure he was greatly wounding me, but I could also feel a certain release as each one let go.

Finally, he was done and told me to get off the table, stand up and move around. I have always been a stiff person, not in the least flexible. Even as a youth, I was never able to touch my toes. But now as I twisted and stretched myself, I was astounded! Not only was the pain gone and my injury completely fixed, but I was so limber I felt like a little child again! I grinned from ear to ear as a tremendous burden lifted from me. I felt like a kid released to play in the sandbox.

He smiled and nodded approvingly. "Now these things can come back," he said. "Once the muscles have been stretched by coming out of place, it's that much easier for it to happen again. But if it does, you just come back and I'll put it in for you again"

Then he collected his fee—$10.

"Wow," I thought as I drove home, "that was the best $10 I ever spent in my life." I was singing on the way home I can tell you that. Not only had I gotten back what I had lost, but I was made even better than before!

I seemed to keep running into miraculous deliverances. At the end of the spring, my life had been checkmated over my book and the end of my Klamath National Forest career. But the hotshot crew had materialized, rescuing me from the doldrums and putting new life back in me. Then overnight everything came crashing down again with this “incurable” back injury. But Lee Bogg had appeared out of nowhere and once more I was restored to wholeness. Where were all these deliverances coming from? Even earlier than that, my life had been spared from the rolling log and the near accident with the plywood board through the rotor blades.

But miraculous deliverances didn’t happen to everybody; other people’s lives like John Brannon’s and Dave Dreyfus’ had shipwrecked around me. I’d seen timber fallers die in the Seiad woods; a fire fighter die in Oregon.... Why was I being favored? The question was very reasonable. What was sad was it never even occurred to me to ask it.

BACK IN THE ACTION

After my back problem was solved, the summer continued its lively pace. Soon we were flying to the airport in Coeur d'Alene, Idaho, and traveling north through Bonners Ferry and Sandpoint to fight a fire within a mile of the Canadian border.

Then we were on a fire in Happy Camp, of all places, back on the Klamath, my old stomping grounds. In fact, we ran into Glen Robinson out on the line one evening. I said an enthusiastic "hi" but I'm not sure he recognized me. He looked spaced out, barely acknowledging my greeting.

Another time, we were called to a fire in the Susanville, California, area on the eastern slopes of the Sierras. The day before we arrived, there had been a midair collision between an air tanker and a spotter plane in the smoke over the fire. The air tanker had limped back to the airport, but the spotter plane lost its rear stabilizer fin and nosed straight into the ground in a meadow near the fire, digging a hole fifteen feet deep in the soft earth. Nobody walks away from those crashes. People say, “When your time comes, it’s over; when it’s not your time yet, you live.” Was that all there was to it? Was it no more complicated than that? But they never explain *who* sets your “time” and what criteria *they* use.

ALL GOOD THINGS MUST COME TO AN END

All too soon the season was over, and it was time to say good-by. It was a sad time, yet I was on top of the world. I was in better physical shape than at any time since leaving high school. I was filled with the self-confidence that comes from being a respected member of a highly esteemed group, and being an integral part of something far bigger than myself. I was happy; I was victorious; it had been a great summer!

Before we left, Dale wanted to meet with each of us individually. We were puzzled, but it turned out he wanted to review our performance over the summer.

"Well, Hobbs," Dale said, when my turn came, "you had a good summer, worked hard, stayed out of trouble...."

Then my eyes jumped in their sockets as I saw him studying a little notebook that he used to write in a lot—that we always wondered what was in it.

"However, back on the lake project on June 27th, when we were stacking logs and debris to burn...." He looked up from where he was seated, "You were screwing off with Tony and Hubby and not getting any work done."

I was speechless, in shock that he'd remembered that incident so long ago. It seemed like last century. But there it was, all written down in his book where he'd been recording all our goof-offs the whole summer. *That's* what he'd been writing!

"Still," his faced softened, "you've had a good summer. Take care of yourself and maybe we'll see you next year." He stuck out his hand and I shook it, relieved that the past was over and done.

After a chorus of "see you next years," I was off in my pickup, heading for Etna.

Some were offended that after such a good year, Dale suddenly dredged up negative things from ancient history, mostly inconsequential in nature. I was not offended, but I learned a valuable lesson from the incident: the past is not forgotten, though we ourselves may forget it. One day, we will all have to face it again. I hope on that day my Judge can stretch out His hand and say, "Hobbs, you've had some major screw-ups, but you've learned from them, you've come around, you've accepted my Solution. For you the past is wiped out and forgiven. Welcome home!"

WORKING AT UKONOM

Fresh from my triumph on the Rogue River Hotshots, I returned to Eslie's ranch. I was spending a few days there kicking back and relaxing when Jorgen Danielson, who leased the ranch, told me that the Forest Service at Ukonom was hiring people to cruise timber for fire sales in the spring. A major forest fire–that we missed–had occurred that summer that killed thousands of acres of trees. Now the timber sales had to be mapped out so the timber could be sold during the winter and harvested next spring.

I drove down to Ukonom and talked with the timber management officer. Though I didn't have any timber experience, they hired me anyway. They would teach me what I needed to know.

The work was fascinating and enjoyable. The warm fall days were absolutely perfect, the sky was blue, the air was clear and crisp, and the winds were still.

One of the reasons the Forest Service was in such a hurry to get these trees harvested was to prevent an epidemic of bark beetles. But the beetles were already at work! In the quiet, warm afternoons, if we stopped in the middle of a burned out stand of timber and kept absolutely still, we could hear them gnawing on the wood inside the trees! Also, as we walked through the forest of dead trees, tiny specks of sawdust drifted down all around us like fine, light snow, glinting in the sunlight. This sawdust was produced by the gnawing beetles. In a short while, these trees would be useless as lumber, and hundreds of thousands, perhaps millions of dollars of wood would be lost forever. We were truly in a race against time.

I loved this work because of everyone we were helping. Our one crew was providing employment for the loggers and profit for the U.S. government. In addition, a significant amount of money from every timber sale went to support county schools. We were providing lumber for the nation and benefiting the forest at the same time by pruning it to make it healthier and more productive in the future.

A BRUSH WITH EVIL

Along about this time, Uncle Eslie had a crisis. One Saturday when I took him to town to get his mail, there was a letter from his estranged wife, Gertrude. She was living with their daughter,

Yvonne, up in Yakima, Washington, but in the letter, she announced her intentions to move back in with Eslie. This news shook him to the core of his being.

In my brief experiences with her, I had found her to be pleasant enough, but she could be sharp and she definitely had no tact. She cut Eslie no slack at all, treating him like a dimwitted child. Her strong personality completely dominated him, raising in him a fierce resentment, all the fiercer because she allowed him no opportunity to express it.

Immediately, Eslie plunged into a deep stew. The more he sat smoking his pipe and thinking about it, the more agitated he became. He kept asking my opinion and advice, but whatever I said didn't make any difference. Nothing I could say alleviated his worry, nor helped him make up his mind about what to do.

The author and Eslie Cory

Watching him over the course of the day, I could hardly believe the effect it was having on him. From that alone, it was obviously not a good idea for her to move in, so I told him he needed to politely but firmly inform her that she was not welcome. But he seemed thoroughly cowed—there was no way he could stand up to her—which ate away at his self-esteem, making him all the more resentful. That night, Eslie began talking in his sleep.

Now Eslie was a strange study. His personality had been thoroughly repressed over the years, so much so, that in all my years of knowing him, I never heard him once raise his voice. I've seen him get angry and his eyes flash, but never shout, scream, or throw a fit. I've seen him *try* to raise his voice, for instance if he was trying to call someone far away. At these times he would gather up all his strength and put everything he had into it, but only manage to raise his voice a few decibels.

Once when the county was widening the road, some of Eslie's trees had to be removed. The workers, accommodatingly, left them by his garage so we could cut them up for firewood. I started cutting on the biggest one, which was waist high. After I had cut off one round and was standing on the downhill side, suddenly the whole tree started to roll towards me. I was facing away and didn't see it, but Eslie did and tried to shout out a warning. But he was unable to—he literally could not raise his voice even to save my life! Luckily, I caught the motion out of the corner of my eye and leapt clear just in time. I marveled at how completely his repression went.

This repression was complete except when he was asleep! During sleep, a totally new personality could come over him in a strange, even eerie transformation. In his sleep, he could rant and rave. He could whine, get angry, shout, even threaten with utmost ferocity. In his sleep, all that had been repressed over the years could come boiling out with frightening force, revealing a seething cauldron underneath the mild exterior.

This much was already known to me. I had experienced it on occasion, though it didn't happen often while I was living with him. But when my brother Jesse was there one summer painting the house, Jesse experienced it a lot.

Jesse is not a cowardly person. Nevertheless, after enduring Eslie's almost nightly ravings and shouted threats to kill him, Jesse left the bed I slept in downstairs in the parlor, and took refuge in one of the upstairs bedrooms where he could lock the door. That muffled the sound, and Eslie would have to walk up a long flight of stairs and break through the locked door before he could do anything to him. Not that we had ever known Eslie to do more than rant and rave in his sleep. Still, Jesse moved upstairs.

That night I awoke from a light sleep. The night was young, before midnight, but Eslie was starting to go at it again. That's what awakened me. I lay there and listened for awhile. It sounded like the pent-up anguish and resentment he felt over Gertrude had stirred him up big time.

Eslie always revered his mother. The only room in the whole house that was locked was the last upstairs room at the end of the hall. In it was his mother's wedding dress: his most treasured and carefully guarded possession. He had a large picture of her hanging in his bedroom. A picture of his dad was there too, but he seldom spoke about his dad.

His father had died in 1926 when Eslie was twenty-four years old. I'm sure it was a far greater shock when his mother died only a year later. Eslie had spoken on several occasions of having weird, "Twilight Zone" experiences of his mother returning to their house and playing the piano after her death.

This night, however, I was startled to hear him suddenly call out in a voice so loud and clear that it filled the house: a voice that was a perfect blend of the whine of a spoiled brat and the imperious demand of a dictatorial adult. "MOTHER! GET IN HERE, FIX ME MY BREAKFAST!"

I wondered if that's how their relationship had really been, and if so, what strange psychological twist of mind had since elevated her to saintly status. It was freaky, but I didn't know what to make of it. I didn't hear anything else significant right away, so I slipped back into slumber.

Everything up to this point, I know really happened. But in what follows, it is harder to discern the reality from my own dreams.

But whether in fact or in my dreams, Eslie's rantings started up again, this time against me! I became the object of his wrath for no apparent reason, and his threats against me spewed out of his mouth in a torrent, filling his room. Then he rose from his bed. Not content to rant against me, he was coming to kill me, to choke my miserable life out of existence. Slowly he came out into the living room on his tottering legs, then through the open, sliding doors, and into the parlor where I was sleeping.

I was transfixed by fear and unable to do anything to stop him or defend myself. I was like a mouse watching the snake circle round and round, frozen by terror, waiting for the strike.

Still spewing out rage, Eslie approached my bed, his shaking hands reaching for my throat. When they were only inches away, suddenly, something within me stood up and pushed him back—like a straight-arm in football; like someone with greater authority had shouted out a commanding "NO!"

With a mighty shove, I thrust him, his rantings, and his murderous intent away. Then I got out of bed and gathered it all up: the threats, the anger, the malicious hatred—all the incredible evil that had spewed from his mouth against me. I gathered it all up into a ball. And it was the slimiest, blackest, foulest, most revolting YECCCH! I have ever seen. I am convinced it was a revelation of pure evil.

I carried the disgusting ball to the door of Eslie's room, reached through the opening, and deposited it inside. When I put it down, the black, slimy, ball turned into Eslie's obsequious dog "George," which sidled away from me, meekly wagging its tail between its legs. Then I returned to bed.

The next morning I was blown away at the remembrance of the night before. I was flabbergasted that Eslie would try to attack me, even in a dream! I was angry at him over the whole deal. I hadn't demeaned or belittled him; I'd only offered him advice when he'd asked for it. I was so shocked that I took off in my pickup and drove far up into the mountains where I sat overwhelmed for a long time.

I don't believe that Eslie was trying to kill me, I just dreamed that part. I don't think he ever physically got out of bed and came after me. But I believe I did suffer attack: from evil spirits empowered by Eslie's ranting. They were using him to project their power into this world, and when they got strong enough, they came after me.

What were they trying to accomplish? To kill me? I don't think they could. But they were trying to get into me just like they had gotten into him. They were trying to get a foothold in my life through fear. When Eslie was about to choke my throat in my dream, I think they wanted to trigger a sudden fear reaction within me–a *panic attack*. That would have given them the opening they needed to get a foothold in my life.

What happened instead? Did I suddenly stand up against them at the last minute? Although that's how it seemed in the dream, as if I had beaten off the attack single-handedly, I don't believe that's what happened. How could it? I had no power against them. I was frozen in fear. I believe what happened was at the last instant, when their hands were closing on their helpless victim, God sent an angel who thrust out his hand and pushed them away, returning all the evil that Eslie had spewed out back to his own room where it could harm no one but him.

Once more, in an hour of desperate need, this time from a dangerous spiritual attack, a Power far greater than my own had intervened and rescued me. *When* and *how* could I ever discover who this Power was? Could I meet it? Could I know it? Unknown to me, my search was coming ever closer to the answers to these questions. In fact, in less than a year, my life would be totally transformed by the incredible answer.

Gertrude did in fact move in with Eslie. There seemed no way he could stop it. But the move was so disastrous that after a week she packed up and returned to Yakima.

A GLYMPSE INTO THE ABYSS

The sunny, warm days of October turned into November and the rains began. Ukonom normally gets 50-115 inches of rain each winter, depending on elevation. But this year was different. This November the storm door got stuck open and the storms kept coming, one after another almost every twenty-four hours for the entire month. I think it turned out to be the wettest November on record.

But rain or no rain, the cruising and tree marking went on. I worked every weekday of the month, and it rained on us every day except two.

With the continual rain and the increasing hours of darkness brought on by the advancing season, my time there gradually became more depressing and lonely. There was nothing to do in the long evenings at the barracks. The regular employees disappeared to their homes, and the occupants of the barracks steadily decreased as the remnants of the fire crew and slash-burning crews were sent home. Only the three of us working on the timber sales remained.

One of my fellow crewmembers was a young guy named Mike. He was in his late teens and friendly, though in some ways goofy and slightly weird.

I thought maybe he had some psychic powers. Twice while in my room in the silent barracks reading, I was sure I heard his voice calling me: "Dave." It was a low call but very distinct.

Both times I got up and went to the door of his room and said, "Yeah, what do you want?"

"Nothing," he replied.

"But didn't you just call me?"

"No, I never called you."

I was sure it was his voice but finally decided the call came in my mind rather than in my ears. The fact that his voice could speak in my mind was what made me wonder if he was psychic.

He was often out in the evenings prowling around the station in the darkness. He had some marijuana, and occasionally I would go out with him behind the ranger station on a bare little hill, if it wasn't raining, and smoke a joint with him. But it didn't ease the loneliness.

In my loneliness and depression, I began thinking about my life with dissatisfaction and looking for changes. It would have been a good time for someone to share the Gospel, but no one did.

My sister back east had gotten into meditation through the Maharishi and his Transcendental Meditation movement (TM). From the letters she sent me, it sounded attractive. Maybe I could use meditation to calm my soul and give meaning to my life—get in touch with a higher consciousness or a higher power, or whatever else could give me peace. For awhile, I seriously considered asking her how to get started, but never quite got around to it.

Mike had made contact with some of the local "pot-heads" and one evening, they invited me to go driving around with them and get high. We ended up stoned at the new cement bridge over the Klamath River.

We parked just off the bridge and walked out onto the span. The road was deserted—as was everything else around Ukonom—and the river, swollen by the continual storms, swirled in a rushing, muddy torrent below. It was night and the rain had stopped. In the sky above, the wind pushed ragged clouds across the face of the moon that occasionally shown through brilliantly on the raging waters below, showing them brown and glistening. When clouds passed in front of the moon again, the waters faded into an indistinct, blackish mass of surging motion.

The rest of the guys were joking around as guys will, lightheartedly pretending they were going to throw one another off the bridge.... But I was horrified. In my stoned condition, standing above that dark torrent was like standing above the mouth of hell itself. I sensed that were I to fall into those angry waters, not only would my physical life be swept away, but my soul would be lost forever in the dark abyss of eternity.

I don't know how I sensed this, but something inside me confirmed it as truth. You could chalk it up to marijuana-induced paranoia, but to me it was a chilling brush with an inarguable spiritual reality.

I wish I could adequately paint a word picture of what I experienced that night, of the insecurity of being on that bridge over the irresistible force of the turbulent waters below—the absolute *insignificance* of my own human power compared to the colossal power of nature that, if given the chance, would take my life in an instant without giving it a second's thought. Not to mention the much greater Power that had to be behind the power of mere nature! But those with me on the bridge, who saw everything I did, seemed to sense nothing of the insecurity of our lives above a fearful eternity.

FINISHING THE BOOK

December 1973

I had left Eureka and the coast in the late spring of 1973 an overburdened, beaten down "old man" of twenty-six, crushed by the writing of my book and its irresolvable problems. The very thing I had hoped would be my ticket to fame, prosperity and happiness, had instead almost been the vehicle of my destruction.

As I had driven over the ridges from Arcata to Willow Creek, I had stopped and opened the book for one last time, hoping finally to get the understanding that would crystallize the story in my mind. Instead, it was as if the pages were shouting at me in a great mocking chorus for my inadequacy. I couldn't bear to read a single word.

What had that Ohio doctor meant by his questions: "Who are you trying to please? Who is the book for? I see you holding the book up to somebody for their approval, but who is it?"

Totally defeated, I had pushed that all from my mind and entered back into my other world of fire fighting. And the results had been beyond what I could have asked or imagined.

There was not a doctor in the whole world who could have given a better prescription of therapy than the one provided in the hotshot crew. In the place of the book and its problems came a program of rigorous physical exercise, new friends, travel, fires, victories in life, even a rejuvenated back.

The single biggest factor was the camaraderie of the crew. We were like a team that trained hard, played hard and topped it off by winning the Super Bowl. When I left Union Creek ninety days later, I felt like a new man: strong, energetic, and confident, on top of the world. It was the most amazing turnaround I had ever experienced. Even the back injury and the loneliness at rainy Ukonom were but brief glitches in the road to my recovery.

Out of the Fire

Driving from Ukonom to the coast, my thoughts at last turned to what was waiting for me there: the task of finishing the book. Could I resolve the book's problems now that I'd been completely away from it? Or would that terrible headache come back again?

With some trepidation, I resumed work on it, returning to my customary place of writing in the student lounge in Sproul Hall on top of the hilly, Humboldt campus. I liked to work around people because it eased the loneliness I felt from my solitary task. Their presence, studying or quietly talking, was a soothing tonic of normalcy that kept me from drifting too far into the dark recesses of my mind.

I soon found nothing had changed. I had no more answers to the conflicts and central questions regarding the book than I had before. I still couldn't resolve the questions of where I wanted the book to go or what I wanted it to say, and I still couldn't bear to throw any of my "inspired" writings out, even though they took the book off in contradictory directions.

Since I couldn't resolve any of the problems that had plagued me in the chapters I'd already written, I just added new chapters! At some point, I wrote the final chapter, the title of which became the title for the whole book, *Waiting for the Dawn.* It was a dream sequence in which the main character dreams he's a large bird, perhaps an owl. Loosened by his wings from the constraints of the earth, he is able to soar wherever he wants and gain new perspectives on the earth below. But it is nighttime in the dead of winter, so no matter where he flies, all beneath him is cold and dead. Finally he spots one little point of light—a campfire—way off in the distance. Flying to it, he finds many other creatures drawn like him to the light, heat, and promise of life contained in the fire. Like them, he settles down just outside the fire's glow "waiting for the dawn" to renew life on the earth.

I still like that chapter, because, though it was a dream sequence, it was rooted in a transcendent reality. By resolving the contradictions in my character's life at a deeper level, it bypassed the impossibility of rational explanation, while remaining satisfying to the spirit. But more than that, it also expressed where I was in my own life, and offered me hope of future resolution. I too was "waiting for the dawn."

The "Waiting for the Dawn" chapter marked a departure from my usual writing in that it was a dream sequence and thus able to break free from the narrative of the events of the character's life and get into deeper realms. To my surprise, it proved to be the opening of a new fount of inspiration that began to give me ongoing, spiritual visions for my book. It was as if the book, stalled out in the natural, had begun moving ahead in the spiritual.

I immediately recognized the value of this material. It was powerful stuff. There was inspiration in it that didn't come from my own mind. These were not things I sat around and figured out. It was as if in response to my struggle for something of value to write, a well of flowing inspiration had opened up to me.

While sitting in the student lounge one evening, I got an amazing vision of war in the heavenlies between the forces of God and Satan. It was not a thought sequence or an idea, but an experiential happening. I was still aware of my surroundings, yet I could "see" this vision in my mind's eye just as surely as if I were watching it on a movie screen. But I was not producing it and therefore, was not in control of it. I realized this at the end of the vision, when Satan and his forces stormed through the gates of heaven, destroying everything in their path. Try as I might, I couldn't make it end any other way.

My own brain and imagination had broken down and "run out of gas." Now I was getting inspiration from another source, powerful and compelling, just what I was longing so desperately for. Yet I was not in control of it. I could either accept it and write it down the way it came, or reject it and go back to my own bankrupt ideas. Needless to say, I wrote it down the way it came. I knew beyond the shadow of a doubt this new source of inspiration was my ticket to the success and recognition I craved. People would pay to read this stuff!

The only bad part was the after effects. Each time I received one of these visions, it left me devastated inside. It turned me toward darkness, depression, and despair. Especially after the heavenly war vision, I felt compelled to go down, find a bar in Arcata, and drink. I started frequenting a certain bar in downtown Arcata that had a daily "Happy Hour" from 5:00 to 6:00 p.m. It became almost part of my daily routine to go to this bar and drink one, two, or even three drinks during Happy Hour and then go over to John and Jeannette's for supper.

John and Jeannette, who had become my closest friends, saw this dangerous turn of my life with the sudden onslaught of compulsive drinking, and were very worried. Jeannette tried to drop hints in subtle and not-so-subtle ways. But I was oblivious; it all seemed so natural to me.

I did remember the story of the writer Jack London from high school literature class, about how he wrote such great stories until he drank himself to death. "So this is how it happens," I thought, "you get inspiration at the cost of personal destruction."

Luckily I didn't have far to go on my book before considering it finished. I remember the first time I finished it. The relief was so great that that night I dreamed I was flying, soaring at will wherever I wanted to go. It was a great dream.

But the next day, I was back at it again, still not satisfied, still not ready to let it go. I added, revised, and finished it a second time, only to pick it up again. There seemed no way out and I was afraid things might degenerate into the deadly paralysis of the previous year.

THE AUTHOR AND LINDA AT ESLIE'S, DEC. 1973

ERIC, KELLIE, LINDA, AND ESLIE, DEC. 1973

Before it could get that bad, I decided to publish it myself. I had sent it around to various publishers but I knew instinctively none of them would want it; it was too much a conglomeration of disparate material. I just wanted to see it in print. That would be part of the process of being set free, because once printed, it could no longer be changed. I found a large printing shop in Eureka that would print 500 copies for $1000, which I had in the bank from my summer's work. I borrowed a camera and drove to Etna to take some pictures of Eslie to use on the front and back cover, and it was done.

I had a lot of deep psychological and spiritual things happen during this time as I was struggling to complete the book. The most poignant was a dream I had one night where I was trying to cross some train tracks by climbing up a signal tower and crossing on the beam where the signal light was attached, coming down on the far side.

It was night of course. The tower was slippery and dangerous. As I got higher, I grew increasingly fearful, my muscles tightened, and my progress slowed to a crawl. Finally, I reached the point where the cross beam was to be attached that would take me over to the other side. But I was stunned to find that there was a break in the beam—part of it was missing! There was an unbridgeable gap between the precarious perch I had climbed to and where the horizontal beam came out from the other side. After all that danger and struggle I still couldn't get across.

Was this dream saying that in spite of all I had gone through to produce this book—all the hard work and the psychological danger—it still wasn't enough and maybe *never* could be enough to please the mystery person I was holding it up to?

THREE WOMEN—SUZANNE

There were three women that impacted my life in major ways that winter. The first was Suzanne.

Suzanne was a divorced woman with two young sons who had attended our Universalist Church in Kent, Ohio, for a number of years. She had a doll-like face: large, expressive eyes, round cheeks, full lips, all framed by a head of full bodied, richly brown hair. She was intelligent and artistic—a graduate English student at Kent State University teaching private, classical guitar lessons. She was warm and friendly personality with a gentle spirit and a good sense of humor. Her beauty, charm, intelligence, and attainments in life, plus the fact that she was almost ten years older than I, put her in a category of women that I labeled "Nice but Unobtainable."

However, I was older now, more worldly-wise, more tuned in to the world of women.

When I went home for Christmas in December I met Suzanne again and spent some time with her, and it was as if we were seeing each other for the first time. She was close to our family, mainly to my father, as they were both involved with the university.

So we were around each other, spent some time together intentionally, and seemed to kindle some sparks. Then I had to leave. I had no idea when I left what all this would mean, if anything. But again, seeds had been planted.

Not long afterward, Suzanne called and said she wanted to get away for awhile. She wanted to come out and spend some time with me. “Would that be all right?” It was like a bolt from the blue. Would that be all right? Yes, of course it would! She would be arriving in five days. I could scarcely believe it.

Suzanne seemed to have a naturally curious and inquisitive mind. Many people spend so much of their time locked into their own little worlds that they have little time left for the worlds of others. Suzanne wasn't like that. She wanted to explore worlds other than her own. She would be here for four days, and in that time she wanted to see and experience everything about my world.

I took her to the college and showed her everything of interest there. I took her out to the ocean, to my secret beach in Trinidad. We toured Eureka and Arcata and everything to be seen there. I took her into the redwoods where I used to walk from the college and meditate. But even that wasn't enough.

We took an excursion into the interior where we visited with Eslie, and I showed her the ranch. We went downriver to Seiad and I showed her the ranger station where I had worked for so many summers. All the time she was looking, asking questions, experiencing. Her interest was flattering but sometimes disconcerting. It can be scary to expose so much of yourself to someone who is still mostly a stranger, and who hasn't yet earned the right, by a commitment to you, to see it.

But all in all, it was a wonderful four days together. I was especially delighted to discover that her inquisitiveness went to the very depth of my being. But then it was time for her to go. Now what?

"Well, it's been nice; I've had a great time, let's get together and do it again sometime."

As for an ongoing relationship?

"I admire a man most who is not emotionally dependent. We both need to avoid an emotional dependence on the other."

Me, an emotional basket case, a desperately insecure and immature individual, not get emotionally dependent?

"Let's just treasure the time we've had together and leave it at that. Who knows, down the road maybe it will happen again."

It was like the Gale Garnett song so popular in the 60s:

I will never love you, the cost of love's too dear.
But though I'll never love you, I'll stay with you one year.

I'll sing to you each morning, I'll kiss you every night.
But darlin' don't cling to me, I'll soon be out of sight.

But we can sing in the sunshine, we'll laugh everyday,
We'll sing in the sunshine, then I'll be on my way.

That was where she was coming from. As for me, I was desperately looking for acceptance and emotional security. I was looking for someone to give myself to totally, in exchange for love and long-term commitment. We could hardly have been more different in what we were looking for, and in what we wanted to avoid. But, as with Linda and Judy, sex now bonded me to her—that supreme, physical relationship designed to make two into one. Once again I was bonded to someone going in a totally different direction. Suzanne came into my life, stirred up a host of desires, emotions, and hopes, then left.

It was hard pouring out my heart to her in letters every other day and then receiving one in return every two or three weeks. I think Suzanne might have been surprised by all the things she stirred up in me and didn't know what to do with them. I have no doubt she cared for me, but not enough to alter her lifestyle. Like Linda, she had been married once, and didn't seem eager to go there again anytime soon.

When my book was printed, I sent her a copy, eager for her affirmation.

Shortly after that, in the early spring, I decided to take another trip home to visit the folks, and her, of course. My unemployment benefits had run out, and I was free to travel.

It was a difficult time. She had read my book, and had a much clearer vision of it than I had at the time. She tried to be gentle, tried to be positive, but I was crushed. I so needed affirmation; I was so insecure.

She didn't want to have sex; she wasn't on any contraception. "Couldn't she just take a pill, *the* Pill," I wondered? I was ignorant of the working of the Pill, and thought she was not being upfront with me. All in all, I saw a terrible side of myself: immature, selfish, demanding, angry, and even lurking in the darkness of my soul—violence.

My relationship with Suzanne aroused in me very strong, contradictory, and even dangerous emotions. In that sense, my relationship with her was personally destructive. Our relationship brought me face to face with my worst parts: the lust, insecurity, selfishness, and jealousy.

Caught in the grip of these dark emotions, under the power of things I couldn't control, what I had entered into with such excitement now turned into a personal nightmare. I did something I can't remember ever doing before in my life—I prayed.

I was lying in bed at home one night, after a particularly painful visit, feeling all this *stuff* running around inside of me, overwhelmed by the impossibility and complexity of the situation.

I don't know what I believed about God at the time, though I had believed in some sort of god/God ever since using drugs. But regardless of religious theories, I knew one thing: whoever God was, *I needed Him.* In sincere desperation, in the darkness of my room, I looked up to heaven and prayed, "God, please help me."

And God did help me. He lifted me from the seething emotional cauldron I had fallen into and returned me to a place of sanity. After that, Suzanne and I were able to spend some good days together. We went on some outings and did some things with her boys.

The problems were not solved, but the emotional conflict I was going through and the darkness of my inner being abated. And we didn't talk any more about my book.

But God was not through answering my simple prayer: "Please help me." As events proved, this was only the tip of His iceberg.

THREE WOMEN—CLAUDIA

Claudia was the youngest of Fred and Bonnie Cranston's four children. Fred Cranston was the physics professor at Humboldt State that my mother had first contacted for help when I was arrested for drugs. Larry and I went on to become good friends with the whole family. It was Larry who married Carol, their oldest, after beating me out for her hand.

Through all my years of association with the family, Claudia had always been on the periphery of our attention. She was the typical ungainly teenager, the hidden flower not yet ready to bloom. We all liked Claudia, in a slightly patronizing way. She was sincere and had a good heart, qualities I had not yet learned to fully value.

I hadn't had much contact with the family for several years when Claudia contacted me out of the blue, wanting to talk. It turned out it was regarding a religious conversion she had recently experienced. I told her I would talk with her if she came out to my house, testing her because I had always heard how prudish these religious people were. To my surprise, she agreed and came out and talked with me on my waterbed about her new faith in Christ. I can still picture that most incongruous scene in my mind—Claudia, the simple, sincere, enthusiastic believer sitting cross-legged on my waterbed with me sprawled beside her in my darkened bedroom with the "mood" lighting on and the "artistic" nude wallpaper on the wall, sharing Christ with one so vile and depraved, that, if given half a chance, would have taken advantage of this sweet one he used to relate to as a kid sister. But then, her newfound Lord had said, "I am sending you out like sheep among wolves. Therefore, be as shrewd as snakes and as innocent as doves" (Mt. 10:16).

She told me that Bonnie too had "believed." They were going to a "Spirit-filled" Baptist church in Arcata only a few blocks from where they used to live on the edge of campus.

Sad to say, my intentions toward her were less than honorable. I saw her as a woman now, and fair game for conquest. I had become increasingly predatory, as my search for love became more and more a search for sex. She was truly a lamb among wolves.

As far as the testimony of her new faith, I dismissed it out-of-hand. After all, I was the older, more mature, and wiser one—the worldly-wise "great intellectual" who knew it all and couldn't take counsel from one so young and inexperienced on the path of life.

She spent some time with me after that, following me around, wanting to go with me wherever I was going, showing her care and concern and hoping I would embrace this Christ she had found. But in my pride and hardness of heart, the only thing I tried to embrace was her, thinking this might be the opportunity to get another relationship going.

My obtuseness finally drove her off—she who was trying so hard to help me, who loved me so sincerely. Still, secretly I admired her and what she was trying to do, and something within me, even in my hardened state, would have been deeply disappointed if I had succeeded in my shameful, amorous designs.

It was very distressful for Claudia. She cared so much; she so wanted me to "get saved" and share in her discovery. But I was an impregnable fortress of pride and unbelief. In sorrow she gave up.

But she could only see the outside. Inside, far from the eyes of men, her witness did speak to me: less in the words she used than in the pure love of her shining life.

THREE WOMEN—KAY

Kay was my other roommate that winter, living in the third bedroom. Kay was above average in height, slender, and fresh-faced. She wasn't even a student, but worked as a nurse/receptionist in a medical office. She had a boyfriend who despised me because I tried to put the make on her.

Kay was bitten by this religion "bug" too, about the same time as Claudia. She also tried to "convert" me. She gave me a newly released book that was being talked about everywhere: Hal Lindsey's *The Late Great Planet Earth.* It dealt with his interpretation of the prophetic Book of Revelation by fitting it into the current world political scene. It was fascinating reading. I had never imagined the Bible spoke so clearly to our present day, nearly 2,000 years after it was written.

Another time, she encouraged me to watch a Billy Graham crusade on TV. I did watch it alone in the house at the time. At the end, when Billy invited those watching at home to ask Jesus Christ into their hearts by repeating a prayer, I said the prayer, more out of curiosity than anything else, but nothing happened.

Kay kept trying to talk me into going to a church in Eureka to hear a preacher by the name of Jim Durkin. She described him as a powerful preacher with a compelling message, and she had been going there often to hear him. Finally, one night she prevailed upon me to take her to the evening service.

Imagine my surprise when we pulled up to a run-down building in a run-down part of Eureka and I saw the name, Deliverance Temple! This was the place just across the street from where I used to live on Cedar Street five years ago. At the time, I thought it must be a Jewish synagogue.

We parked and went inside. Everyone we met knew Kay and greeted her warmly. After she introduced me, they also greeted me warmly. I was not prepared for such an outpouring of warmth, but tried to accept it graciously without losing my cool.

The place was nearly as run-down inside as it was outside. However, it was filled with exuberant young people of all kinds. Some were hippies with flowing beards on the men and flowing dresses on the women. Others were clean-cut and traditional-looking like Kay. The one thing they all had in common was joy. We went upstairs to a tiny balcony overlooking the sanctuary.

Jim Durkin, the preacher, was a most singular man. His age was hard to tell. From his energy level he could have been in his mid 40s, but his face was deeply lined, as if, whatever the number of his years, they had been extraordinarily difficult ones. His hair was turning white and his disheveled clothes were topped off by a battered, brown leather jacket. "This is the preacher?" I marveled. I was used to preachers with smooth skin and nice clothes. This fellow could just as easily have been someone sleeping on a bench at the bus station. However, looking around at the drab surroundings and the motley crowd, I had to admit that he fit right in with the church.

For the first part of the service we stood and sang songs together, not the traditional hymns I was used to, but modern love songs to God like:

Father I adore you//Lay my life before you//How I love you

While they sang, most would close their eyes and raise their hands, swaying rhythmically and smiling ecstatically. They really did look like they were in love with Jesus.

When Jim Durkin got up to preach, it was like nothing I'd ever heard. He had a most forceful way of speaking, building in power until he was almost shouting at the top of his voice. Then, just when it seemed he would overwhelm you completely with the force of his argument, he would suddenly stop dead in his tracks and whisper into the microphone words that I could barely catch though I strained with all my might to hear them. Now this was preaching! I was spellbound for the length of the message. He was easy enough to understand, but the style of the preaching rather than the wisdom of the words was what made the deepest impression on me.

After the message, the young man who had led the singing earlier, got up and led us in singing "The Lord's Prayer" from the Sermon on the Mount. I was familiar with the words, but I had never heard them set to music.

The song had a beautifully flowing melody with rich, harmonic chords underneath. It was constantly modulating from major to minor and back again. "What a nice way to combine it with the words," I thought. Toward the end, it came to a pause after the phrase, "and deliver us from e-vil."

Then suddenly it launched into the last section, "for thine is the kingdom..." I could feel the pulse of the song quicken as it pushed upward toward an unseen goal high above. Meanwhile, the chords were pinched, diminished ones, crying out to be released from the pressure. With each phrase, it took a run upward, "for thine is the KING-dom," then fell back. Another run "and the POWer," still fell back, unable to break through.

But the third time, when it hit "and the GLO-ry," something in the chords changed, something happened to the logjam that was holding us back. Suddenly, in a burst of revelation, I could see where the music was heading! There in the distance was an impossibly high note we were striving to reach. Instantly, I was totally involved in the music. How could we possibly get there? Goose bumps broke out on me. From "GLO-" the music came back down to "ry." The chords started falling into place, though they were still crying out for release.

"YES!" I said in my heart, "YES!" I knew where the music was going and my whole being was fixed on that one high note. The music had come back down as if for one more run, "for..." But this time, instead of running up towards the high note, the music made one breathtaking leap, crossing the chasm in a single bound as the chords fell into place underneath. WE HIT THE NOTE!! That impossible high note! We hit it head-on and my spirit soared with it in exaltation. "EV-V-V-V-V-V..." I didn't want to let go of that note. I wanted to soar on it just like the word said, "forever." Then, after what seemed an eternity on the note, the melody floated down effortlessly like the softest feather to the "er," placing the period on the sentence and the thought. Then the quietly sublime "a-men" and it was over.

I was oblivious to the altar call and the rest of the service. I drove Kay home at less than twenty-five miles per hour. I had been so deeply impacted by the service that I couldn't function normally for awhile. There was a serenity in my soul such as I had never experienced. In that moment I had touched eternity.

And yet life went on. The feeling wore off. I never went back to Deliverance Temple, though I never forgot it either.

Not long after that, Kay moved out, going to live with other Christian young women like herself. She was deep into this religious thing, and seemed quite happy and excited about it.

She told me that Jim Durkin had more than just the church in Eureka. He also had a Christian discipleship ranch at an abandoned lighthouse called Lighthouse Ranch where young Christians went to live out their newfound faith. His ministry also owned a free advertising tabloid called the *Tri-City Advertiser*. She said he was also affiliated with another Christian discipleship ranch somewhere inland, in California's Central Valley.

I wished Kay the best of luck, glad that she was so happy, that she had found something in life to give her joy and meaning.

A FOURTH WOMAN— AN ANONYMOUS SAINT

There was another woman who briefly crossed my path in the winter of 1974, but who affected my life far more than I realized at the time. To this day, I don't know her name. It was one of those unplanned and mysterious experiences that life sometimes serves up without warning or explanation.

I had been quite affected by Ken Kesey's book, *One Flew Over the Cuckoo's Nest*. It was about an insane asylum and its inmates who were subjected to oppression from the management in their enforced captivity due to their supposed insanity.

Meanwhile, only a mile up the road was a new convalescent hospital, the last stop for the elderly who could no longer live alone. I wondered what it would be like to be left there to die. I thought it might make the subject for a good book.

On a whim, I decided to go there and do some research. Looking back, it seems quite unusual. But there I was driving up to the facility out of the blue. I don't know what I asked for initially, maybe some patients to visit or talk with. I know I didn't tell them I was there to do research on a book! They took me to some patients who were basically vegetables—scary in their comatose state—but I didn't get far talking with them! Finally, I ended up in the dayroom where the healthier ones sat during the day, talking, watching TV, or playing cards. Here were people a little more normal.

They were glad to see someone from outside, and asked a lot of questions about me, my family, and my life. And I, in turn, asked them questions about their past and about their life at the facility. I visited several times.

On one of these visits the ladies learned that I had been a music major in college. One of them asked if I could play the piano. When I admitted I could, they asked me to play their piano in the dayroom. After I played some of the popular songs of the day, one of the ladies excused herself and returned with an old, well-worn hymnal. "Here," she said, "can you play any of the songs in this?" Instead of choosing one myself, I asked her to pick one she liked and promised to give it a try.

She turned to an old hymn called "Blessed Assurance." It was probably the first time I had heard the song. But it had a catchy, lilting melody in flowing 9/8 time and I soon caught on to its simple chords. It ministered to her so much that she had me play it several times.

Blessed assurance, Jesus is mine!
Oh, what a foretaste of glory divine!
Heir of salvation, purchase of God,
Born of His Spirit, washed in His blood.

Of course, she wanted me to play all the verses. And as I played them the words touched me too with their simple assurance of God's love, the believer's relationship with Him and the comfort that flowed from that. I was struck by the Christian's hope for the future:

for a glorious existence beyond this life.

Perfect submission, all is at rest,
I in my Savior am happy and blest,
Watching and waiting, looking above,
Filled with His goodness, lost in His love.

I played others but I especially remember that one. It caused her to take out a handkerchief and daub at her eyes.

I sensed the impact I had on her and her friends just from playing their favorite hymns. When it came time to go, I asked her if I could take the hymnal home with me to practice the ones she liked, so when I came back again, I could play them better. She paused for a moment, looking at her beloved hymnal and considering whether to part with it or not. Finally, she said slowly, "No, I'd hate for anything to happen to it. But you come back and play from it any time you wish."

I assured her I would.

Before I left, I let her and a couple of her friends pray over me. They earnestly asked God to bless this young man who had come to play their hymns and brighten their day. It was touching.

But, as though she had a premonition, as abruptly as my visits began, they ended. I don't know why. I never decided not to go back. But in the busy-ness of life I never did.

PULLED BY DARKNESS, PULLED BY LIGHT

The winter of 1973-'74, saw a great battle being waged over me, over what kind of person I would be, though I was totally oblivious to it at the time. But there were powerful forces pulling me in different directions. I've already mentioned the inspiration that started coming as I was finishing my book. It had vitality; it packed punch—far different from my own lightweight ramblings. But the price was a frightening increase in darkness in my life: an internal devastation of spirit after sessions with this revelatory agent that drove me to drink, despair, and a dark abyss.

Then there was the affair with Suzanne. Just like with Linda, there was an initial burst of joy and intense feeling, of sexual and soulful bonding. This was followed by the same long letdown: the unanswered letters, the lack of commitment, the dashed expectations, and the irreconcilable differences. But this time the period of joy was much shorter, and the letdown much quicker and steeper, until it plunged me to a dangerous low of bitter frustration and suppressed violence. But from that had also come a prayer of pure desperation: "O God, please help me."

But then there was the gentle pull of light, a softer influence seeking to permeate my life. There were people like Claudia and Kay who had found something that made them very happy and met their needs in life. These people were interested in me; they were reaching out to me. There were the memories of the little old ladies at the rest home who had loved for me to come and play for them. There was that profound church service with that dynamic Durkin fellow and the music reaching for and then attaining that impossible high note.

Once Jeannette called and invited me to their house to watch the classic Cecil B. DeMille movie "The Ten Commandments" starring Charlton Heston. It stretched over two evenings.

I got caught up in the drama of the story, in the large picture of God dealing with nations, and of the small picture of God dealing with individuals. Especially staggering was the ending, where God, after all He had done for Israel in freeing them from Egypt, bringing them through the Red Sea, giving them the Ten Commandments... after all that, just as I was expecting a grand climax, God compelled them to wander forty years in the wilderness until the whole generation died off because of their continued disobedience. Even Moses, the man God used to deliver them, the founder of the Jewish religion and the "Great Lawgiver" of the Old Testament—God refused to let into the Promised Land either, because of <u>one time</u> when he disobeyed God. "Wow," I thought, "this God is one heavy dude!" Once more, as at Jim Durkin's church, I was affected deeply.

There was a great religious stirring going on in our community of which I was only vaguely aware. I would have been even less aware if it hadn't been for people like Claudia and Kay who were eager to tell me about it. But not all of its influence was positive.

I read the *San Francisco Chronicle* every morning with breakfast. Since time was not of the essence, I read the whole paper and other things like the local advertiser.

But I'd forget this advertiser was put out by Jim Durkin's group. I'd be reading through the ads, and all of a sudden come across a scripture from the Bible that had been snuck in there unannounced. This used to annoy me no end because it would catch me off guard. I'd be reading along: "The family of Marcus Allen wishes to express thanks to all who sent flowers during their bereavement over the loss of their beloved James."

"Hmm yes, 'beloved James.' OK let's see what's next...."

"From the rising of the sun unto the going down of the same, the Lord's name is to be praised."

"What, what, what...? Why those rascals! Blindsided again!"

Also they sent out street witnesses to share Christ with whomever they happened to find in the community.

One warm spring day I happened to be at a park in Eureka. This young man walked up and began talking to me, something like this:

"Hey man, are you going to heaven?"

"Who are you? I don't even know if there is a heaven."

"But like are your sins forgiven?"

"What's sin? What do you mean 'forgiven'?"

"Well like is Jesus Christ the Lord of your life?"

"What are you talking about, anyway?"

"Jesus, man; Jesus, man; you need to find God."

Meanwhile he wasn't looking at me. He seemed to be looking somewhere above my head and there was a glazed, faraway look in his eyes, like he was from another dimension.

This angered me and I began to upbraid him. "Look," I said, "here I am enjoying this beautiful day and you come up talking 'God' to me. Look at the beauty of nature. Here's God! But you're interrupting my enjoyment of God with your 'Jesus' gibberish."

Instead of answering me or coming down to my level, he kept speaking in those catch-phrases and Christian jargon, all without looking directly at me or focusing on where I was at or what I needed. So after more arguing with him, I left in disgust.

"Man, that guy's on a trip," I thought.

So some of my interactions with this "Jesus Movement" sweeping the area were positive, while some were negative. But even with the negative ones, Jesus was still on my mind.

TAKING STOCK

In May of 1974 I turned twenty-seven years old.

Financially, as far as carving out a life for myself that utilized the world system to the max, I had done it. I had my own three bedroom house that would be paid off in five years. The rent I was getting for the other two bedrooms was paying my house payment plus my share of the utilities. I was living virtually for nothing, my only other bill being the $70/month payment on my new pickup.

I was working five months a year for the Forest Service: three months in fire fighting and two months in other work. While fire fighting, because of the overtime, hazard pay, and per diem allowances, I made enough money to max out my unemployment benefits in the winter. Getting the maximum unemployment benefits gave me more than I needed to live on, so I didn't have to spend any of the money I made during the summer.

The unemployment benefits continued for five months, during which time I could hang around and work on my writing. After the unemployment ran out, I could travel.

I was proud of how I had built a comfortable life for myself by taking such great, and perfectly legal, advantage of "the system."

In addition, I was a budding author who had written and published his first book. This was just the start, I told myself.

On the other hand, I was turning twenty-seven. What had started as a temporary job to support my way through college was now my only job. I had no career or future with the Forest Service. I was only a temporary, and would never be anything more.

I was deathly afraid of a "traditional" career anyway. I had so swallowed the counterculture thinking of the 60s that getting a career and a family were the last two steps on the road to oblivion.

I thought I was perfectly set up to pursue writing as a career. And I was, as far as time and opportunity went. Yet I didn't have anything to say. I didn't know the answers to the problems of my own existence. How could I help others? On top of that, writing *Waiting for the Dawn* had almost destroyed me, and now the new source of inspiration I was tapping into, while powerful, was even more destructive. How could I survive another book?

At the same time, I had dreams of opening up my own publishing business to publish books from people like myself that no other publisher wanted. The fact that I could be totally serious about such a plan with no money, no publishing experience, and no business acumen shows how deeply enmeshed in delusion I was.

As far as the opposite sex went, I was as checkmated in that area as in writing. The only three women I had been deeply involved with were either married or divorced. All of these would be considered adulterous relationships from the standpoint of traditional morality. Each relationship had brought much pain, and none had met my longing for a loving, long-term relationship. Each of the few single women I had pursued chose someone else.

My current flame, Suzanne, was a free spirit who wanted an intimate relationship without emotional commitment. I tried to give her what she wanted, but found my own needs going unmet. I wanted attachment, stability, commitment. After intimate time together she wanted to fly away like a carefree bird, leaving me stranded and emotionally desolate.

But in reality, the fault was as much mine as hers. My needs were so deep there wasn't a woman alive who could meet them.

But the most amazing thing in looking back from the vantage point of time: I was oblivious to all of this! My life was lurching down a dead-end road toward the brink of destruction, and I thought everything was going great.

In spite of the fact that writing one book had almost destroyed me and had opened me up to destructive demonic forces, and despite the fact that I had no message or answers to share with my fellowman, I was still hoping that somehow a writing career would materialize, just because I had time to write.

Even though my career with the Forest Service was tenuous at best, with no long-term future, and had shut down on me once already, and in spite of the fact that I had no other training or skills to fall back on, yet I had no worries about the future.

Thus as the fateful summer of 1974 rolled around, I was feeling pretty good. I was careening toward the edge of the cliff, feeling just fine about myself.

SONG IN A THUNDERSTORM

As I drove my pickup up Highway 299 from Arcata to Redding on a late spring afternoon, I noticed that a thunderstorm was brewing over the mountains. Somewhere past Weaverville, the skies turned dark and threatening. Thunder rumbled and the first drops of rain fell. Before I reached Redding, a full scale thunderstorm was in progress in the mountains around me, hurling occasional showers at the truck as I drove by.

I came out of the mountains into Redding, leaving the storm behind, and turned north on Interstate 5. I figured I would be in the clear now, but as I re-entered the forested mountains around Shasta Lake, the storm resumed, even intensified. The rain was coming down all around, bouncing off the road in explosions of glistening white droplets. The sky grew so dark that cars turned on their headlights. Because of reduced visibility, I slowed down to forty-five.

Thunder boomed off in the distance.

It's 100 miles from Redding to Yreka, a couple hours drive on a good day. On this particular day, in the storm, it seemed to go on forever. I was shut into my own little world in the cab of the truck with the rain beating down all around me and the windshield wipers creaking steadily, driving through the gloom that had turned the once sunny afternoon into premature evening, the only sign of life being the phantom-like shapes of cars passing in the mist—yes, I was truly alone.

It was a heightened sense of the aloneness that I used to feel especially at night, alone in the dark, seeing the lights of civilization yet feeling a great sense of exclusion. Lights in houses pointed to the warmth of fellowship and security inside of which I was not part. Streetlights or outdoor lights only emphasized the absence of life as they illuminated the world's emptiness. Now I was doubly alone, with very few lights of any kind along the winding, nearly deserted freeway.

I was also a writing loner. I had no network of friends with whom to share ideas, to provide mutual encouragement and critique my work. The thought came to me that if I really wanted to make it in writing, I should go someplace where things were happening, such as, New York, Hollywood, or San Francisco. But I was stuck, like my small-town protagonist in *Waiting for the Dawn*, not bold enough to pull up stakes and move to an impersonal, fast-paced city.

I was constantly expecting to drive out of the other side of the storm. Thunderstorms in the West are generally localized affairs. They might be over one mountain range, or a band might pass through. But to drive for miles and hours in a continual thunderstorm was unheard of—it just didn't happen.

In the enforced solitude of the pickup's cab, my thoughts turned from writing to women. I had experienced intimate relationships with three women and each relationship had been more destructive than the last. I wasn't learning or growing from these relationships. I was just repeating past mistakes in a greater way.

I had spent years hoping that Linda would change course and come back to me. I had spent months in Eureka waiting for Judy to show up. Now I was hoping for Suzanne to miraculously change from a free-spirited woman to a one-man, stay-at-home partner, devoted to me.

Though I wouldn't have thought it possible, the rain seemed to increase in intensity. As I passed through mile after mile of river canyon, it was a continual cloudburst. I had to slow down even more as the road got harder to see. It was all under a layer of water now that couldn't run off fast enough. The whole world seemed to be a gray blur. I was only doing thirty-five, hoping it was fast enough to keep my things dry in the back of the pickup. I could still hear thunder and see occasional flashes of lightning. It didn't look like I was leaving the storm behind at all. If anything, I was driving deeper into it! "How can this be?" I wondered. I sunk back into reverie again as the miles slowly ticked off and the windshield wipers kept up their monotonous beating.

I had spent seven years going through college, had a bachelor degree with two majors, but wasn't doing anything with them. In fact, I had run aground during the college experience. The tide had gone out, carrying my classmates to jobs, careers, families and growth, leaving me behind stranded on a sandbar.

The lightning seemed to be getting closer—the flashes were more vivid, the thunder louder, and the time span between the two, shorter and shorter.

So while seeming to have conquered life and the system, I had really checkmated myself without even knowing it. I had no future, unrealistic goals, and was still living a Peter Pan existence, afraid to grow up and face the real world.

I had wanted to change the world, to make a difference in people's lives, and I had. I'd started Linda off on drugs, which had launched her into the party lifestyle from which she'd never returned. I'd helped Linda find life beyond her husband, a transition so successful that other women who wanted to ditch *their* husbands looked to *me* for help! I had....

Suddenly there was a blast of lightning and a stupendous crash of thunder! After driving through the thunderstorm for two solid hours, all my effort, all the miles, had only brought me into the very heart of the storm!

As suddenly as the lightning, came the vivid revelation of my own inadequacy and the failure of all my efforts, which had only brought me into the middle of life's storms, compounding my problems instead of solving them.

But with this revelation came a change. Somewhere deep within, a chasm was crossed, a new direction taken. Spontaneously, I began to sing an old hymn: "Just a Closer Walk with Thee." Alone in the pickup in the rainy dusk, not caring if the words were right, at first tentatively, and then belting it out at the top of my lungs, I sang:

Just a closer walk with Thee,
Grant it Jesus hear my plea,
Daily walking close to Thee,
Let it be, dear Lord, let it be.

I am weak but Thou art strong.
Jesus keep me from all wrong.
I'll be satisfied as long
As I walk dear Lord close to Thee.

It was going so well and I was pouring out my heart and soul, but I was running out of verses. So I improvised. With a lump in my throat and tears in my eyes I continued:

Through the years of toil and snares,
If I falter Lord who cares?
Who with me my burden shares?
None but Thee, dear Lord, none but Thee.

Through the years of pain and woe,
If I falter Lord who'll know?
Who will keep me on the go?
None but Thee, O Lord, none but Thee.

Through the years of toil and strife,
Who will keep me from the knife?
Who will lead me on through life?
Only Thee, dear Lord, only Thee.

As I continued singing, improvising new verses, then going back to the beginning and starting over again, the storm began letting up. It was just raining now, not pouring. The road was wet and black, but it was no longer white and obscured by the bouncing of the raindrops. The lightning and thunder receded, the rain gradually decreased to light rain, then to a drizzle, then stopped. By the time I came out of the mountains at Gazelle, it was over, and the sun was peeking from behind the clouds before dropping over the mountains to the west.

Though outwardly things returned to normal, yet something profound had happened inside. And it proved to be the opening salvo of a spiritual tsunami I was heading into that would change my life forever.

BACK TO UNION CREEK—MEETING MIKE HARRIS

June 1974

Now it was on to Prospect and the Union Creek barracks. This time, I wanted to arrive early and get the pick of the bunks, not repeating my mistake of last year and ending up next to the door. The first thing I did was go to the back corner of the barracks to a little alcove separated by a partition. There were two beds. I grabbed one for myself and put some of my stuff on the other one to save it for Tony, who had asked me last fall to save him a bed. Then I gadded about greeting people and renewing friendships.

When I went back to my bunk later, I noticed someone else had claimed the bunk I was saving for Tony, setting my stuff on the floor. This annoyed me. I mean the guy was right there with his back to me, moving his stuff in like he owned the place!

I was about to open my mouth and straighten him out when he turned around and smiled broadly. "Hi, I'm Mike Harris," he said, thrusting out his hand. He was broad of shoulder, medium in height, with a round, handsome face that seemed to shine.

ROGUE RIVER ROUGH RIDERS, SUMMER OF 1974
(SEE APPENDIX FOR NAMES OF CREW MEMBERS)

Disarmed by his friendliness, I never could get out my complaint about him taking the bed I had reserved for Tony. So he was in, Tony was out and would have to fend for himself.

Mike told me that he had been on the crew two years ago. With Mike back, a bunch of old war stories from his past were dredged up by the Levers, Lacey, and some of the older hands. It seemed Mike had been the greatest hell-raiser on the crew. With his good looks he was a natural womanizer, and he loved to drink and party and get wild.

They told of one night in particular at the barracks where Mike, reeling from beer, grabbed his chainsaw and ran through the barracks, revving it up and flinging oil from the chain onto people in their beds. In the uproar that followed, Mike disappeared from sight though they could still hear his chainsaw outside the barracks. Then they heard the saw bite into wood.

By the time people rushed outside, Mike had sawn a tree one-third of the way through by the back corner of the barracks. He thought he was going to drop it towards the lawn away from the barracks, but when examined the next morning, the tree actually had a distinct lean *over* the barracks. If it had fallen, it would have come crashing down on top of the frame building with the people inside! Luke Lever pointed out the tree to us. There it was, still standing, with Mike's cut one-third of the way through it!

But that was then. This was now, and Mike had changed. "Hey guys," he smiled. "Guess what? I found Christ."

Mike Harris, a "Jesus Freak?"

This created a problem for Lacey and some of the old guard who had previously known him. If some new guy had shown up, claiming to be a Jesus Freak, they could easily have dismissed him as being an oddball, and kept him on the fringes of the crew, as some of the others who were not popular. But Mike had been one of *them*. In fact, he had been the essence of all the things they admired most—the hardest drinking, the rowdiest, the most womanizing, yet also the hardest working and most filled with the crew spirit of them all. And now to have *him* show up with Jesus stickers all over his car, and smile warmly at them and say, "Guess what? I found the Lord..." well it was hard to deal with.

He was still friendly and outgoing. He hadn't clammed up or gotten religious or spooky. He didn't suddenly change his speech and start talking about "Gaw-w-d" like a pansy preacher. He didn't look off into space like that park preacher, using jargon that... who knew what it meant? Mike still had his good qualities, just not his bad ones. So when Lacey offered him a chew of Copenhagen, Mike smiled and said, "No thanks, I don't do that anymore." If pressed, he might say, "I don't want to abuse my body with that stuff."

It was the same with drinking. When offered a beer, he might occasionally accept, but most of the time he would smile and say "No thanks." When pressed, he would say, "I don't have to drink to have a good time now, and with Christ, there's no hangover." Then he'd chuckle, because everyone knew about the mass hangovers the crew had after a big party.

So Mike was a real perplexity to those who had previously known him. The crew still liked him and wanted to include him in full crew fellowship, but now he was different. He stood in opposition to the tenets they held dear. His very life contradicted them, yet he never said a word of judgment against them. He never railed against their "debaucherous life-style." He just lived his life side by side with theirs as if to say, "Hey guys, look, I've found a better way."

DOC

Most of last year's crew came back, so things fell into place quickly. "Basic Training" under Lacey was hard as usual, but it was just part of what you had to go through. After that, it didn't take long to get the handful of new guys a place on the line and teach them our system of progressive line building. After only a few digs, we were declared ready to go.

Soon we were back in the southwest again on a large brush fire in New Mexico.

We had a character on our crew called "Doc" because he was a medic from the Vietnam War. Doc also "had religion" like Mike, but he was a Mormon. It was interesting to see the differences between his brand of religion and Mike's. Doc was a more "in-your-face" kind of a guy, whereas there was a sereneness about Mike. In fact, Doc was a lot like the rest of the crew minus the bad habits—a cleaned up version of the rest of us. Mike was truly different. He had inner peace.

Anyhow, back in fire camp, I don't know how it happened, but Doc, still the rowdy, made the statement that he could bite the head off a live lizard—which were all over the place. At first, it was just something within our crew, but then some Mexicans from a nearby crew heard the boast and started to inquire. Soon after that, Luke Lever, seizing the moment, climbed on a crate and announced to all the crews milling about that Doc was going to bite the head off a live lizard. Then he started taking $1 bets that Doc would do it. It wasn't clear whether he was taking $1 bets or just charging people $1 to see it. But whatever, money soon began flowing in from everywhere.

When he had cashed out the crowd and raised the expectancy to a fever pitch, the time came when Doc had to step up and do it or lose face. So, gamely, he stood on the grate, put the live lizard's head in his mouth and took a mighty bite down on its neck. Without waiting to see what happened, he spit it out, turned and walked away. He hadn't severed the head cleanly; it was still dangling by a tendon or two. But he was not about to put it back in his mouth and finish the job. We all gave a roar of approval signifying that he had won, and, in spite of some grumbling from the Mexicans, we carried the day, and thus it went down in the lore of the hotshot crew.

FIREWORKS DOWN SOUTH

It didn't take Mike long to start "sharing Christ" with me. I had rejected most of the Jesus Freaks who had tried before as too weird to be taken seriously. But Mike was different. He was the first Jesus Freak I could relate to as an ordinary guy.

But that didn't mean I automatically accepted his message. He started out by telling me that I was empty, that there was a hole inside me that only Christ could fill. I couldn't buy that. All my old defenses went up immediately. "But I'm happy," I insisted, "my life is going just fine!"

After what had just happened in the thunderstorm on my way up from Redding, the fact that I could blithely claim everything was fine in my life shows how deeply in denial I was. I was not willing to admit to the inner turmoil of my life, to Mike or even to myself.

"I don't need this Christ stuff," I thought. "I'm content just the way I am. Still, it does seem to have done some good for him."

When it came time to decorate our hard hats, Mike painted his with yellow letters on the back, "I Belong to Jesus."

Some thought *that* was going too far. Someone even defaced his hat with lewd remarks. That hurt him, but he repainted it, put the smile back on his face, and kept going.

Next, we were sent to a couple of fires in Southern California: first on the Angeles National Forest; then the Los Padres, near the ocean.

The Los Padres fire had burned like wild for awhile, and all kinds of crews had been ordered. But by the time we got there, the weather had changed and the fire was mostly out.

We were on a main ridge with lots of spur ridges coming off it, and there were crews milling around everywhere with nothing to do.

Finally, to escape the crowd, Dale took us over to the next spur ridge and told us to fan out and "hunker down" in the brush while he hung with the bosses till they figured out what to do with us. So we spread out along the top of the spur ridge in the brush and rocks, talking, playing cards, and spitting Copenhagen.

I started out in an open area of rocks by myself. But I got bored and walked about fifty yards up the ridge and joined others in a clump of brush.

I had been watching the cumulus clouds build all day in the direction of the ocean. As the day wore on, the clouds got thicker and turned darker. A thunderstorm was forming right before our eyes, and as it formed, I realized it was moving in our direction! We could hear the ominous rumble of thunder as the storm became energized. Then off in the distance, I saw the first down strike.

It kept coming right at us and increasing in power. We were all interested now, especially as there was no place to hide. There were no trees, and we felt completely exposed on top of the ridge to this approaching fury from the heavens.

As the storm drifted closer along the ridge, I noticed there was a down strike on every spur ridge it came to. When it was three ridges away: Boom! A down strike on top of the ridge. Then, a few minutes later: Boom! Another down strike two ridges away. Only a few minutes later: Boom! A crashing down strike on the next ridge over, where we had been earlier. Now the clouds were towering ominously overhead. Some rain began to spit down on us.

"Oh man, it's coming right at us; we're next!" I cried out in anguish. I looked around desperately, but there was no place to go. Should we make a mad dash for the bottom of the ravine? Being up and exposed like that might draw the lightning to us. But here there was nothing: not a hole to crawl into or rocks big enough to crawl under. Just the stubby brush, dirt, and slab rock on top of the ridge. I felt like a paratrooper caught in an enemy spotlight, floating helplessly, waiting for the machine gun bullets to find him.

For a breathless moment, as the dark clouds drifted over us, we waited. Then the gloom was broken by a blinding flash with a simultaneous crash of thunder. The down strike hit the rocks about fifty yards away, right where I had first been hunkering! After that one shot and a sprinkling of rain, the clouds drifted on toward the next ridge.

"Wow," I thought, "when I decided to move over here, I had no idea it might be a life-or-death decision." Once more disaster was averted and my life spared by circumstances beyond my control. Maybe Mike was right; maybe I needed God more than I thought.

NEW LIFE AROUND THE BARRACKS

I got to spend a lot of time with Mike in our little alcove in the far corner of the barracks. He told me the story of how he got saved, how last year he'd been working for the Forest Service all winter, living in a barracks with a lot of time on his hands. He'd been seeking the meaning of life: why was he here, and what was he supposed to be doing? Somehow, he got the idea that if he read the Bible all the way through, he would find the answer. So he started at the beginning in the book of Genesis, and was reading it every night.

One Friday night, he came to a verse in the Psalms that said, "In your presence is fullness of joy; in your right hand there are pleasures forever." Something about that verse clicked; suddenly he knew that Jesus was the answer to everything. With that revelation, he said he felt something like a vial of warm oil poured out on the inside of his body, flowing down and covering every part of him. Then he began speaking in a strange language he didn't understand that continued off and on all weekend. Shortly afterwards, in March, he was baptized in the Rogue River with snow on the ground.

After that, he joined a church in Gresham, Oregon, near Portland. One of the great things about his church was that every week, they sent him a cassette tape of the Sunday service: the worship and the message from his pastor, Jerry Cook.

I couldn't help but listen to his tapes every week. Having grown up in church myself, I was vaguely familiar with parts of the Bible, but this Jerry Cook could explain it so clearly. Most of his sermons revolved around "The Kingdom of God."

He spent several weeks on The Sermon on the Mount. His explanation of meekness—"Blessed are the meek, for they shall inherit the earth"—impressed even Lacey, who overheard the tape as Jerry explained that meekness was not wimp-iness, or weakness, but "strength under control." "Anybody can be meek if they are too weak to have another option," Jerry said." But true meekness is when you have the strength to be aggressive, but choose not to exercise it."

Lacey said he'd never heard it like that before. Jerry certainly made those old Bible passages come alive with new meaning!

I began to look forward to Mike's weekly tape, and always asked to listen with him, because he made so much sense.

NORTHERN OREGON NIGHT SHIFT

As the summer wore on, I was being drawn more and more into the orb of Mike Harris. The deciding factor was not his theology or his tapes or his arguments, though they all played a part. The bottom line was that in the deepest, most secret place of my heart, I recognized that Mike had something that neither I nor anyone else on the crew had, and that something was attractive. What he had was an inner peace and tranquility that pervaded everything he did. A genuine joy flowed out of that quietude, and behind the joy was a sincere love: for us, the Forest Service, and for his God, whom he believed was summed up in the person of Jesus Christ. Even more, he had faith: simple but unshakable convictions about right and wrong. All of these qualities I found attractive.

He wasn't defensive about the taunts and gibes of the crew. He usually met them with a good-natured comeback. Even those who didn't agree with him had to respect him.

I compared him to the other two on the crew who had religion: Doc and Dale Alter. Which of the three did I want to follow? Doc was defensive about his Mormon beliefs and lacked that inner peace. He still needed the approval and acceptance of the rest of the crew, while Mike rested secure in the acceptance of his God. Doc was a cleaned-up version of the rest of the crew. He didn't drink, swear, or chew, but he could be offended easily; he could be argumentative, and he definitely was hot-tempered.

Dale, on the other hand, was only rumored to be a Christian. Some said that he and his wife attended a small, off-brand church in Prospect. He was certainly straight-arrow enough, but it seemed to be strictly a private matter with him, nothing that he desired to communicate with anyone else. If the claims of Christ were true, shouldn't His followers be out telling others?

As I watched Mike's life over the course of the summer, I gradually came to the conclusion that this guy genuinely *had* something, and whatever it was, I wanted it. Out of all the people I'd observed in the Forest Service and at college, I'd finally found the one who had what I was subconsciously looking for! It was not a matter of personality, which I couldn't alter, or upbringing, which I couldn't change, or even how he lived his life, which I could have copied on my own. Mike was truly different inside. He had an inner serenity and a pure love that couldn't be faked.

So, while I never came right out and told him, "I want what you have!" I did allow myself to be drawn in and seek it for myself. As he had sought and found it so gloriously last winter, so I too began to seek—tentatively at first, but seek nonetheless.

We talked a lot about what it meant to be a Christian and follow Christ. He showed me different scriptures on discipleship and giving up all to follow Him. He talked about dying to self, giving up my own life—my wants, my plans, my ambitions—and giving myself completely to Christ. In this process, he said, the old self actually dies in a spiritual sense, and a new self is formed in its place—the new birth. This new birth is actually Jesus coming in to live His life through us, like a verse he shared: "Therefore, if anyone is in Christ, he is a new creation; the old has gone, the new has come!" (2 Corinthians 5:17, NIV).

We also talked about the Holy Spirit—that as Christ comes to live inside us, it's in the person of the Holy Spirit, who teaches and leads the believer.

About this time, I felt the need to buy a Bible for myself. All summer I'd been listening to the messages and trying to follow along in Mike's Bible, but I really needed my own Bible, not only for the messages, but to read and study. After all, the Bible had played such an important part in Mike's finding God.

There were no Bibles around Union Creek or Prospect. I would have to go to Medford. So when a rare day off came, I decided to pick one up. Mike prayed with me that the Lord would guide me by His Holy Spirit, and as I drove down the hill toward Medford, I got a mental picture of myself driving into town on the main street. When I got near the heart of town, I would turn left on a side street. About halfway down the first block would be a store on the left side of the street where I could buy a Bible.

I believed so much in the concept of being led by the Spirit that I resolved to do just that: to follow this mental picture or "vision" just the way it had been shown me. So I drove into Medford on the main street and continued down to where I felt this mental picture had indicated. "This has to be the street to turn on," I thought. I turned left and parked along the right curb. Then, wanting to be led completely by faith and the Holy Spirit, I didn't even look at any of the store signs across the street. I was determined to go as close as I could to the very spot, guided only by the vision. So I crossed the street, went about half a block down the other side, came to a store and stopped. "Ha, this must be the place," I thought and looked up at the sign.

I expected to see a sign for a Bible bookstore or something. Instead, the sign read "Woolworth's." I felt a tinge of disappointment, but determined to carry through. I went in, looked around, and asked a sales clerk hesitantly if they sold any Bibles.

"We sure do!" she boomed, "Right over there; we have a whole section of them."

There they were, right next to the greeting cards. My spirit soared; it had worked! I had been led through prayer and the Holy Spirit!

I was so excited that I bought three Bibles: a hardcover one like Mike had; another version in paperback; and a pocket New Testament to carry with me on fires. On my return, Mike shared in my excitement about my purchases. Now I could follow along in my own Bible.

It wasn't long until the fire call came again, to Northern Oregon. There was a fire in the rugged mountains right above town. We left immediately, arriving late in the afternoon. They put us on night shift to guard the line.

Night shift is no fun because your biological clock is all fouled up, and you're usually passively guarding line or watching something burn out. You have to fight to stay awake.

Another reason night shifts are no fun: the next day they let us bed down in a nice grassy park in town with plenty of shade. But the weather was so hot that by 10:30 in the morning it was already over ninety, too hot to sleep even in the shade! We were tired but unable to sleep, cross and cranky in the miserable heat.

"Hey, this might be a good opportunity to read my pocket New Testament," I thought. I started reading in the gospel of Luke. I read the whole gospel, but it left me slightly uneasy, I'm not sure why. I just thought Luke to be rather cold.

Then I decided to read the book of Revelation, the last book in the Bible. This was the one I had heard so much about in Hal Lindsey's book, *The Late Great Planet Earth.* "I'm looking forward to this," I thought. But the book overwhelmed me with its depiction of strange, mythical creatures, global wars, cataclysmic events and terrible, earth-wide destruction. "Boy," I told Mike, "there's a lot more to this religion stuff than I bargained for."

On the last day of the fire, as we were leaving, somebody handed me a newspaper with a headline announcing that Richard Nixon had just resigned as president. It was August 8, 1974.

MAKING CHOICES

All summer, I found myself making mental comparisons between the life of the other members of the crew and this strange new life being modeled by Mike Harris. One thing that especially highlighted this difference was the "crew party." We would go out and get some kegs of beer, set up a barbecue and a stereo on the lawn, invite girls and lady friends, and then party hearty.

JOHN LACEY AT A "CREW PARTY"

Since Mike lived in the barracks and was part of the crew, he didn't avoid these parties. He would drink some sodas, eat the food, mingle with the crowd, tell old fire stories on Lacey, and generally have a good time while everyone else was getting wasted.

When the next morning rolled around, he would be up early, cheerful as usual, ready for the next day. Sometimes he would get up even earlier, go out in the woods and pray. But the rest of the crew would be hurting. The misery of the hangover can be quite complete, usually in direct proportion to the craziness of the night before. It occurred to me that Mike's way was definitely better. He seemed to have as much fun at the parties—eating and drinking, talking and laughing—but also avoided the suffering the rest of the crew experienced the following morning.

Then I found another area of comparison. After coming back from a fire, we would have a slack day of standby at the barracks to wash clothes, rest, and retool for the next one. I got into the habit of spending these afternoons with Mike in our alcove, listening to the latest tape from East Hill, reading from my own Bibles, and discussing these things with Mike. These had become enjoyable times to me, pleasant islands of stimulating fellowship.

But there was another way to spend time on those slack days. Emerson would come over and invite me to go into the woods behind the barracks with him and Hubby and "smoke some weed." We'd meet, get stoned, and talk about life from that perspective.

Most of the crew was straight and didn't do drugs, except for us and the "inner city affirmative-action" guys. So whether it was with Mike discussing religion or with Emerson smoking grass, in both cases, I was coming apart from the normal life of the crew into another world, a special world that only the initiated could share.

I noticed that while I was with Mike and partaking of his Christian world, I had a consistently good time. On the other hand, with Emerson, while I still enjoyed being stoned, there was little comparison with what it used to be. And then that old nemesis paranoia would come and rob me of the little enjoyment it still offered.

One time in particular I remember going right from having a good time with Mike in the barracks discussing the things of God, to smoking dope behind the barracks with Frank. The difference was so stark, I thought, "Why am I doing this? Why do I keep leaving something that brings me joy to do something that makes me fearful?"

After the next fire I was lying on my bunk having another good time with Mike and his tapes. God seemed so real and loving and good. Then I heard a scratching at the window. It was Emerson scratching on the screen. "Hey Hobbs, ya wanna go out and...?" His face told me all I needed to know.

I was about to automatically follow him when I stopped and remembered the trade he was asking me to make. I somehow knew those two worlds were incompatible: I couldn't take this world with me behind the barracks, smoke pot, and discuss the things of God. Nor could I get stoned out there and come back in and fellowship with Mike around the things of God. No, it was one world or the other. Emerson was asking me to trade Mike's world for his. "But why leave this world where I'm having such a warm time of fellowship, and go out with him to the cold uneasiness of being stoned?" I thought.

Suddenly, it all became very clear. I *didn't* have to. There was no reason in the world I had to. I could choose to keep this world instead. Amazed at the simplicity of it, a little unsure that it could really be so easy, I smiled at Frank and said, "No thanks. I think I'll stay here." Frank shrugged and left, and my good time continued unabated.

Later, I was lying on my bunk thinking about this. I had

sprained my ankle playing volleyball, and the crew had left on a work detail. I realized I had to make this choice permanent, anything less could allow the negative influence of the drugs to come seeping back into my life. After all, I'd quit marijuana once for several years and then gone back to it. In a burst of resolve, I made up my mind to get rid of the stuff forever! It seemed like such a bold stroke.

But what should I do with the stash of weed in my locker? At first I thought, "I'll just sell it, or maybe give it back to Emerson." But if it really was so bad, then that would be shifting its evil influence to another person. I couldn't do that. Looking back, I'm amazed at how quickly morals and conscience had sprung up in my life! No, the only morally clean thing to do would be to throw it away. But where to throw it? If I poured it out on the forest floor, what if some of the seeds happened to sprout and grow new plants? This was getting harder than I thought. Then a thought occurred to me. They had just ripped up the lawn between the barracks and the cookhouse, prior to reseeding it. "I'll dump the stuff there and scatter it over the dirt," I thought. "Even if they did sprout, none of the seeds could ever amount to anything, because they mow the grass and keep it short." So I hobbled out to the door with baggie in hand and scattered it to the wind over the old lawn. It was an irrevocable step. I never used drugs again.

EMERSON, THE AUTHOR, HUBBY AND DECKER AT THE LOG PILE

THE BIG ONE

About the middle of August, we were called to central Idaho. The fire was near the top of a range of mountains. The fire camp was at a ranger station down the hill, with the kitchen set up across the road in a beginner's ski area.

We were sent up near the top on the first day to put line around some smoldering spot fires across the road that passed the ranger station. Because of the elevation, there was a lot of grass and only scattered clumps of trees.

You would think that this open terrain would make the job of building fire line easy, but the grass came with a tough sod that required great effort to break up.

Though the elevation was high and the air cool, the sun was hot and the soil was dry and dusty. Soon, we were covered with dirt and sweat. It was a lot of work for what seemed like little accomplishment.

The next day, we were sent below the fire to dig a line along its bottom. This time, we couldn't see the fire at all, but it was supposed to be somewhere above us. We were to dig a fire line straight across the slope. This meant it all had to be trenched to protect against burning, rolling material. There was no fire to get us pumped up, and the end of the dig was so far away, we didn't even know where it was. It was just us, our tools, and the Idaho mountainside.

The soil was soft and digging was easy. But our problem was the endless roots from the trees. Each one had to be cut out so we could take our trench through. Often one of us in the hoe section would have to call a pulaski back to handle roots that were too big even for our sharpened hoes to cut through.

The hours slowly ticked off as the sweat ran down and turned the covering dust into mud. The sun climbed in the sky. The drinking water in my canteen assumed body temperature, making me almost gag to drink it. Tempers got short as fatigue set in. The temptation was to leave too much for the next guy and just shuffle on. So those at the end of each section were always snarling, "Bump back! Bump back! You're leaving too much!"

But Lacey was our savior! Ever the champion of crew spirit and "gutting it out," Lacey seized the day. This was the ultimate opportunity to "pit up." He grabbed a hoe, slung his radio behind his back, stuck a big chew of Copenhagen in his mouth, and started swinging away. Seeing Lacey in his glory was an inspiration to all of us. Lacey lived for such occasions. It was a rare day of total victory for him when the sweat line on his shirt from his right "pit" and the sweat line from his left "pit" met in the middle of his chest. Then he was "totally pitted up."

At last, late in the afternoon, we reached the end. There was still no sign of the fire, but we tied in to an old logging road that marked the end. Then we turned around and retraced the line we had dug, tired but triumphant. Somebody paced it off on the way out—over a mile of under-slung line dug that day! The greatest line-digging day in the two years I was on the crew.

That evening, after eating supper, we went back to our camping area and lounged on our sleeping bags, savoring a few moments of rest before night fell.

Then one of the fire overhead personnel came up and started talking to Dale. He said the wind had come up at the higher elevations and was fanning the fire, especially on top of the mountain. The fire had jumped the line one place in particular and was heading into new ground. They were asking us to pull a double shift and go up there and stop it.

We were all tired and really looking forward to crawling into our sleeping bags. But this was our job. So there we were, some grumbling, some pumped up for glory, and some just resigned: all heading up the hill again in the fading daylight in the back of a National Guard troop truck, feeling the chill in the air now that the sun was down.

The scene that greeted us at the top of the mountain was wild pandemonium. The wind was howling over the ridge and the fire was being fanned as if by a giant bellows. Every bit of fire was burning with incredible intensity. The noise level from the wind, the fire, the chainsaws, and people shouting was deafening. The only way you could communicate was by screaming at the top of your voice. There were a handful of Forest Service people already there with pickups and chainsaws, but their frantic activity was accomplishing nothing. They were trying to build a new line through a brush patch, but the line was only half built and the wind-whipped flames were already upon them.

After quickly scouting the situation, Dale had most of us drop back and start building a line through a stand of young fir trees beyond the brush patch. There was not much undergrowth there, just a light carpet of pine needles, so building the line would be easy. Yes, building it would be easy, but holding it...? He sent the sawyers ahead to where the forest began, to start cutting the trees and brush for our line when we got there. He sent others into the thicket beyond our line to scout for spot fires from the sparks that were continually blowing over our heads.

From the very start, it was a valiant but losing effort. Even as we were getting our line built through the young fir trees, spot fires were springing up around us. Each spot fire, when it flared up, had the same wind-fanned intensity of the main fire. We didn't have the manpower to stop building line and fight these spot fires that were constantly springing up. Instead, we relocated the fire line beyond them, to get them back inside the line. Thus we were continually being driven back.

Then a hair-raising thing happened—a spot fire started up *in* one of the fir trees about twenty feet off the ground! I had never seen this happen before—a green tree, with no fire under it to dry the branches, starting to burn from one spark and continuing to burn with no help from any other source. Green trees aren't supposed to burn like that! But this one sure was burning, and high enough that we couldn't reach it with anything to put it out.

We had to call a saw-guy back to cut the whole tree down. But as the tree was falling, the wind fanned the fire into a roaring conflagration. By the time it hit the ground, there was no question of putting it out—half the tree was going up in flames! So again, we had to fall back and reroute our line beyond the tree.

"This is not working," I thought. "The fire is going to keep pushing us back. There's no way we can stop it." Still, gamely, we pressed on.

Things were getting strung out. People were spread thin all up and down the line. Each one had some crisis to deal with. Some were shouting one thing; others were shouting another. Our order and cohesiveness was breaking down under the noise, the confusion, and the rapidity with which things were happening.

Again, the fire spotted in the top of a tree. Again, we had to call a sawyer back. Again, the tree, as it fell, exploded into flames. Again, we had to relocate the line around it.

Then suddenly, unexpectedly, the whole situation changed. The fire stopped threatening the line, and stopped spotting over the line. We tied in our newest line to the old line, burned it out, and it was over—"The Battle of the Bulge" was won!

The crew started celebrating like crazy. "We did it! We did it!" they screamed. If we had had guns we would have been firing them into the air. People were shouting, laughing, and hugging each other. "We're the best in the west! We're the greatest! Etc.

But I wasn't celebrating. I was puzzled. What had *really* happened? *We* hadn't stopped the fire; we *couldn't* stop the fire. We'd been working up here like crazy for hours without making any progress toward stopping the fire. The fire was unstoppable.

Then what *had* stopped the fire?

As I was pondering this question, I heard how Mike Harris had almost been killed by a falling tree. In the noise and confusion, he walked right under a tree cut by the other saw team. It had hit him on the head, on the back of his hard hat, right on the saying, "I Belong to Jesus," the whole back of the hat was smashed in. Undoubtedly the hard hat had saved his life.

The next day, after the emotional frenzy had passed, I found Mike alone and asked him, "What happened up there last night to stop the fire?" I narrowed my eyes and looked at him suspiciously, "You didn't say a prayer up there or something did you?"

And Mike told me this story. "Dave, you know, last night... well for awhile I hadn't felt the presence of the Jesus. It's like I've been walking afar off. Spiritually things have been dry. When that tree hit me, it knocked me to the ground unconscious. As I was lying there dazed, all of a sudden I felt the Lord's presence very close again, just like before.

"Sensing His love and closeness I began to pray, 'Lord, we can't stop this fire; you know we can't. It's too much for us Lord. I pray you would stop the wind that's pushing it and keeping us from controlling it.' Within a minute, Dave, the howling wind died down completely. Then it started blowing gently back the other way."

"Wow, that's it!" I exclaimed. I hadn't noticed the wind dying down. That's why I couldn't figure out why the fire stopped. "You prayed, Jesus stopped the wind and the fire quit."

I was utterly in awe. I had just seen a miracle with my own eyes. I had seen the Almighty Eternal God intervene in time and space in our own world in response to prayer.

That incident on the hill that night revolutionized my concept of God. Through drugs I had come in touch with the spiritual realm enough to believe there must be some kind of God. Then there was that time when I'd secretly cried out to God in prayer over Suzanne, and the situation had improved. But I still had only the fuzziest concept of who God was.

Now my faith took a major leap forward. I had just seen that He was a personal God who could get actively involved in His creation. He was not some God afar off, impersonal and unattached. Rather He was loving and caring, powerful enough and willing to get involved in our world, right here, right now.

After being on the fire for four days, soaked with sweat, and covered with dirt and grime, we were a mess. By this time we were mopping up, with powdery ashes and soot being added to the layers of filth. We were raunchy and stunk to high heaven.

That evening, after supper, I entered an outhouse by the eating area. I was sitting inside, taking care of business and pondering these things. But I stunk so bad and felt so grodie it was hard to stand myself. It seemed the Lord could only be glorified by my getting clean. I wasn't about to embrace that pseudo-scripture "cleanliness is next to godliness," but God Himself was holy, after all, and that was the ultimate clean. Everything about Him was pure, and we were called to be His children. Emboldened by these thoughts and by the powerful answer to prayer I had just seen up on the mountain, right then and there I prayed, "Lord, please provide some way for us to get clean out here."

Someone from the crew must have seen me go into the outhouse even though it was dark, because the words were hardly out of my mouth when one of the crew came by and banged on the door, "Hey Hobbs, guess what? They just set up some portable showers below the kitchen in that grove of trees. See you down there, man."

Portable showers? Here on this fire? Portable showers were very rare. In all my eight seasons of fire fighting, there was only one other time that they were available and that was in Southern California. There hadn't been any mention of them on this fire, and I wasn't thinking about them. But out of my need and the conviction that it would be pleasing to God, I prayed, and the prayer was immediately answered.

God not only answered my prayer, but He must have known well in advance what I would be praying for, because the plan to set up the showers had to have been put in motion at least a day before. God had overseen all the arrangements and preparations so the moment I did pray and ask, the answer would be ready immediately. "Wow!" I thought, "This is tectonic plate-movin' stuff!"

I shouted out a "Thank you Jesus!" hurried back to our camp, grabbed some clean clothes and rushed down to the glen. There was a shower tent with a huge kerosene unit to heat the water as it was being used. I jumped in and started luxuriating in the steamy water. A shower never felt so good!

The high wind that caused such problems on top of the mountain a few days before, signaled a change in the weather. Though it stayed dry, each day got colder and colder. The morning after my hot shower, when we showed up to eat breakfast, there was ice on the tables. They had hosed them down before breakfast and the water on the tabletops had frozen into solid ice. Needless to say, it wasn't an enjoyable way to eat breakfast. Once the sun came up though, it warmed quickly.

That day we were kept in camp instead of being sent out to the line. The fire was in the mop-up stage and the danger was past. After going to the plans tent and talking with the overhead people,

Dale came back and called us together.

"They've given us a choice," he said. "We can stay here on mop-up and be guaranteed twelve working hours per day, plus hazardous duty pay until the fire is declared controlled. Or we can be released. In that case, we might go home, or we might get sent to another fire with some more action. What do you want to do?"

Well, as usual, nobody could agree. Some shouted one thing; some shouted another. Different factions arose trying to win supporters. After many opinions, with no agreement in sight, Mike said to me, "Why don't we go off and pray about it."

So he and I and a fellow we called "the Indian" went back into the brush and hunkered down under a small tree. There we prayed, taking as our basis the scripture that says, "Where two or three are gathered together in my [Christ's] name, there am I in the midst of them" (Matt. 18:20), and, "if two of you shall agree on earth as touching anything that they shall ask, it shall be done for them of my Father which is in heaven" (Matt. 18:19).

We laid the problem out before the Lord, confessed that He knew all things and must know which one would be best for us. Then we simply asked Him to work it out.

We had barely finished praying when a mighty shout rose from our camp. We hurried back and inquired what it meant "We're going home!" they said. "They've just released us!"

CHANGES WITHIN AND WITHOUT

After that fire in Idaho, I was a different person. I couldn't deny the things that had happened to me. I had seen them with my own eyes. I now had some of the most precious knowledge that anyone can possess: first hand, experiential knowledge of God. I had seen His hand move three times in answer to prayer: once reversing the wind and stopping the fire in response to Mike's prayer; once with miraculous provision of a shower in response to my prayer; and once with perfect timing working out our release in response to the three of us praying together.

Unknowingly, I had passed the point of no return, but I hadn't made the final commitment yet. The baby had left the womb and was headed down the birth canal, but it hadn't yet cleared the opening into the world.

In response to issues raised on Jerry Cook's tapes, Mike showed me chapters six and ten in Hebrews, where it talks about the possibility of being born again and then turning back. I hadn't made that final commitment yet, though I was seriously considering it. What the Bible was saying was, "Be sure you really mean it when you do it, otherwise you'd be better off not doing it at all."

I considered these things deeply. I really wanted what Mike had, and I had a growing excitement for the possibilities of a relationship with this awesome God. The downside was dying to self. From that moment on, I would be living for Christ: "I am crucified with Christ; nevertheless I live; yet not I, but Christ liveth in me" (Gal. 2:20 KJV). Christ would be calling the shots in my life. He would determine my career: where I would live, who I would marry, or even *if* I would marry! But then, maybe that wasn't so bad. I didn't exactly have a stellar track record in that department! Who could make a better choice for me in these areas than the One who knew me better than I knew myself. God, after all, was the perfect Father. Wouldn't He always want what was best for me?

I remember once standing in the barrack's bathroom looking at myself in the mirror, saying, "Hobbs, I think you're ready to die!"

And then there was the issue of sex. Mike said he hadn't had sex since March when he was saved. That was five whole months! With regard to sex, I believed in the maxim, "Use it or lose it." So this could either be a great stumbling block, or an opportunity for great faith. In this difficult area, I had both the example of Mike who seemed to be doing just fine, and his encouragement: "Yes it can be done; it's not even that bad."

All this time, I was changing. I was seeing things more from a spiritual perspective, and I was now better able to sense the presence of the Spirit of God. When we talked about the things of God or prayed together... well it was just like Jesus said, "Wherever two or three are gathered together in my name, there am I in their midst." I could actually *feel* Jesus' presence—not see or hear Him, but definitely sense Him. After being in His presence for awhile, the spirit of the average crew member—which I had been like until a short time before—seemed so crude, coarse, and out-of-whack by comparison.

I remember one time in particular. It was evening, and we were home at the barracks. Some had gone to town, some were outside, and some were in the other barracks next door. Mike and I were the only ones in our building. We were sharing some precious things about God, and His presence was there with us in a warm and loving way. We might have been talking about Jesus loving us so much that even if He knew we were the only ones who would ever accept his sacrifice, He would still have come down from heaven and died on the cross—just for us! It was one of those moments so special we didn't want it to end.

Then, right in the middle of it, we heard the back door open and the clomping boots of someone coming in. Suddenly the thought of the spirit of the crew intruding upon us seemed so awkward and out of place that I think both of us cringed and held our breath, bracing for the usual stream of profanity or a loud belch or some other vulgarity to break the spell. But then, while still out in the bathroom area, the boots stopped. I know there's no way to prove this, but in my spirit, I sensed an angel standing between that crewman and the inner door to the bunkroom, preventing his entry. There was a long pause, absolute silence. Then there was another muffled rumble of boots on the floor and the screen door made a quiet slam—he had left! And we returned to sharing Christ again.

I was out playing volleyball one afternoon. Normally my language was as bad as any. If I missed a shot or hit one out-of-bounds I'd cry out "Jesus Christ!" in utter disgust. Or I'd "god-damn" this or "god-damn" that or shout out "s_t!" all to the crew's approval. But this afternoon, for the first time I was actually hearing myself say these things, and I was shocked! They were no longer empty expressions of disgust. I knew who Jesus Christ was now--His goodness, His love and His character. How could I use His name as an epithet of anger and contempt?

I was being drawn to Mike's God. I was reading the Bible, listening to tapes, praying with Mike, and praying some on my own. Changes in my outer behavior were happening along the way. But I wasn't even looking for that. I was looking for the Living God and a supernatural life in Him. These other changes—the cleaned up life—seemed to come with the territory.

MAKING THE ANGELS REJOICE

It was a still, warm, late-August evening. The crew was at the barracks and things were quiet. "Let's go out and pray together," Mike said. Pat, another crewmember, came with us. Pat was another one of the hoes, a young man, who was also being drawn to Christ. We went out behind the barracks to the "log pile," a jumble of short, thick, cull logs that had been piled together to be burned. In the past, I had gone there to smoke dope with Hubby and Emerson. Now we were going to seek a different spirit.

We each found a log to sit on in a rough circle and began to pray together. The sun had gone down but it was not yet dark. It was balmy and peaceful, without a breath of wind stirring—an absolutely beautiful, late summer's evening.

Mike prayed first. After praying in general for awhile, praising the Lord for His goodness and thanking Him for His mercy and how He had brought Mike to the crew that summer and blessed his witness, Mike changed gears and began to pray about me. He thanked the Lord for me and for bringing us together in friendship for the summer. He thanked the Lord for the opportunity to share with me, and for how receptive I was to the words of Christ.

Then he took a slightly different tact, lifting me up, commending me to God. He said something like, "Lord I just want to offer David up to you now. He's heard your words and responded to you, and he's come to understand what it means to give himself to you and live his life for you. Lord, I think he's ready to totally commit himself to you for now and eternity, to surrender his will to you completely and allow you to come and live inside him...."

As I was listening to him pray, especially the part about the total commitment, I was thinking, "Yes, I guess that's right, that's basically true." I thought he was going a little overboard in this total commitment and complete-surrender-forevermore stuff, yet I was agreeing with the gist of his words in my heart. I had no idea anyone would or could be listening in to my thoughts; I had no idea that a verbal contract was being made and that I was signing on to it.

But tentative though my assent may have been, as soon as I agreed in my heart to his words, something strange started happening inside me. The best I can describe it is to relate it to a roller coaster I rode once at an amusement park. At the beginning of the ride, our car was slowly pulled up the first, biggest hill at a stunningly steep angle. We were pressed back against our seats while the roller coaster's big diesel engine kept pulling us higher and higher on a ratcheted chain, a click at a time.

That was what I was now experiencing spiritually. Something was pulling me higher and higher in the spirit, at a stunningly steep angle, a click at a time. I didn't know what it was or where it was taking me. Higher and higher I went, so high I was frozen inside my "car," afraid to look down. I wondered if this Power would pull me right into heaven itself!

I finally got so high, I freaked out—I had a rush of fear—and the Power stopped and let me go. Instantly, I was released in the spirit, higher than I'd ever been on drugs, higher than I'd ever been before. In this rush that started with fear but ended with wonder I felt my body freaking out. My heart was pounding ninety miles an hour and inside me it felt like a hurricane was blowing.

Outside, meanwhile, not a leaf was moving, not a breath of air was stirring, not a thing was happening, except Mike might still have been praying. In a moment of profound revelation I realized, "God has completely turned my world upside down, but He's done it from the inside. He doesn't have to use nature or the external world to reach me. He is in a whole different dimension, able to see and minister directly into my most hidden, inner self. "

That was how God revealed Himself to me. I understood His transcendence, that He was the Creator, outside of and in total control of His creation. In that moment, I knew there was a God, I knew I had just encountered Him, and I knew that this God of power deserved my total service and devotion all the days of my life—not because I had seen His glory in the heavens, or heard the thunder of His majestic voice, but because I sensed His absolute power and control in the innermost part of my being.

It was the most profound experience of my life that forever altered the course of my existence. The dedication of my life to this God followed as naturally as heat follows the sun.

I had known deeply moving experiences before, especially with music, where on occasion music stirred me to the very depths of my soul, causing me to "dedicate myself to music." Those experiences had faded with time, and the "dedication of my life to music" no longer held any meaning.

Music, after all, is not personal. To truly give yourself to something, it has to be personal; it has to have the capability of receiving your offering and responding back to you. But when I encountered the Living God and dedicated my life to Him, He saw and heard; He received the offering of my life. From that moment on, He was with me. I was never alone again.

I don't remember a lot after that. I was on cloud nine. I told Mike that I had met God and had been born again.

That night in our bunks with the lights out, I was still aglow, filled with love and good feelings. I felt like I was lying in the arms of Jesus. I remembered what Jesus had said, that when one soul repents on earth, all the angels rejoice in heaven. It was as if I could sense that happening right now—I was feeling the far-off joy of the angels. "Hey Mike," I whispered, "Are you still awake?"

"Yeah," he whispered back.

'I think the angels are rejoicing in heaven."

"I'm sure they are."

A HARD HEART AND THE KINGDOM OF GOD

For a day or two I was in heaven. Then one morning I woke up and the good feelings were gone. I wanted to love the Lord as I had been doing, but my heart felt strangely unresponsive. "What's wrong?" I wondered, and took it to the Lord in prayer. He showed me a mental picture of my heart. It was hard as stone. The understanding He imparted to me, if I can verbalize it, was: "Over your lifetime your heart has become hardened like stone, so you can't love Me as you'd like." His antidote: "Let My Spirit gradually drip upon your heart, and as water wears away even stone, so my Spirit will wear down and dissolve the hardness of your heart."

The next Sunday, Mike got the idea of going down and attending a church service in Medford—he hadn't been to one all summer. We left as soon as work was over, not even waiting to eat so we could get there on time. It was the first church service I'd been to since being saved, and only the second "Jesus" kind of church service I'd ever attended. It was a small nondenominational church with mostly young married people in it. During the worship service, I saw other people raising their hands in worship. I'd seen people do this in Jim Durkin's church too, but had never thought of trying it myself. I wanted to, but felt so self-conscious. Finally, glancing furtively around and seeing no one paying any attention, I took a step of faith and raised my hands tentatively in worship to God. It was a little weak, but I was glad I had done it.

After the service, Mike and I went out to a Mexican restaurant for dinner. We splurged and had a couple of beers with dinner and talked about the church service and the Lord.

Afterward, Mike drove us back to the barracks. It was after 9:00 p.m., but we passed the time in warm and animated discussion about the kingdom of God.

As we were driving along, a quiet, subtle change happened to me that was so different from the mighty wind howling through me when I got saved. It was like being stoned; but there was no paranoia; there was no craving for food. It was a pure high that changed my outlook on everything. I was no longer outside looking in. I was inside looking out. "Mike," I said, "Mike, I ... I ... I think I'm in the

Kingdom of God."

Whereas being saved was a powerful, one time experience, this was an ongoing experience, a continual high. From that time on, my head was no longer in the same place. I saw things differently; I thought differently; I reacted differently. Before, I had been *in* the world and *of* the world, now I was still *in* the world, but I was no longer of the world.

The Bible—which at one time confounded me, and then lately had started making more sense—now fairly jumped out at me. I could understand exactly what Jesus was talking about: "The wind blows where it wishes, and you hear the sound of it, but cannot tell where it comes from or where it goes. So is everyone who is born of the Spirit" (John 3:8 NKJV). It meant the others on the crew could see some of the external evidence of what had happened to me, but they could never see the spiritual reality that had happened inside me, just as we are unable to see the wind or understand where it comes from or where it is going.

I don't remember much about how the rest of the crew reacted to my accepting Christ and following in Mike's footsteps. They had probably seen it coming. It probably made some nervous, while others may have been secretly encouraged that maybe there was truth to it after all; maybe there was hope even for them. But outwardly, they all had to deplore losing "another good man" to religion. But if I had any regrets over losing respect from the crew over my decision to follow Christ, it dissolved instantly when I found this incredible scripture that practically flew off the page concerning me and the crew.

> **For you [David Hobbs] have spent enough time in the past doing what pagans choose to do—living in debauchery, lust, drunkenness, orgies, carousing and detestable idolatry. They [the crew] think it strange that you do not plunge with them into the same flood of dissipation, and they heap abuse on you. But they will have to give account to him who is ready to judge the living and the dead. (1 Peter 4:3-5 NIV)**

A WIDE OPEN FUTURE

Then we were back in the fire business again. This time, it was up to southern Washington State.

Everything was new for me. Even the world looked wonderful and new. Riding through the rolling terrain in a bus returning to the airport from the fire, even the grassy hills looked incredibly beautiful and majestic. Like the verse said:

> **Therefore, if any man be in a Christ, he is a new creature: old things are passed away; behold, *all* things are become new. (1 Cor. 5:17, KJV, emphasis mine)**

Even though it was only the first of September, already the change of seasons was at hand. Leaves were turning yellow and there was a certain autumn crispness in the air. "Looks like it might be an early fall," people said.

We entered into September and the weather turned cold and blustery. It looked like the fire season was over.

Though the crew was supposed to last until September 15, hanging around that long would be like beating a dead horse. Dale said it was all right if I left early. Others too were anxious to go, so there was a general "move towards the door."

It was hard to leave Mike. It looked like I might be the only immediate fruit of his labors in the Gospel that summer, though we still had high hopes for Pat, and for the other seeds that had been planted in people's lives.

But in looking back over the summer, I realized that God had sent Mike to the crew this year more than anything else for one person—me! I was the one he had come in and bunked beside. I, more than anyone else, was the one he had poured his heart out to all summer; and I was the one who had most fully accepted his message. I was leaving changed and on fire for God.

PAT (L), MIKE HARRIS (CF) AND THE AUTHOR (R) AT THE LOG PILE

"You know," Mike said to me, "after I got saved in March, I had already been accepted by the hot-shot crew. But I had a hard time deciding if I should still come down here. I knew what the crew would be like—the bad language, the drinking, and the wild lifestyle. I prayed about it, and felt God say to me, 'Go, I have fruit for you in that place.'"

The thought that God cared about me so much to send Mike up there to endure the bad manners of the crew for the whole summer just to bring me into the Kingdom brought a lump to my throat. Especially as I remembered how coarse and rough I'd been, how I'd preached against God in high school, put a "God Is Dead" sign in my college dorm window, led others into drugs... my pride and haughtiness, always thinking I knew it all and was superior to everyone else... my immorality.... I was choked up thinking about a love that could overlook all that.

"What do you think? If a man has a hundred sheep, and one of them goes astray, does he not leave the ninety-nine and go to the mountains to seek the one that is straying? And if he should find it, assuredly I say to you, he rejoices more over that sheep than over the ninety-nine that did not go astray. Even so it is not the will of your Father who is in heaven that one of these little ones should perish." (Matt. 18:12-14 NKJV)

WHEN HE WAS ON THE CROSS
By Mike Payne

I'm not on an ego trip; I'm nothing on my own,
I make mistakes, I often slip, just common flesh and bones.
But I'll prove someday just what I say, that I'm of a special kind,
'Cause when He was on that cross, I was on His mind.

A look of love was on His face, the thorns upon his head.
The blood fell on that scarlet robe, and stained it crimson red.
Though His eyes were on the crowd that day,
He looked ahead in time.
When He was on that cross, I was on His mind.

He knew me, yet He loved me;
He whose glory made the heavens shine.
So unworthy of such mercy.
Yet when He was on that cross, I was on His mind.

EPILOGUE

By a series of God-ordained circumstances, I ended up in a Jesus people commune in the Marysville-Yuba City area of California—that turned out to be that "other Christian discipleship ranch" affiliated with Jim Durkin in Eureka (pg. 256). I lived communally for five years. During that time, the Lord brought a lot of inner healing into my life. I served the Lord for six years—as Jacob did for his wife—and watched almost all my friends get married and start families. Then, in the seventh year, God brought a pure and holy young woman into my life. Because each of us had put God first, He gave us a wonderful marriage that has produced three sons; just what I was always looking for, but never knew how to find.

The End

Appendix

MIKE HARRIS' STORY

I guess I should start at my mother's death, when I was six years old. Just before she died, she made my father promise that he would raise me in the church. At that point, my dad had never been to church and was living a lifestyle indicative of that. But when Mom died, he immediately started going to church and began taking me.

Church for me was not a positive experience. We attended a small Christian Church and we went through a pastor every year or two. Some pastors ran off with money, some I questioned their salvation... it was just a bad situation. By the time I went to college, I'd made up my mind that "if this is Christianity, I don't want anything to do with it."

So I went my own way for the next seven or eight years. This was back in the late 60s and early 70s, when "going your own way" meant you were in the hippie scene and all that went with it, including drugs. This was part of the whole process of trying to figure out who I was; trying to make sense of life while attempting to enjoy myself at the same time. But always this emptiness was inside, and somewhere deep within, the conviction that there was something better in life.

I graduated from Portland State College in December of 1971 and left right after Christmas to travel in Europe for six months. There was a guy from the fire crew—Bill Gitlin—who had gone to London a few months prior and was working in a pub. My plan was to meet Bill and travel with him. When I finally found him, he said, "Why don't you stick around? My girlfriend is coming and she's bringing another girl with her; maybe the four of us could travel together...."

I said, "Why not?"

When Kathy and her friend arrived about a week later—Surprise! Surprise! It was a girl that I'd had a blind date with four years earlier. She was from Medford, Oregon, and her name was Patti. We had experienced a terrible time on that blind date, hadn't had any contact since, and here we were meeting in London.

Patti and I got along better this time, so we ended up traveling together for about five months. When we returned from Europe, I again went my own way and got a job as a chemist for Coca Cola, which I hated. All this time I was still involved with the same old stuff and becoming emptier by the day, still dealing with a deep sense that there had to be more to life than what I was experiencing.

In the fall of 1973, I decided to quit my job with Coke. Just on a whim, I called the Forest Service in Steamboat Oregon—the place where I'd worked right out of high school for four summers. Usually the fall is when the summer help is laid off, so there's little chance of getting a job. But I called anyway and asked, "By chance is there a position open? I really want to get out of Portland and would love to come back and work in the woods."

The guy I knew there, who hires, said, "Well, Mike, not ten minutes ago, one of our timber cruisers quit. We were just talking about replacing him, and if you want the job, it's yours."

I gave my notice at Coke, and a week later I was down at Steamboat Ranger Station working for the Forest Service. The job lasted till April the following spring.

Now I had this thought: "If I read through the Bible, I'll know what it means to be a Christian." Where this thought came from, I have no idea—something I heard growing up that stuck, prayers of those who knew me, the Holy Spirit drawing me to Him: maybe all those things.

So I got my Bible out and started reading in Genesis. It was terrible—especially through Numbers, Leviticus, and Chronicles. Every night, I would struggle through these passages and I thought, "My goodness, this Christianity stuff is really boring."

Anyway, I worked in the woods and was still doing drugs, drinking a lot, and carousing around.... But at night, often in a stupor, I would get my Bible out and start reading where I'd left off the previous night.

I was on a Forest Service basketball team, and we traveled around playing other Forest Service districts. On March 2nd, we were in a tournament in Medford. While there, I decided to look up my old girlfriend Patti. I hadn't heard anything from her for probably a year and a half. When I went to her house, Patti was at the store, but her mom told me she should be back any minute.

I was sitting there reading a magazine when Patti came in the room. *Immediately* I noticed something had happened to this woman. I mean she was radiating! She had this huge smile, and you could feel her coming into the room before you could even see or hear her. I said, "Patti, what in the world happened to you?"

She began sharing how she'd had an experience with Christ and how He'd become real in her life. This was exactly what I wanted, so I asked her how she did it.

She said, "Well, I got to a point where I needed Him beyond all the things I was doing or wanting to do, and I asked Him and He was there."

I replied, "Well, I've been reading the Bible every night all winter and... it just hasn't worked for me."

She said, "Well, I'm going to be praying for you, because my experience is available to you too."

We had a basketball game that night and afterwards the guys went out and got all liquored up, but Patti's words continued to haunt me.

The following day, I saw Patti again and she said, "Why don't you come and stay at our house" (I was going to be in Medford for a couple more days and was staying in a hotel).

The first night at Patti's I remember lying in bed in her brother's bedroom reading my Bible. It had taken me since September, reading every night, but now I was finally in Psalms. As I was reading the 16th Psalm, I came upon the verse that says, "In his presence, there is fullness of joy; at his right hand there are pleasures forevermore."

Something really caught me on that verse, and I read it again and again, maybe ten times in a row. Each time, it became more personal and more real. Now this is going to sound far out, but to the best of my abilities I'll try to explain what happened. There came an incredible sense of a light in the room, and it was very pure... not a light that was brightness. It was a light that was pure—something other than what would come out of a light bulb. Suddenly I had an intense feeling of unworthiness. Then it felt like someone had taken hold of my insides and was wringing them out like an old wash cloth: wringing out everything. I had an unbelievable sense of emptiness. There was nothing inside me anymore. I was completely empty. I started crying, half out of fright and half out of this amazing feeling of emptiness. And then in the midst of my crying, the pure light that was in the room seemed to flow into me and fill me. At that exact moment, I knew without a shadow of doubt who Christ was. I knew that He was real, and I knew that I would live the rest of my life for Him.

I didn't sleep the rest of the night. I remember lying in bed making up sermons to tell my friends about this amazing reality that I had experienced in Christ.

The next morning Patti joined me for breakfast. I shared with her what had happened, and we cried together.

Now her brother, who was involved in a Christian ministry in Eugene, called Shiloh, was home to get some dental work done. I spent all morning talking with him and asking a lot of questions. Later that day, we went out to the Rogue River, and even though there was snow on the banks, we went out in the water and Mike Clark baptized me. My stint for the Forest Service at Steamboat ended a couple of weeks later.

For the past six summers—excluding the summer before when I worked for Coca-Cola—I had worked for the Rogue River Rough Riders: a [hotshot] crew based in Prospect, only fifty miles from Medford. That winter, I had reapplied and been accepted back for the upcoming summer of '74, starting in June. Until then, I moved back to Portland.

On my way to Portland, I stopped in my home town of Sutherlin and shared my born-again experience with my dad. It was an amazing experience. As soon as I walked in the door, he asked me what had happened. He could see the change in my face and my expression. I shared what had happened to me, and we cried together. I began to think that crying was something that Christians did quite often!

On my way to Portland, I met a missionary who was going to Africa. I ended up giving almost all my money to him. So I arrived in Portland nearly broke and got the cheapest apartment I could find. For the next two months, I lived in that little apartment, going for walks once in a while, but mostly just reading the Word every day and also books on Christian life.

In June, I went back to the Rough Riders. I had bought a 1955 Chrysler Windsor and filled the whole back window with Jesus stickers. I made it my mission to go back to the Rough Riders and convert all those guys to Christianity—those rough talking, rough living, drinking, chewing, spitting, fighting kind of guys whom I had been part of for the previous six years.

I came rolling up in my big Chrysler with all these Jesus stickers and hopped out, "Here I am guys, let me lead you to the Lord." Of course, people were very skeptical. I was laughed at and not taken seriously. It was just another trip Mike was on.

When I was in Portland, I'd made contact with East Hill Church. In fact, Easter, 1974, was the first time I attended East Hill and also the first time I'd been to church since I was a kid. Everything clicked. It was the right place for me to be.

I had arranged for tapes from East Hill's pastor Jerry Cook to be sent to me over the summer, and I would listen to them in my bunk. A couple of guys, including Dave Hobbs and Pat Young, would listen to these tapes with me on occasion. We'd talk, and over the course of the summer, Dave, Pat, and several other guys began spending more and more time around my bunk. I was even asked to pray at our meals over at the cook shack—I guess I became the token Christian of the group.

Even though Dave, Pat, and I talked a lot, for awhile not much happened. At first, I was very pushy with my Christianity. I'd had such an incredible experience myself that I thought, "Everyone needs to have this experience." My life had been changed completely, and I knew this same reality was there for anyone who asked for it. But then I thought back to all the times people had talked to me about Christianity and I was so turned off I wouldn't listen. The timing had to be just right for me.

So I cooled my jets for awhile. I began thinking it was more who I was and how I lived rather than what I said. For the next month or so, I just did my job and was one of the guys, but I didn't participate in the swearing, drunkenness, or carousing.

The summer went on. I can't remember many of the fires that year, but I do remember one particular fire in Idaho that happened toward the end of the season. We had been on the line all day long and had just gotten back to fire camp. As we prepared to eat dinner, the fire boss came in and told us that some big winds had come up on the sector on which we'd been working, and the line was in danger of being overrun. He asked if we would be willing to go back out again. After some grumbling, we got our gear together and went back to the fire line.

It was dark by then and the fire was raging up the side of the mountain. To stop it, we had to take out a whole section of small timber. Since the fire was crowning, the only way to stop it was to get the trees down quickly, before it got there. Four guys were working the saws. Jeff Leever and I were each falling trees and another two guys were bucking up the logs and rolling them out of the way. The rest of the crew was digging the fire line.

The only light was from the headlamps on our helmets. Jeff and I were dashing from one tree to another. I'd just cut one down and was running to the next when BOOM! Lights out. A tree that Jeff cut had landed on my head. I still have my hard hat that's all caved in at the back. So there I lay unconscious. I think some of the guys thought I was dead because the tree had struck me squarely on top of the head.

I remember coming to a little bit. I felt like an accordion that someone had squeezed tight: all my spine, vertebrae, and insides were compacted together. Then I felt that same amazing sense of God's presence: the same light and warmth I had experienced back in March. Suddenly I felt that accordion being stretched out again, and things popping back into place. I opened my eyes and stood up, to everyone's amazement, and a few minutes later, I was back to work again cutting the trees down.

A little while later, I prayed with several of the guys. We asked the Lord to stop the wind from blowing. Almost immediately, not only did the wind stop blowing up the ridge, but it began blowing gently back in the opposite direction. I don't think there was anyone on the crew that didn't get touched by the reality of a living God that night.

Shortly after the fire, Dave and Pat gave their hearts to Christ, and for the remaining days of the summer, we had a great time praying and talking together.

I'm sorry I can't remember too many of the details of that summer. But I do remember that all my intentions were to bring Christ to every one of those guys and to see that whole crew saved. But God had a different plan, and I learned a lot about who I was and His life in me, which goes on to this day and will continue until His return.

Micheal C. Harris,
Sept. 26, 1991

THE ROGUE RIVER ROUGH RIDERS, SUMMER 1974

1. Mike Harris 2. Dale Alter (foreman) **3."The Indian" 4. "Hubby" 5. "Tex" 6. Decker 7. "Luke" Leever 8. The Author** (with pipe) **9. Frank Emmerson, 10. Don Bailey** (asst foreman) **11. "Doc" 12. Pat 13. Jeff Leever 14. John Lacey 15. Benny Colon 16. Steve Norton**